HUDSON, ROCK
B   cop.1
HUDSON,
ROCK
Clark, Tom
Rock Hudson, friend of mine.

ROCK HUDSON
Friend of Mine

ROCK HUDSON
Friend of Mine

By Tom Clark
With Dick Kleiner

Pharos Books
A Scripps Howard Company
New York, New York

First published in 1990.
Library of Congress Cataloguing-in-Publication Data
Clark, Tom, 1930-
Rock Hudson, friend of mine / by Tom Clark with Dick Kleiner.
p. cm.
ISBN 0-88687-562-5 : $18.95
1. Hudson, Rock, 1925-1985. 2. Motion picture actors and actresses—Unit-
ed States—Biography. I. Kleiner, Richard.
II. Title.
PN2287.H75C58 1990
791.43'028'092—dc20
[B] 89-27196
CIP
Printed in the United States of America
Interior design by Bea Jackson
Jacket design by Nancy Eato
Pharos Books
A Scripps Howard Company
200 Park Avenue
New York, NY 10166
10 9 8 7 6 5 4 3 2 1

To Emily who wishes I hadn't.

Contents

PREFACE • xi

CHAPTER ONE • 3

Friend of Mine

CHAPTER TWO • 30

Rock Hudson

CHAPTER THREE • 43

Early Years

CHAPTER FOUR • 71

Family

CHAPTER FIVE • 86

Entertaining Royally

CHAPTER SIX • 93

His Friendships

CHAPTER SEVEN • 109

Travel

CHAPTER EIGHT • 141

Making Movies

CHAPTER NINE • 154

On Television

CHAPTER TEN • 172

The Heart Attack?

CHAPTER ELEVEN • 181

In New York

CHAPTER TWELVE • 197

On the Stage

CHAPTER THIRTEEN • 219

Aging Gracefully

CHAPTER FOURTEEN • 224

The Split

CHAPTER FIFTEEN • 242

Illness

CHAPTER SIXTEEN • 264

Saying Goodbye

INDEX • 271

Preface

This is the book I swore I would never write.

But it is the book I had to write for Rock Hudson's sake.

Those of us who knew him well have been so disappointed in other things written about Rock that we feel a truer picture should be shown.

Since I knew him as well as or, probably, better than anyone else—our relationship spanned more than twenty years—the task has fallen to me.

This is not a conventional biography of the man. I can only tell you about the Rock Hudson I knew from 1964 until his death, as well as some of the things he and his mother told me of his early years.

It is really not a biography or autobiography of a person. It is the autobiography of a friendship.

ROCK HUDSON
Friend of Mine

CHAPTER ONE
Friend
of Mine

Rock Hudson and I had a close and intimate relationship for more than twenty years. Before we met, we had each had many acquaintances and a smattering of good friends. As Henry Adams said, "One friend in a lifetime is much; two are many; three are hardly possible."

Rock was one of those once-in-a-lifetime friends, for me, and I know the same was true for him. Rock was the kind of man you would expect to have many friends—he was open, gregarious, outgoing. But that was the surface Rock. He was open and gregarious only so far, outgoing and friendly only up to a point. After that point was reached, he would generally withdraw into a crackproof shell.

Many people knew him; very few knew him well.

I was one of those fortunate few. Mark Miller and George Nader were two others Rock considered *very* close and warm friends.

We were alike in that respect; I, too, had very few close friends. And we were alike in many other respects. Our differences were the kind that united rather than divided. Our childhoods had been different, but Rock envied me my childhood so much that he kept wanting to hear about it. It was almost as though, in my retelling the stories of my near-idyllic childhood, he might somehow make up for the difficult early years he had suffered through.

We often compared our youthful experiences. Our fathers, for example. His real father had walked out on him and his mother when Rock was a small boy. His stepfather had been a bully and a drunk, a child- and wife-abuser. My father, on the other hand, was one of those *Life with Father* sort of men—the solid, small-town business-man who was always ready to go fishing with his son and who always came home from work at a certain time and who told bedtime stories and was a real pal to his son. The storybook kind of dad.

My dad was still going strong when Rock and I became friends, and he sort of adopted Rock. Rock loved my dad, too. Whenever my folks would come to California, from Oklahoma to see me, my dad and Rock would get together and talk. I think Rock was trying to make up for lost years, fatherless years, by having a father-figure to talk to. He borrowed my dad, and my dad was very willing to be borrowed. He thought highly of Rock.

Rock and I had many other things in common, too, but that business of loving my father was high on the list.

Of course, there were areas where we differed—the amount of education we had had, for example. But Rock's lack of advanced formal education and the fact that I was a college graduate brought us together more than kept us apart. He had dropped out of high school when he went into the Navy; I had finished the University of Oklahoma. And yet Rock had this craving for knowledge, a craving that had made him read the *Encyclopaedia Britannica* from A to Z—and he had done that several times. He envied me my college diploma and, although I think he knew a lot more than I did about many things, he still felt inferior because of his lack of a formal education.

He went out of his way to cultivate certain habits and pastimes which he equated with being intellectual. He was an avid cross-word-puzzle solver, for example, and he also read a great deal and played chess and bridge. He believed, accurately I suppose, that crossword puzzles, reading, chess, and bridge are all indications of an intellect that is at least slightly above average. (Of course, that depends on the degree of difficulty of the puzzles and the quality of the books one reads). But Rock was also a whiz at Double-Crostics, a higher and tougher form of crossword puzzle.

It was, in fact, Rock's love of bridge that brought us together.

I was working as a publicist at MGM, near the end of the glory days of that once-mighty studio. There were still some vestigial traces of that glory, and that might hanging on, but they were fast disappearing. The studio was, in the early 1960s, rather like an ancient dowager who clings desperately to her faded glamour but knows that she is already an anachronism. But still the ghosts of all the old stars haunted the sound stages and there were some people still around who had been part of the great days. For a movie buff like me, it was exciting and verged on the genuinely romantic.

One of those living ghosts was my boss, Howard Strickling, the legendary publicity man who had run the publicity department for a hundred years and had survived the turmoil of a dozen changes of administration. He still struck terror in the hearts of his staff, but he was a publicity genius.

Since I was single, I was the designated partygoer in the office. Somebody had to represent MGM at every fancy party and affair and premiér that Hollywood proudly threw virtually every night. There was always something going on somewhere. Strickling would say, "Clark, you don't have anything else to do tonight; you go to this, will you?" and toss the invitation on my desk. It wasn't really a request—that "will you?" was merely a formality—it was an order. So I would grab a date (plenty of starlets the studio wanted to showcase were around) and go to whatever it was that night.

One night in 1964, I went to something or other and then, afterward—it was an early-evening affair, probably just a cocktail party—I went to Pat Fitzgerald's to play bridge.

Pat was an old-time Hollywood press agent, a good-hearted lady who lived up near Mulholland Drive, the road that snakes along the top of the mountains that separate Los Angeles from the San Fernando Valley. She had called me and said she needed a fourth for bridge and could I come over. I had said yes, but it would have to be after the party Howard Strickling had assigned me to attend. That was OK; Pat and her bridge cronies always started late and finished much later.

I looked forward to it. You know how it is with us bridge players: we will drop everything for a good game. So I rushed through my command appearance, flying the MGM flag enough for Strickling to be pleased, and then rushed up the mountain to Pat's home.

She and her good friend Lynn Bowers, another publicist, were playing; I have forgotten who the third person was. I was the fourth. The cards were already dealt by the time I go there, and my drink was poured and waiting.

"You dealt, Tom," Pat said. No time wasted on superfluous preliminaries. Not with real bridge players. You just dive in. So I sat down, took a sip of my drink, picked up my cards, and bid whatever I could.

We played an hour or so and then the front-door bell rang and Pat got up and opened the door, and there was Rock Hudson.

He had been shooting at Universal, over in the Valley, and was on his way home and had stopped by on the off-chance that there might be a bridge game going on. Like me, Rock was a bridge nut and would go anyplace at anytime and do anything for a game. In Hollywood, there aren't too many bridge players. Rock had, apparently, taken to stopping off at Pat's just because there might be a game going on.

"Great! You're playing," he said, walking in. Pat introduced everyone. Rock pulled up a chair and began kibitzing as Pat, Lynn, the other person, and I continued playing.

I had grown up being crazy about movies and movie stars but, since I had been working at MGM, I had gotten to know many of them pretty well—Greer Garson, Glenn Ford, Lana Turner. Movie stars, as a class, no longer impressed me by their very presence. I liked them generally, and still do, but the fact that the great Rock Hudson was sitting next to me, watching as I played bridge, did not send icy fingers up and down my spine.

We played a while and he was a good kibitzer: he didn't say a word. But I could tell he was dying to get his hands on the cards (I would have been, in his place), so when we got to the end of a rubber I asked him if he would like to play a couple of hands while I went to the bathroom.

"Great," he said. "Thanks a lot."

So I got up and he took my seat, and I never did get back into the game that evening. I finally went into the other room and watched some television until the game broke up and we all went home.

That was our first official meeting. It wasn't anything earth-shattering. No rockets went off. I didn't give it a second thought and I don't imagine Rock did either.

It wasn't the first time I had seen Rock, however. There had been an earlier occasion when our paths had crossed.

When I had decided to move to California from Houston, where I had been working, a girl I had been dating who was a huge Rock Hudson fan extracted a promise from me.

"If you ever run into Rock Hudson out there in Hollywood," she had said, "I want you to drop everything and call me. No matter where you are or what you are doing, you call me, hear? Promise?"

"Oh, come on, Jeannine," I had said. "That's silly."

"Silly or not, you *MUST* promise me you'll call me if you ever run into Rock Hudson."

So I had promised. And, of course, it happened. I was having dinner one night at Chianti, a restaurant on Melrose Avenue, and I was sitting there with some friends and in walked Rock with a group of people; he was with Claudia Cardinale. I remembered my promise and got up and went to the men's room, where the phone was, and put in a call to Jeannine in Houston.

She was very excited. She asked me to describe what he was wearing and who he was with and every detail I could possibly mention. As we were talking, he walked into the men's room and gave me one of those polite smiles you give somebody else in the men's room.

I immediately switched conversational topics and Jeannine realized what was happening.

"Oh, don't tell me he's right there with you," she squealed.

"That's very true," I said.

"Oh, I can't stand it," she said, and hung up.

That was the only time I had ever seen him until that night at Pat Fitzgerald's.

And, for a while after that, nothing much happened. Our paths crossed a few more times—in the Hollywood social scene, that is inevitable—and we would smile at each other and murmur the proper polite, meaningless phrases, and that would be that.

I found it pleasant to be recognized by Rock Hudson. After all, I was still the kid from the sticks and so that sensation of rubbing elbows with stars was still new enough to give me a nice feeling. Maybe they no longer impressed me as they had at first but, nevertheless, I couldn't help but think how my old buddies and girlfriends back in Oklahoma City would drop dead if they could see me now.

We who work in Hollywood come to take all the glamour for granted—and, no matter how some may scoff, it is a glamorous place, full of glamorous people. (The dictionary definition of *glamour*, remember, is "excitement, adventure and unusual activity such as to arouse envy," and that certainly fits the Hollywood the fans envision.) We tend to forget, very quickly, how much we ourselves envied those who were intimates of the stars before we became intimates ourselves.

But still there were a few stars I grew to like as people—Rock became one of that number—and a few I still had up on some heroic pedestal. One of the latter group was Ava Gardner. Like so many young men of my generation, my adolescence had been full of wild crushes on beautiful movie stars. In my case it was either Lana Turner or Ava Gardner, depending on which one I had seen most recently. Rock and I later compared teen crushes, and we had shared those same two romantic fantasies as youths.

At MGM I had come to know Lana and, while I liked her and she certainly was gorgeous, familiarity bred a kind of disillusionment. But I had not yet met Ava Gardner, so she was still up there on a cloud somewhere in my daydreams.

One evening Rock called. We had met a few more times since that evening at Pat Fitzgerald's, brought together mostly by our mutual love of bridge, so it was not surprising to hear his voice. It happened to be one night I was free. No assignment from Howard Strickling to cover some affair. I had been looking forward to a quiet evening at home—the maid had been there that day, so the house was clean, there were fresh sheets on the bed. I had eaten dinner, taken a shower, put on clean pajamas, found a book, and went to bed around 7:30, all set for a lovely evening of reading and dozing.

Then Rock called.

"Me," he said. He always started his phone calls with "Me," and never said "This is Rock Hudson" because he hated that name so much he could never bring himself to say it. We all knew that "Me" was Rock Hudson calling.

"Hi, Rock," I said.

"Need a fourth. How about it?"

"No, not tonight. I'm in for a quiet evening at home for a change."

"OK, that's too bad," he said, and hung up.

Twenty second later, the phone rang again.

"Tom, honey," said a sugary voice, dripping with magnolias and invitation. "I'm so sorry you-all couldn't come over to Rock's tonight. I was so looking forward to meeting you, after all the sweet things Rock said about you."

"Who is this?" I asked.

"Why, it's Ava."

"I'll be there in ten minutes," I said, already half into my clothes. I was there in maybe twelve.

Rock answered the door, a sly grin on his face.

"Where is she?" I said, pushing my way past him.

"In the kitchen," he said, and I raced down the hall and into the kitchen—and there she was, in all her considerable glory. She was wearing a cocktail dress that must have cost ten thousand if it cost a dime. No shoes. A cigarette, dangling out of one corner of her mouth. A tumbler full of straight scotch in her hand. And, with the other hand, she was stirring something that was bubbling in a pot on the stove.

"You must be the famous Tom Clark," she said. "Why, I do believe you are even better-looking than Rock said you were."

Ava and I became friends that night, a friendship that lasted, professionally and socially, for several years.

As the days and weeks and months passed, Rock and I spent more and more of our time together.

We found ourselves traveling together, playing together, having fun together. And by 1973 we began to realize that we really ought to live together, too. It made good sense. I had a big house and he had a big house. I had dogs and he had dogs. Even when we weren't physically together we were speaking on the phone. So it just seemed like the logical thing to do. And one day Rock broached the subject we had both been thinking about.

"Let's live together," he said.

"Why not?"

Why not, indeed? When it came to a your-place-or-mine decision, we opted for his place. Mine was big; his was bigger. I had fewer possessions to move. Besides, nothing short of an earthquake of around 6.5 on the Richter scale could have blasted him out of that house of his.

So I moved into his big house and stayed there for the next ten years. We separated, for what we both felt would be only a brief interlude, in September 1983. By then, although neither of us knew it, he already had in his system the virus that killed him. He began to get sick and we never got back together until he was very ill. Then, when I understood that he was dying, I came back to nurse him. I was with him until the end—and after.

There was a professional as well as a social reason why it was logical for Rock and me to be together. By a series of coincidences, our professional paths had crossed several times in the years since we had first met.

While I was still at MGM, I had worked on the movie *Ice Station Zebra*, in which Rock starred. That was in 1967. I left MGM and worked at the Disney studio for a time and, in 1973, when Rock suggested I move in with him, I had moved on and was working for a private public relations firm headed by Rupert Allen. And one of Allen's clients was Rock Hudson. So we were working closely, and it would be helpful if we spent our off hours together as well. Most of my years in Hollywood had been spent as a unit publicist. In those days a unit publicist was a vital cog in the Hollywood machinery. In that era, when big studios controlled most film production, the studio publicity departments would assign someone as unit publicist on every production. The unit publicist would theoretically be with that production from the day the first shot was filmed until the premiere, which could often mean six or eight months. The unit man or woman would arrange press visits and interviews; prepare releases on anything that happened during the shooting; put together a press book and press kit, which would be sent to major newspapers and wire services; assemble photos to be released to newspapers and magazines; supervise any radio or television coverage; and continue doing that for that one picture up to and including any festivities at the premiére. (Too often, that didn't work out as it was supposed to—we would be hustled off one picture and onto another—but that was the way the system was supposed to work, and often did.) It was a big, important job, and a good unit publicist could do a lot toward making a picture a box-office success.

Gradually, time and budgetary considerations have eroded that big job. As the studios lost importance and more and more productions became independent, producers hired outside, freelance unit publicists, and so the job became freelance in character. It also began to be a big-paying job and that sowed the seeds of its own demise. More and more indy prods (as independent producers began to be called) elected to do without unit publicists entirely. Instead, they retained outside public relations firms who would, in turn, assign one of their staffers to handle the production. Because it might be a different person each week there would be no continuity, and because it often would be a junior, inexperienced person there would be no skill. Today the majority of films are made without any unit publicist on the premises at all. But in my days at MGM, being a unit publicist was still the plum job in the office.

MGM, like all studios, was full of feuds. Maybe it is true that creative people in general are so temperamental that minor disagreements become major feuds. Strickling and producer Marty Ransohoff had one of those fallings-out, so Ransohoff refused to accept any of the MGM publicity people on his films. Since his next film, *Ice Station Zebra,* was going to be an MGM production, this caused an immediate and moderately large problem.

I had just finished a picture on location in Jamaica and had stopped off in New York on the way back to California. Rock was in New York too, and we met and he and I and his agent at the time, Dick Shepard, decided to fly back to Los Angeles together.

On the plane, Shepard said that Rock was about to start *Ice Station Zebra,* and both of them wanted me to do the unit. I explained that the producer wanted no MGM publicity people around because of his feud with Strickling.

"Marty will have no choice," Shepard said, "if we insist on it."

"That will just get him angrier," I said. "Don't do anything until I talk to Strickling."

When I got back to the studio, I met with Strickling and he figured a way out of the dilemma. He had survived dozens of shake-ups at the studio, and a man doesn't survive all that in-fighting without acquiring a good ability at compromising.

A deal was worked out. I would be assigned to the picture—but not as the official unit publicist. I would only be there to do Rock's publicity. Ransohoff hired an outside unit publicist, so his anger was assuaged, and I was there, too, so Strickling's ego was stroked. And I was able to see that Rock's interests were taken care of.

After that picture I was hired away by Disney to do the unit on *The Love Bug,* and I did a few others at that studio, too. I worked on *Bedknobs and Broomsticks* and then I was put on a quickie called *The Boatniks,* with Stefanie Powers and Bobby Morse. When they hired me, the Disney people had asked me to provide "a new perspective" to selling their films—which were at that point losing money. I tried to do so, but I got shot down.

One scene in *The Boatniks* had a bunch of young people—including girls in bikinis—frolicking on a speedboat. I took a still of that and asked the studio advertising department to build their ad campaign for the picture around that shot. When the studio executives saw the mock-up of the ad, they nearly had a stroke.

"You can't do that," they howled. "This is a Disney picture! No bikinis in our ads."

"But the scene is in the picture," I said.

"Doesn't matter," they said.

I realized Disney and I were not made for each other, and I left. But it had been a profitable time for me, because I went there with a big stock option, which I had exercised, and I was able to build a house with the money I realized from that venture. In 1971, then, I took Rupert Allen's offer and joined his firm, which was called Allen, Foster, Ingersoll and Weber. The four partners were Rupert Allen (most famous for being the chum and confidant of royalty, such as the English royal family and Monaco's Princess Grace and Prince Rainier), David Foster (who left soon and became a successful producer), Rick Ingersoll, and Lois Weber, who was the New

York representative of the firm. I dealt mostly with Rupert Allen. He hired me and gave me my first assignment, which was to handle one of the firm's most important clients: Rock Hudson. Rock was so important to the firm's business that I was not alone in representing him. I worked closely with another publicist, Emily Torchia. Emily had been at MGM too; in fact, she had become a legend in her own time.

When you think about a female publicist or press agent, your mind probably conjures up a vision of a tough gal, probably blonde, who drinks like a fish and swears like a trooper and uses her sex as a tool of her trade, like her typewriter. Emily Torchia could have passed as a Sunday-school teacher or your favorite aunt. She was (and still is) a sweet, demure, kindly, old-fashioned lady with the values and morality of a Quaker. Yet she was perhaps the best publicity person in Hollywood for many years. At MGM, Lana Turner wouldn't turn around without first consulting Emily. Rock Hudson adored her—and so do I.

Ice Station Zebra had been a long shoot, but it turned out to be a very successful film, at least with the moviegoing public. It was strictly an adventure yarn, and those rarely get any positive reviews from critics. Unless a film makes some pretense of being arty, critics usually brush it off. But it was an important film in Rock's career, a turning point of sorts.

During the filming Rock and I had some serious discussions about where he was going with his career. I wanted him to do television. Offers for him to do TV were flooding in, two or three a week. But he was from the old Hollywood school, which held that TV was a minor art form at best and that no true motion picture star would be caught dead in a television show. Most of them hoped that, eventually, television would just go away. It is hard today to remember back to when that philosophy flourished among the Hollywood set. But in the sixties the established movie stars felt TV was beneath them. They wouldn't do it.

"But, Rock," I would say. "TV is here to stay. If you don't do it, you'll be left behind."

"Good, then I'll be left behind," he would answer. "I'm not going to do it. Whose deal is it?"

Then came an offer to do a TV movie, something called *Murder by the Book*. It was a terrific script (even he agreed on that) and he happened to be free, and he liked the people involved, so he did it. His first television, and it turned out well. He enjoyed filming it, and they took pains and time with it, so he didn't feel as rushed as he expected he would.

When NBC aired it, it had enormous ratings, so both NBC and Universal, which had made it, asked him if he would do a series based on the character he played in *Murder By the Book*. At first, predictably, he said no. But NBC and Universal wore him down, and I helped in that erosion process.

One of the things that persuaded him to do the series—which became *McMillan & Wife*—was when the network said they would make it part of a wheel. That meant three other shows would alternate with *McMillan.* So Rock's show would only be on once a month, not every week, allowing for a longer, slower shooting schedule and making it more like shooting a feature film than a TV show. They also gave him approval of cast, director and script and approval approval, and they threw in a whole bunch of money, too.

McMillan & Wife became a big hit, overseas as well as in the United States. Rock began to get invitations to go abroad to make promotional appearances. He began accepting many of those invitations and, of course, I went with him.

It was the beginning of ten or twelve years of traveling all over the world. Rock and I both enjoyed traveling—especially when we could travel in style, which we did. We were always in the front of the bus—or the plane or train or ship or whatever. We always were received with red carpets and wine. We stayed in the finest hotels, ate at the best restaurants, met the crustiest of the upper crust.

Our first trip together was to Australia, with a stopover in Tahiti, of which more later. That jaunt set the tone for future trips. We found we got such a boot out of traveling together that we seized on any excuse after that to be off and going.

Traveling with Rock Hudson was always an adventure, always a special experience. He took his worldwide celebrity for granted, but for me, riding along in his considerable wake, it never ceased to be pretty heady stuff. But Rock was always ambivalent about his stardom, and especially about the perks that went with it.

We went on a few cruises and, of course, Rock was automatically asked to sit at the captain's table. It happened on the Greek ship *Stella Solaris*, but that time he said no. He said he preferred to eat with his friends. But he sat with the captain when we cruised on the *Royal Viking Sea* and when we crossed the Atlantic on the *QE2*.

In Rome once, they asked him if he would like an audience with the Pope. People would kill for that privilege, but he said no. Graciously but firmly. They couldn't understand that, and he couldn't articulate his reason (he said his schedule didn't permit it) but the real reason was simply that he hated all that pomp and cringed at being singled out for that kind of special privilege. In his innermost soul, he felt unworthy.

I remember, when *The Exorcist* had just been released there were lines around the block waiting to get in. Rock and I were both very eager to see it, but he just couldn't wait in line for a couple of hours—he would be mobbed. So I called the theater manager and asked if he could sneak us in. He said he'd be delighted, but when we got there and he took us in, we found he had roped off two entire rows—with velvet ropes, yet! Rock was so embarrassed he pleaded with the manager to take the ropes down and let people into the rest of the seats.

A few years later, when *E.T.* was the hot film around town, I called the manager of the theater where that was playing. This time, he said if we came to the first show, he would put us in the balcony—he didn't open the balcony for the first show, so we would have it all to ourselves. That was fine with Rock, and so we sat in the balcony, all alone, and watched that delightful film.

I think he would have preferred to be overlooked rather than to be singled out for all that favoritism.

Rock looked elegant and could (and did) behave like he was born to the purple, but underneath I know that he was squirming all the time. He was so good an actor that no one (except me and other very close friends, such as Mark Miller and George Nader) ever sensed his discomfort, but he was much more at ease with average people. Hoity-toity made him very uncomfortable. He always had the sense that they knew he was an imposter, because he had come from such a humble background. He masked it beautifully, but he was never happy with high society, or even medium-grade society.

Still, he coveted certain perks of the privileged classes. And, because of who (or what) he was, those privileges were forthcoming. In London, he thought he would like to become a member of the Royal Driving Club. One phone call and he was an honored member. Another call and we both belonged to the distinguished old London theatrical organization, the Garrick Club. Without even a call we were given a membership in the ritzy White Elephant Club—and, to this day I still get my annual membership card.

When we were in Kyoto, Japan, in 1973, Rock expressed a yen to see the Royal Palace. At that time it was closed to tourists. Rock's wish became a royal command. The palace was opened for us, and we were given a special tour.

A few years after that first trip to Australia, we went to South America, to Rio de Janeiro and Buenos Aires. It was during that trip that Rock suggested I leave Rupert Allen and go to work for his company, Mammoth Films. He offered me the title of vice president, and most of us are seduced by high-sounding titles like vice president. But there was more than the title to Rock's offer. There was a good salary, interesting work—looking for properties Rock could appear in and perhaps, eventually, properties for other actors as well, and guiding his career. And it meant that we would be spending more time together, which seemed like an enjoyable prospect to both of us.

More and more we had come to realize how much we shared. We had both been married, unsuccessfully. We both had a stepparent. We both loved dogs. We already knew that we were both bridge players, but we also discovered our mutual enjoyment of crossword puzzles and reading good books and going to the theater and listening to a wide variety of music. We both enjoyed eating well. We both liked to garden. We both liked to go to bed late and get up early. The list of pleasures we found we shared went on and on.

We were leading a terrific life. It was a life in which only the best would do. Whatever it was that we did or experienced, we settled for nothing less than the best. Eventually we had an apartment in New York too; it was fully furnished so that, at the drop of a whim, we could pick up and leave L.A. and fly to New York and find everything we needed already there.

Money was never a problem. Rock was a millionaire by then, and although he might be tight with a buck when it came to things like tipping and paying his household staff, he was very liberal when he was spending money on himself. And, since I had become part of his life, I enjoyed the fruits of that largesse.

Actually, I was appalled when I first moved into the house and found out how much—or, rather, how little—he was paying the people who worked for him. Joy, the housekeeper, was making sixty dollars a week and had been making sixty dollars a week for years. The others were also making ridiculously low salaries. I don't think it was because Rock was tight so much as the fact that it simply never occurred to him to give them raises. As soon as I pointed out to him that he wasn't paying them enough, he immediately tripled all their salaries without batting an eyelash or a checkbook.

Rock never carried a dollar, or even a dime, on his person. I would pick up and pay every check and take care of all the tipping when we were together. He was delighted to turn that responsibility over to me. Money was, in his view, a necessary evil, and he hated having to handle it. So, generally, he didn't. I took care of the daily out-of-pocket expenses and his business manager paid all the bills that accumulated.

Like most rich people, Rock economized in some strange ways (he didn't like to buy clothes for himself, for example) but he could be supergenerous in other ways.

Giving gifts—large, bountiful gifts—was one of his great pleasures. He knew, for instance, that one of my boyhood dreams had been to write a novel. (I had long since given up that dream, recognizing the limits of my writing skills.) Rock kept encouraging me to write more and, as a symbol of that encouragement, one Christmas he gave me the biggest, fanciest, snazziest electric typewriter that IBM made. It had everything on it, a memory and I think it even had power windows, but I never mastered the knack of operating the darn thing. He threw in about twenty books on how to write a novel and a novel-writing course at UCLA. I read the books and took the course, but never did write the novel. I didn't have the dedication you need, or the talent, or both.

When Rock went shopping to buy gifts for friends, it was a major undertaking. He would spend hours compiling his list, going over it several times and asking me for suggestions. Then off we would go to shop for all the gifts on the list. That sometimes presented a problem, because if he was working during Christmas shopping season, it would be difficult for him to find the time to go to all the stores he wanted to visit. Once, during the *McMillan & Wife* period, his friend Marion Wagner, who had a fine shop in Beverly Hills, arranged for the I. Magnin department store to stay open after hours just for Rock. So, when Rock's shooting day was over, he and I and Marion went to Magnin's, got in through a side door as arranged, and were met by a Magnin salesgirl. The four of us had the store to ourselves, and Rock raced from department to department, picking out gifts and checking names off his list.

"I'll have that, I'll have that, I'll have that," he said, and the poor salesgirl could hardly keep up with him as he pointed at whatever caught his considerable fancy.

When he shopped, money was not only no object, it was not even a consideration. He never looked at price tags or even asked how much anything was. If he liked it, he would just say "I'll take that," and that was the end of it.

Once he wanted to buy something for Nancy Walker on her birthday. She was working with him on *McMillan* then, and they were old and good friends. We went into Marion Wagner's store on Rodeo Drive in Beverly Hills and he spotted a lovely silk blouse and told Marion to wrap it up. As he was looking around, he saw a pretty scarf and tossed it to Marion.

"Throw this in, too, will you?" he said.

"Wait a second, Rock," Marion said. "That scarf is —."

He stopped her.

"I don't care what it is. It's a nice scarf and Nancy will like it. So just throw it in."

Marion shrugged and wrapped the scarf up, too. When the bill arrived, we learned that the scarf was hand-painted, I think by Dali, and cost $750.

Rock looked at the bill when I showed it to him and said, "Well, maybe I should ask the price of things." But he really wasn't disturbed by what that scarf cost. And he was right—Nancy loved it and still wears it to this day.

* * *

When I think about Rock today—and I think about him often—the first thing that springs to mind is his laughter. We had that in common, too, that love of laughing, that ability to find humor everywhere. Life was fun to both of us, and the people in it were fun, and so we had a marvelous time laughing at things that happened every day of our mutual lives.

When something really tickled him, he became so hysterical he literally could not control himself. You've heard of people breaking up; Rock positively shattered. Naturally, some of those times occurred when they shouldn't have. In church, for example.

Neither of us was particularly religious. Rock had had a bad experience as a boy in a Catholic church, which turned him off organized religion. And yet he believed in God fervently. We would go to various churches from time to time, not out of any religious commitment, but simply because we enjoyed the ceremony of it.

We would occasionally go to a noted Catholic church, St. Vincent's, in Beverly Hills. All the Catholic stars attended that church. Loretta Young, who is devoutness personified, was a regular. Rock and I would sit there, entranced, as Loretta swept in, making an entrance like she used to make on her old television show. She would stand at the back of the church, waiting for everyone to turn and focus on her, then float down the aisle to her pew. It was a marvelous performance, but the best was yet to come.

As she knelt to pray, a beam of sunlight would flash through the solid roof and shine on her head, and she would turn her face upward, basking in that celestial spotlight. We could never figure out how she did it, but Rock would always start to laugh, and that made me laugh, and the two of us would have to dash out.

It got so we never called the church by its real name. To us it was always St. Loretta's.

Emily Torchia, also a devout Catholic, kept trying to entice us to go to her church. She accomplished that once by telling us of a special attraction. She lived in Culver City, near MGM, and that city had an ever-increasing Mexican population, so her church was going to have a Mariachi Mass. That sounded unique and interesting, so Rock said we should go, and we went.

There were mariachis, as advertised, in the choir loft with their instruments. But they were all drunk as skunks—and you haven't lived until you've heard a bunch of drunks play mariachi music in a church loft. This was a few days before Christmas, moreover, so the highlight was a rousing, alcohol-stained mariachi version of "Silent Night."

Rock and I looked at each other and, of course, we began to laugh. We literally could not stop. Even staid Emily joined in. The three of us had to get up and leave, with the mariachis staring angrily at us.

Another time when it is not politic for a star to get the galloping guffaws is during an interview with a reporter. Emily set an interview for Rock with a distinguished reporter for *The Christian Science Monitor*. It was to be in the Polo Lounge, that most fashionable restaurant/bar in the Beverly Hills Hotel. Rock and Emily showed up at the scheduled hour. Rock had his favorite booth, but this day it was occupied—a man was sitting there alone—so they moved on to the next booth and waited for the reporter to show up. Finally, the maitre d' came over and said, "Mr. Hudson, there is a gentleman waiting for you. I took the liberty of seating him at your usual booth." So Emily and Rock moved over and introduced themselves and Rock, for the first time, took a close look at the reporter waiting to interview him.

He was wearing the tackiest, cheapest, most ill-fitting toupee the world had ever seen. It was so obviously a hairpiece, and such a poor one, and worn so sloppily, that Rock couldn't contain himself. He had to excuse himself and went to the men's room, where he burst into great, galloping guffaws. He knew if he went back to the booth he would start laughing again.

So he had Emily paged and told her he just couldn't do the interview. She had to go back and tell the reporter that Rock had been taken suddenly ill and had had to leave. Rock was still chuckling when he got home and told me about it. Emily and the reporter had a nice lunch and the interview was rescheduled, but this time Rock knew what to expect so he was able to control himself.

He would often break up on the set, too. Nancy Walker could do things that sent him into hysterics. So could Maggie Raye (as his good pal, Martha Raye, is called by her close friends). And Doris Day was no slouch at making Rock break up, either. Doris and

Rock were doing a film which dear, sweet Delbert Mann was directing; something struck both Rock and Doris as funny, and away they went. It was a simple shot, theoretically, but with the two of them totally out of control, it took hours. And Mann, normally the most even-tempered gentleman in the world, got madder and madder. And, of course, the madder he got, the funnier they thought it was.

On one of our trips to South America, Rock was honored at a luncheon in Buenos Aires. Television was covering the event live, and all of Argentina was watching. A beloved old Argentine comic, the Jimmy Durante of Argentina, was called on to sing. They had warned us in advance that the old man had become a hopeless drunk and so, when he came over to our table and began singing right into Rock's face, we were prepared for the fumes that poured out of his mouth.

He started to sing "Tea for Two" in English, and when he got to the word *tea*, his false teeth flew out. The television cameras, which had been on him, immediately switched over and zeroed in on Rock to save the old man embarrassment as he tried to grab his teeth, strum his guitar, and keep on singing all at the same time. I knew this would cause Rock to break up, and I didn't want to see it happen, not on national television, so I got up and fled. But Rock, ever the trouper, kept a stiff upper face and didn't laugh, not as long as the camera was right in his nose. As soon as the camera turned away, he broke up and ran out and joined me and we collapsed into each other's arms, laughing until we fell down.

It took us ten minutes to get to the point where we could go back inside to the luncheon.

Rock used to say that there was nothing better for the human spirit than to laugh—especially when you're not supposed to. Of course, being human, he didn't think it was quite so funny when the laugh was on him.

We had that apartment in New York, and we spent a lot of time there. When we were in residence on West 81st Street we felt like genuine New Yorkers. We walked all over the city. One day we were strolling down Madison Avenue; as we were crossing 62nd Street Rock suddenly turned to me and said, "Hey, Tom, will you please tell me something? You've been to college, so you should know—what does the word *iony* mean?"

"Iony? I never heard of that word.

"Oh, come on," he said. "You must have seen it—it's all over the city. I see it everywhere. I - O - N - Y And the O is always a little red heart."

When I realized he was referring to the "I Love New York" stickers, I could not control myself. I just started laughing and had to sit on the curb, because I was laughing so hard I couldn't stand up. He still didn't know what had struck me so funny, but he understood that I was laughing at him and he didn't appreciate that. When I finally was able to gain command of my voice and managed to explain what *iony* meant, he didn't find it at all amusing.

For years afterward, if he ever did anything especially intelligent, I would bring him back down to earth by simply saying that one word, *iony*.

Rock was emotional. He laughed easily, got angry quickly, and cried often without reason. He'd cry when they played "The Star-Spangled Banner" at football games. The flag, the anthem, the whole patriotic bit really tugged at his poor soft, romantic soul.

He didn't cry at movies, however, even the calculated tear-jerkers. I supposed that was because he knew the film trade so well that he understood how it was all make-believe and how the emotion was deliberately spooned on.

But I remember once we were watching some dumb television game show when a young teenage boy was a contestant. He won a car and told the MC (and us) that he was going to give it to his mother, who had recently been widowed. Well, that was all dear old Rock had to hear; he was a sucker for motherhood. The tears began to spring to his eyes and I think he would have given that kid a scholarship to life right then if he had been able to.

He was a complex person, but aren't we all? He projected such an image of virility, and he certainly was virile, but he also had that soft, sentimental side. His interests varied widely and encompassed many often-contradictory things.

Before we met, he had gone through a nautical period, when he had hung out with the Hollywood boating set—Bogart, Wayne, those fellows. He often went through phases of interest—his personal fads—and, although he had outgrown yachting by the time we met, he still kept charts of all the oceans in the house. He would frequently drag them out and pore over them, apparently mapping out in his mind trips he would like to take, islands he would like to explore. I think he might have gone back to boating sometime in his future, but it was too time-consuming a hobby for anybody who worked as hard and as long as he did. I believe he dreamed of that someday, sometime, but it was a someday and a sometime that never happened.

But even if he was an armchair yachtsman, he was an active gardener—a passion we shared. We had a fabulous garden at the house (two full-time gardeners helped make it so) and we both like nothing better than spending an hour or so out in the garden, puttering.

My own particular joy was rose bushes. At one point I had one hundred and sixty roses, mostly different. Until I introduced him to the pleasures of rose cultivation, Rock hadn't paid much attention to that particular flower, but I was able to infect him with my enthusiasm and he became a rabid rose raiser, too. I had grown up with roses and, to me, growing a magnificent rose is the most rewarding thing you can do in the garden.

Rock would often come home from work—especially during the summer months when the days were longer—and spend an hour in the garden, weeding and pruning and cultivating before dinner. It was, he felt, a great way to unwind after a tough day at the office.

The house was also equipped with a pool, of course (I say "of course" because almost every home in Southern California that isn't a tenement has a pool—and even some tenements have them), and we also had a steam room and a fully equipped gym. But Rock was not a nut about exercising. In fact, he didn't like any of that very much.

The problem was a lack of discipline in his personal life. He had all the discipline in the world professionally—never late to the studio, lines always memorized, totally the pro—but none when it came to things like staying in shape. Fortunately, his physique and his metabolism were such that he automatically stayed in reasonably good shape, although he did have a bad back, which bothered him frequently. The steam room and the gym were there, but we rarely used them.

Rock got along very nicely on only three or four hours of sleep a night. I would be a wreck, but he would bounce out of bed after a late and raucous night, bright-eyed and bushy-tailed, raring to go. He would be ready to go to work at six in the morning, and work a full day and do close-ups and look terrific.

Many times I've gone to dailies—quick prints of the previous day's shooting—knowing that poor Rock had had a wild night before those shots were made and expecting to see the effect of the hangover plain on his face. And there he would be, beautiful as ever, looking clear-eyed and fresh-faced. He was, in that sense, remarkable. Great recuperative powers.

Most nights we stayed up late. We would listen to music (our record collection was incredible) and just talk. There would always be a drink in hand, too. That record collection was the result of our combined efforts. Between us we had amassed a collection that had every Broadway show ever recorded, every movie score, the complete works of every important pop singer, a good assortment of country and western music, most operas, and the finest symphonies and concertos and other classical works. The collection was worth a lot of money, and much of it had been mine originally. They were housed in a whole group of record cabinets that had been built into the screening room which we called the theater. (It's gone now. Even my own records have disappeared, like so many of my things. When Rock died, Marc Christian—of whom you will hear more—quickly departed and so, coincidentally, did a lot of things that belonged to me, such as my records. Christian admitted to Mark Miller that he took my records, and still has them. In fact, at the time of Marc Christian's lawsuit against the Hudson estate, the estate filed a counter-suit against him. One provision of that suit was that he be required to return the things he had taken. Without telling me, however, the estate's lawyers dropped the suit, apparently in the mistaken belief that Christian didn't have a chance in the world of winning his suit. By the time I found out that the suit had been dropped, it was too late for me to start a suit of my own, because the statute of limitations now protected Christian.)

That was our favorite way of spending an evening. One of us would put a record on, or a stack of records, and we would just sit in that very comfortable room and talk while the music provided a marvelous background, and we would have a drink or three. We would usually eat late, James, the cook/butler/general factotum, would have made the dinner and all we would do was heat it up whenever we felt like eating.

Sometimes we would screen a movie in the theater. We weren't much for television, but we loved old movies. Rock had to have only the finest equipment, so he was constantly updating the projection room as well as the sound system. Every time a new system was developed, he would have the old one ripped out and the new one installed. And, each time, we would have to spend days figuring out how to work the new one, because neither of us was particularly good with mechanical devices. Just about the time we mastered one system, a new one would come along, and here we would go again. Rock was a lot like a kid with toys; he loved to unwrap the new gadgets but became bored with them very quickly.

The most important thing in his life was, without any question, his work. He loved acting, loved the camaraderie of the studio, loved being a star. He enjoyed the adulation he received and, unlike many stars, never found it unbearably intrusive. There were times, of course, when it became a problem, mostly because of unfeeling fans who would interrupt his dinner at restaurants in their quest for an autograph, but even that he tolerated well.

If he was doing a picture or a television series, he was all business. He had no patience with actors who appeared late on the set, or who didn't know their lines, or who caused problems or delays. Unprofessional behavior upset him enormously.

He always knew his lines. Perhaps because he was a quick study, he found memorizing lines fairly easy. When he was doing a play, later in his career, I would help him memorize his lines. But when he was in a picture he rarely looked at the script until the day of the actual shooting. Then, as he drove to the studio, he and his dialogue coach—he always insisted on a dialogue coach—would go over the work for that day. By the time they reached the studio he would have the lines down pat. Jimmy Dobson, his favorite dialogue coach, worked with him on several films and on *McMillan & Wife*.

The stage roles were by far the most difficult for him. In a film they might shoot two or three pages a day, at most, and perhaps ten or twelve on a TV show. But for a play, he had many long speeches to commit to memory, especially in the two-character *I*

Do! I Do! and in the very lengthy *John Brown's Body*. But Rock handled even those assignments with relative ease.

On all his scripts he would write notes to himself, as many actors do. After his death, the New York apartment, where the scripts were kept, had been sealed and locked. Rock had given me all of them, but that didn't seem to matter and all of those scripts were quickly sold at auction. I could have cried when the *John Brown's Body* script was sold, for it contained notes he had written and some I had written, as we had worked together closely on his role in that show.

Outside his work, I believe Rock's next greatest passion was sports. We shared that enthusiasm. In fact, I had picked out the college I attended (the University of Oklahoma) primarily because of the high quality of its football team. But then, like Rock, I acquired the football allegiance to the teams in our adopted hometown, Los Angeles. We both became rabid rooters for the Trojans of the University of Southern California and, in the ranks of the pro teams, the NFL's Los Angeles Rams.

We had season tickets to both USC and Rams games. And Rock really got into his rooting, yelling, and screaming like the most excited freshman. In fact, during his *McMillan* period, the producer of that show, Paul Mason, came to me one day and said, "Listen, Tom, you have to do something about Rock and his football games. He can't go to both the USC game on Saturday and the Rams game on Sunday, because he's so hoarse on Monday and Tuesday that we have to dub in every word he says." So from then on, if both USC and the Rams were playing at home on a weekend, we had to make a decision, and we went only to the one game we most wanted to see.

We agreed on most things of significance and, generally, we agreed on politics, too. I am a lifelong registered Democrat and Rock, while he never registered with any party (he always said he voted for a man, not a party) usually went with the Democrats. But not always.

We split in 1980, when he supported Ronald Reagan and I voted for Jimmy Carter. He liked Ronnie as a person. At the time of that election we were in New York, so we voted via absentee ballot. We knew we were canceling out each other's vote, but we always wanted to do our duty as good citizens. He was voting for Reagan, while I was really voting against him as much as I was voting for Carter. I never cared much for Ronnie.

Rock had been very enthusiastic for John F. Kennedy. He liked him as a person, and that was enough, in his mind, to persuade him to support the man. Despite his ardor for Kennedy and, later, for Reagan, he would never permit either of them, or any other candidate or party, to use his name. He didn't feel that the mere fact that he liked a particular candidate was sufficient cause for anybody else to vote for that candidate. I wish other Hollywood celebrities had that sensibility.

About the only thing Rock and I ever seriously disagreed about was his career—what direction it should take and what career choices he should make. After I began, unofficially, to manage that career (I read scripts for him, negotiated contracts for him, supervised how things were going at work for him) I naturally took a close interest in the direction his career should take.

I would try to keep him from doing some of the lousy films he wanted to do, but not always with success. He wanted very much, for example, to do a film called *Avalanche.* He was absolutely determined to do it; feeling that disaster films were hot, he wanted a part in one. I told him that this happened to be a very poor one and, anyhow, disaster movies had run their course. But he had to do it, and he did it, and it was a disaster, all right.

After *McMillan & Wife,* he said he would never do another television series. I tried to explain to him that television was very important to the world and certainly to his career, but he still thought of TV as an upstart art that wasn't really worthy of his attention. Even television movies, he felt, were not quite the real thing.

So, when the script for *Wheels* was submitted to him he wouldn't even deign to read it. To him it was just a TV script, so he waved it away without a second thought. But I read it, and it was a great script, with a great part in it for Rock.

"Rock, you have to do this one."

"Not on your life," he said.

I explained that the script was terrific, the part they wanted him for was terrific, it was adapted from a best-selling book (by Arthur

Hailey); there was a top-flight producer and a fine director. They would give him cast approval—ultimately they went with Lee Remick as the leading lady, and Rock had always wanted to work with her, and Ralph Bellamy was in it, and Rock had long admired him—and, on top of all that, the money they were offering was gigantic. He still said no, but I worked on him and worked on him, and shouted at him and yelled at him and he finally gave in and agreed to do it.

Wheels was a major TV success and shot Rock back to the top of the Hollywood heap overnight. It was, in fact, the highest-rated miniseries NBC had had up to that point and for many years afterward. He enjoyed the experience, too—enjoyed working with Lee and Ralph and later enjoyed the triumph when it was aired. That wore down his resistance to doing television and, afterward, he did much more. He eventually came to respect television—at least the good things on television.

Those arguments about whether or not he should do television were our most serious disagreements, although we did do a lot of yelling at each other over unimportant things. We were both yellers, and little things would set us off. Nothing serious, simply discussions at a high decibel level. Of course, I was convinced that he was being stupid and pig-headed, and he was positive that I was dumb and hot-headed, but we never really lost our tempers or called each other names.

He had his quirks. One was that, fine actor though he was (and even his most severe critics ultimately recognized that he was a much better actor than they had given him credit for being), he was a terrible interviewee. There is an art to being a good interview subject, and Rock didn't have it. He was always pleasant and gentlemanly to reporters, but he hated the process of being interviewed. That was painfully evident to all concerned. He simply never had much to say.

Naturally, as an old public-relations hand, I tried to help, but eventually I realized that nothing could help him. From then on I tried to keep him out of the arena where his phobia would be most damaging: I tried to keep him from doing any of the television talk shows.

Once, however, his old friend Joan Rivers, when she first began taking over for Johnny Carson, wanted Rock on her show to give her a boost in the ratings. She called me and asked me if Rock would do the show, and I said no, sorry, but the answer is no. She bypassed me, however, and got to Rock directly, and because he liked Joan he agreed to do the show. But there was one condition.

Joan was in her Elizabeth Taylor-bashing phase, making joke after joke about Elizabeth, who was overweight at the time. Rock said he would do the show if she promised not to make any Elizabeth Taylor jokes. He adored Elizabeth and she adored him. So he went on the show, and Joan started to say something about Elizabeth Taylor. Rock stood up and started to leave.

"You would actually walk off, wouldn't you?" Joan said.

"I sure would," said Rock.

The audience didn't know what was going on, but Joan said, "OK, I promise. No more," and Rock sat down again.

It wasn't a bad interview, because Joan put Rock at ease after that, and he talked reasonably fluidly. But, still, it wasn't great and I wished he hadn't done it.

Most reporters liked Rock but knew that interviewing him was like dragging words out of a can of alphabet soup. You'd get a little here and a little there, but nothing really solid.

Rock had a special arrangement with one reporter—Dorothy Manners, who had worked with Louella Parsons and then had her own column. She did a Sunday piece each week in the Los Angeles *Herald-Examiner* that was syndicated to many other Hearst papers. And once a year she would come to the house on a Monday-night, and we would watch the Monday-night football game and all get totally smashed and laugh and scream and holler and then she'd go back and write a piece for the next Sunday. There would have been no questions and no answers, just fun and games, but somehow she got enough that way to do a huge story every year.

Rock was always pleasant to the press—actually, he was pleasant to everybody—and had a warm smile, a friendly handshake, a soft sparkle in his eyes. So the reporter would go away feeling good. He might not have much of a story—maybe no story at all—but he or she would have enjoyed the experience. You couldn't help but like Rock.

Everybody did.

CHAPTER TWO
Rock Hudson

R ock Hudson was the kind of man who couldn't stand being less than perfect. I don't mean that he thought he was the greatest thing that ever came along—far from it; he could always keep his ego under control—but he hated to be seriously lacking in any major respect. I think he didn't want to be perceived as being inefficient or ineffective in any particular.

His intellect, for example. He came to feel that he was seriously lacking in intellectual achievements, and this was a terrible blow to him. Once he believed that there was this gap in his make-up, he embarked on a never-ending quest to plug it up.

That feeling of inadequacy had come to him with an embarrassing suddenness. He told me the story one evening when we were sitting around the living room after dinner, drinks in hand and memories at the ready. Something had come up in conversation that he knew and I didn't—a not-infrequent event—and I marveled at the breadth of his knowledge.

"How the hell did you get so damned smart?" I asked, and he laughed and proceeded to tell me how he had gotten so damned smart.

In 1961, he said, he was in Italy, making a movie called *Come September*, with Gina Lollobrigida as his leading lady. In preparation for the Italian experience he had tried to learn to speak some Italian and thought he had mastered enough to carry on a basic conversation. He knew that he was a major star in Italy and wanted to be able to talk to the Italians.

He and Gina quickly became friends. Unlike Sophia Loren, her main rival at the time for the queenship of Italian cinema, who was the product of a grimy slum, Gina came from a middle-class background and had quickly become an elegant lady. In fact, she was, at the time of her work with Rock in 1961, one of the pillars of Roman society. Her home was an exquisite villa, where she entertained lavishly.

In the normal course of events, she invited Rock to a dinner party at her villa, and he was delighted to accept. It was black tie—and Rock, of course, looked as though he had been born to wear black tie.

"Tom," he told me, "I have never before or since seen anything quite as elegant as that dinner at Gina Lollobrigida's. There was a footman behind every guest and the table setting was out of a museum. The villa itself is almost a museum—magnificent art on all the walls and lovely statues in the garden and the rugs and everything else were incredibly beautiful."

Rock had been practicing his Italian diligently with the help of Mario, the driver the studio had assigned him. Driving back and forth between the hotel and the studio, Rock and Mario had talked nothing but Italian and Mario (he became such a good friend that whenever we went to Rome, Mario was always with us) had coached Rock so he could speak the language fairly well. Or, at least, Rock felt he could speak it fairly well.

So, at the dinner, Rock felt emboldened to speak Italian. After all, he was with an Italian group. Gina had seated him at her right; on Rock's other side was a splendidly gowned Italian dowager. Like every other woman at the table, she was decked out in expensive jewelry and her gown had obviously come from some great Parisian or Roman couturier. She oozed elegance.

Rock and Gina talked a while and then, to be polite, he turned to the lady on his right and smiled at her.

"How are you, signor?" she said, in Italian. He was pleased that he understood her perfectly, and he carefully framed his reply in his mind before he said it.

Just as he uttered it there was one of those inexplicable moments that occur at dinner parties, when there is a few seconds of coincidental silence. As nobody said a word, Rock's reply rang out clearly for all to hear. He thought he was saying "I am very well, thank you," but that is not what he actually said.

"I am very beautiful, thank you," he said, and the assembled guests roared with laughter, pointing fingers at him and choking on their vintage wine.

Rock laughed about it when he told me, but it wasn't funny to him at the time. He was mortified.

"I felt like such a stupid hick," he said to me. "I realized just how ignorant I was. And, at that precise moment, I told myself I was going to do something about it. Nobody was ever going to laugh at me again for being stupid."

That was when he set about to upgrade his mind and started his program of intellectual self-improvement. Besides his reading of things like the encyclopedia, whenever we were going on a trip he would make it a point to study up on the place we would be visiting. When we got wherever we were going, he would visit the important spots—not museums so much as historic sites. In Paris, for example, we might go to the Louvre for an hour but we would linger at the Place de la Bastille for half a day. Over the years he acquired a tremendous amount of knowledge that way, and he had the kind of mind that retained what he learned.

He read voraciously; we both did. That was another of the many things we had in common. I always preferred fiction, while Rock devoured biographies. He had an account at Hunter's, a major Beverly Hills bookstore, and they would send him every new biography that was published. Automatically. He read quickly, galloping through a book in an evening or two. Between us, we read every book of importance. Plus, of course, we subscribed to many magazines and newspapers. His favorite was the *National Geographic*. He read every word in every issue as soon as it got to the house.

And yet, with all that learning he acquired, and all the polish and savoir faire that came to be part of his personality, he was still pretty downhome.

He looked great in tuxedo or tails, but he preferred scruffy jeans and an old shirt, maybe even one that was torn and dirty. I kept after him to dress better when we went out, but he said he just couldn't be bothered.

I told him that, as an actor, he was a commodity, and that how he looked was the raw material on which his career was based, at least in large measure. Once he got a part strictly because the wife of a producer had seen a picture of him in a magazine, a picture of him coming out of a pool. He looked so handsome, so virile, so sexy that this lady suggested him to her husband—pillow talk is important in the Hollywood scheme of things—and that's how Rock was cast in the movie, *Pretty Maids All in a Row*.

So I told him he had to look good whenever he was out of the house, because you never know who might be watching. My advice was largely ignored. One of our favorite spur-of-the-moment things was to hop in the car, buzz down the hill to Beverly Hills, go to the little Brighton Cafe, and get one of their delicious meat-loaf sandwiches. It might not be cordon bleu, but it was something we both liked.

So he'd say, "Come on, Tom, I feel like a meat-loaf sandwich."

"You look like a meat-loaf sandwich, too," I'd say. "You can't go out looking like that."

He'd be in ratty old sneakers, a pair of awful old Levis, some shirt with holes in it.

"Suppose somebody sees you looking like that," I'd say.

"Look, we're not going to the Polo Lounge. We're just going to the Brighton Cafe for a meat-loaf sandwich. I don't have to wear something fancy to get a meat-loaf sandwich."

Sometimes I could persuade him at least to put on a shirt that didn't have holes in it. But other times he was adamant, and off we'd go in that holey shirt and the old Levis and the ratty sneakers. He'd be happy as a clam. And I felt like holding a newspaper in front of his face, like those Mafia crime bosses on their way to jail, so nobody would recognize him.

His extreme casualness about what he wore was, I believe, a symptom of his underdeveloped ego. For a movie star, however, a lack of ego is nothing to be proud of. It is a flaw in the character of a celebrity because, by the very nature of the beast, a celebrity should have some ego. A celebrity without an ego is like a shark without a fin—he can't make much progress. Rock Hudson was, in that regard, a celebrity in spite of himself.

He didn't behave like a celebrity should. As a publicist, I had observed enough stars to understand the breed. Having an ego (although I don't mean to the point of narcissism) is a tool of the star's trade. A person must, perhaps even should, believe he is pretty hot stuff to be a functioning star. He has to use that ego to propel himself through the shallow waters of rejection, to be able to survive the shoals of unemployment, to ride out the tempests of lousy reviews.

When Rock did the film *Darling Lili*, for Blake Edwards, he had a terrible time. Edwards and his wife, Julie Andrews, who was Rock's co-star, treated him badly. When Rock called me from Ireland and France to tell me all the gory details, I blew up at him.

"Look, Rock," I said, "you're a superstar. If you acted like one for once in your life instead of acting like some meek little day player, they wouldn't dare to treat you that way. Stand up for your rights and you'll get treated decently."

But he just couldn't do it. It wasn't in his make-up to cause a scene, no matter how righteous the cause or how great the provocation. So he let Julie Andrews walk all over him and he let Blake Edwards treat him like he was that meek little day player.

So, naturally, it became my job to see that Rock Hudson was treated like a Rock Hudson should be treated. During *McMillan & Wife*, if he had some complaint, he wouldn't do the complaining. He would tell me what was bothering him, and I would be Mr. Rotten.

I'd call the producer—Paul Mason originally, and later Jon Epstein—and say "Look, Rock isn't happy."

"Well, why didn't he say so? I can't read his mind. I'll fix it right away. No problem."

But Rock could never make that call. It just wasn't in him. It takes a large ego to throw your weight around, and Rock's ego was tiny.

One time he did make an attempt to throw some weight around and take advantage of his name and fame. It was a disaster.

That happened in Japan. He was on the board of directors of a company a friend of his had founded, and they had a board meeting in Hong Kong. If the meeting had been anyplace else, he probably would have said no, but at that point in his life he had never been to Hong Kong, so he jumped at the chance.

His friend, the company founder and president, mentioned that he was going on from Hong Kong to Japan. That was another place Rock had not yet visited, so he said "Hey, sounds great! Maybe I'll go with you."

"Terrific," said his friend. Rock loved spur-of-the-moment trips like that, so he and his friend packed their luggage, checked out of their hotel, and flew to Japan. At that time, Japan required a visa for entry. Because of the way the trip had been planned (or, rather, not planned) Rock had not had time to apply for a visa. So there he was, at the Tokyo Airport, trying to get into Japan without that required visa.

"I'm terribly sorry," he told the immigration official. "I didn't know that I needed a visa, and I didn't have the time to get one. And here I am."

He smiled his most winning smile.

"So sorry," said the official, smiling back. "Must have visa."

They discussed the matter a few minutes and then Rock decided, well, what the hell, this was one time he would play the star game.

"Sir," he said, "do you know who I am?"

"Oh, yes, Mr. Hudson. Like your firrums very much. Goodbye, please."

So he flew back to Hong Kong, and it wasn't until some years later that he paid his first visit to Japan.

I was never hesitant at using the Rock Hudson name to get places and do things. If we were going out, on one of our frequent spur-of-the-moment visits to whatever restaurant was currently in with the Hollywood crowd, I'd phone and say "I'm calling for Rock Hudson. Can he have a table for two at nine?" They were always happy to oblige; it never hurts a restaurant to have a superstar as one of its customers. They would make room for Rock, even if it meant booting somebody else to a table in the closet.

Rock particularly enjoyed going to a restaurant called Lawry's, famous for prime rib, but Lawry's was one of those places I hate because they don't take reservations at all. No matter who you are, you have to wait twenty or thirty minutes for a table. It wasn't safe for Rock to wait that long in a restaurant bar or lounge; he would be mobbed. So I would call and tell them that Rock Hudson was coming, and when we got there they would have a table waiting and whisk us in a side door, ahead of all the other people. It was the only way.

At all restaurants, and every public place where there were people crowding around him asking for autographs, I would be the heavy.

"Please, folks," I would say, "if Mr. Hudson signs one autograph, he'll have to sign a hundred. And that is impossible, so please be understanding and let him eat his dinner in peace."

And, since most people are decent, they would go away and let him be, although there would often be one or two who would grumble about Rock being too big for his britches, or some such expression.

Rock's taste in food ranged widely, from something as plebeian as a meat-loaf sandwich to the finest cuisine. He simply loved to eat. Naturally, for someone who loved to eat, weight was always a problem. Rock put weight on easily but, fortunately, he was able to take it off just as easily, too. If he was getting ready to do a film, he'd simply cut down for a week or do some exercising (which he hated) and he'd quickly be slim and trim.

Cutting down might have been physically easy for him to do, but psychologically it was always a wrench. He enjoyed high living and he was a party animal.

He did everything to excess. He drank too much, he smoked too much, he ate too much, he lived too much. I don't believe that that excess was a sign of self-indulgence so much as a symptom of his total zest for life and, what's probably more accurate, an insatiable curiosity. He yearned to taste every flavor life offered, sample every item on the world's menu. With him, however, a taste or a sample wouldn't really suffice: he gulped in large quantities. He never did anything halfway. When he did anything, he went all out. Full steam ahead.

He loved to go to parties—invite him and he'd be there—but, even more, he loved to give parties. If he found that a good friend was having a birthday, he would immediately start planning to throw a birthday party. His specialty was surprise parties that he told everyone about so nobody was ever surprised. That didn't matter. Like a big kid, he'd hide behind a sofa or in a closet and jump out and yell "Surprise!," and everybody would have a marvelous time.

I decided to turn the tables on him when he reached his forty-fifth birthday, and I planned a surprise party for him. But this was going to be a genuine surprise, except that blabbermouth Pat Fitzgerald told him all about it a few days before. I didn't know that she had told him, however.

So I went happily ahead with my plans. There was a village of restaurants on Santa Monica Boulevard, and Rock was particularly fond of the Mexican restaurant. I hired mariachis (one of his favorite kind of musicians), planned a great menu with the chef, and invited around fifty good friends.

And, on the big night, I said, "Hey, how about we go down to Verita's tonight. We'll have some of that great Mexican food, tortillas and maybe fajitas."

"No, let's not go out tonight," he said. "I really don't feel much like going out. Let's just stay home."

Well, I had fifty people waiting for us at the restaurant, and all that food and the mariachis and, knowing my guest list, I knew that the margaritas were flowing and half of them were probably already squiffed. And here was the guest of honor saying he didn't feel like going out.

"Oh, come on," I said. "It's your birthday, for heaven's sake.

You can't just sit home on your birthday. We have to do something. Come on, you love Mexican food. Get yourself out of the chair and let's go."

"Oh, well, OK," he said. "We can't have all those people waiting for us."

That's how I found out that he knew about the party, and had known all along. Then we both laughed all the way to the restaurant, and it didn't take us long to catch up to all our friends in the margarita-guzzling sweepstakes.

About four years later, he gave me a surprise birthday party when I turned forty. And he kept it very secret, so it was a total and complete surprise. It was a wild and wonderful evening.

When he reached his fiftieth year, I threw another party. This was at the house, so I didn't even attempt to make it a surprise. I had all the furniture taken out of the two living rooms and turned the place into one huge and gaudy cabaret.

It was a masquerade party; actors naturally love to put on costumes because, after all, playing make-believe is what acting is all about. Carol Burnett and Joe Hamilton (still married then) came as flappers. Juliet Mills and her husband (who had been married at the house in a wedding we had given for them) came as a pair of motorcycle gangsters and even drove in on a motorcycle. Nancy Walker, Olive Behrendt, David Craig, and Roddy McDowall dressed as autograph seekers and stood by the front door asking everybody who came in for their autographs. They all wore sweatshirts with Rock's name on them—misspelled. I borrowed kilts from the wardrobe department at the studio and came as a Scotsman.

When everybody was there, I gave the bandleader a signal and the band began playing "You Must Have Been a Beautiful Baby," and down the stairs came Rock—in a diaper.

When we were touring with *On the Twentieth Century* Imogene Coca was in the company. Rock's birthday was November 17 and Imogene's was the next day. On the night of November 17 that year we were in San Francisco, and I gave them a joint birthday party. I reserved a small ballroom in one of the Nob Hill hotels, hired some musicians, and the whole company was there. It was one more in our series of great parties.

Rock enjoyed life to the fullest but, like most people of that sort, he could fall into moments of depression. They were not deep, dark downs—nothing coming even close to manic—but simply blue moods. When those hit him, I would just leave him alone, let him wallow in the slough of his despair until nature and his basic ebullience pulled him out of it.

During those periods he would simply become quiet and introspective, just retreat within himself. I never did learn what he was thinking at those times. I seriously doubt if it was anything profound. Sometimes I would ask him if, for example, he was concerned about dying and he'd just laugh. No, that was not on his mind—and I doubt if it was much on his mind even later, when he *was* dying. At that time, I believe he was more concerned with his chances of living than with his contemplation of dying.

Few other people recognized those moody moments, because the effect on him was not startling or obtrusive. You had to know him very well, as I did, to be able to tell. When I could see the onset of such a period, I would simply leave him be. It would pass in an hour or so.

Those moods were not brought on by anything connected with his career. While he survived ups and downs, ins and outs, ons and offs in his career, he never brooded about those cyclical experiences. He recognized them for what they were, temporary blips on an otherwise smooth surface. He liked to work and was happiest when he was gainfully employed, but he could easily weather those periods of unemployment.

He often spoke of packing it all in and retiring.

"I'm really sick of this business," he said on more than one occasion. "I honestly don't care any more if I ever act again or not. I'm tired."

I would nod and say, "Sure, old buddy, whatever you say." But I knew he didn't really mean it. Working was the thing he enjoyed more than anything else, and those moments when he talked about retiring were aberrations. All that had to happen was for someone to offer him a movie role—good, bad, or indifferent—and he would jump at it.

But, between parts, while he might make some wild statement

about quitting the whole business, more often he would seize on that time to travel. He would say "Hey, Tom, let's go to Paris" or "You game for a few weeks in New York?" and away we'd go.

That is what made living with Rock Hudson such a sensational, exciting life. Money was never a concern. He had millions and I was very comfortable in my own right. The money was simply there and our only obligation was to spend it. If we felt like a trip to Paris or New York, we didn't have to think twice.

It was only later, when he was gone and I was alone and money was not so readily available, that I reflected back and realized what a great life he and I had had.

At the time, however, neither of us thought much about it. That was our life, period. It was such an ordinary event for us to pack up and leave at a moment's notice, or to buy whatever struck our fancy, or go to the fanciest restaurant and order whatever we felt like eating, that we came to accept that life-style as our due.

We did it all, whatever and wherever and whenever we wanted to. We lived lives that most people never even conceive of in their most elegant, imaginative dreams. We traveled all over the world. And, when we traveled, it was first class all the way. We booked the biggest and most luxurious suites in the fanciest and most luxurious hotels. We hired limousines and drivers, maids and butlers. Nothing but the best would do.

For a kid from Oklahoma City, strictly middle middle-class, I should have had the sense to look at myself and the life I was leading and say "Wow!" And so should Rock, who came from even humbler beginnings and should have said an even louder "Wow!" But neither of us did.

I don't honestly know if Rock ever gave it all a second thought. I know he enjoyed his life, but when he went to bed at night, I don't know if he ever reflected quietly on his intense good fortune. I suspect that he didn't. I suspect that, like me, he just accepted it all and, if he said anything to himself, he said just what I said: "Well, this is how it is."

He could spend thousands of dollars on himself, but he would tip the parking-lot boy who took his car a fast fifty cents. That was until I came along and began doing the tipping for both of us. His cheap tipping was not so much a product of niggardliness, but simply habit. When he first started tipping parking attendants, fifty cents was the going rate. It never occurred to him that the cost of tipping, like the cost of everything else, had gone up.

When I mentioned it to him, he was mortified, but by then I was doing the tipping, so his mortification was never put to the test.

Among our cars was a Rolls. When you leave a Rolls at a Hollywood restaurant, they always have to park it with special care. So they usually put it in a separate place, and that meant, I felt, they had to have a special tip. I used to give them five dollars and, when Rock saw me hand a parking attendant five dollars, he was astonished.

"That's just about what I made in a day when I was driving the truck," he said. But he didn't begrudge the boy the money, he was simply unaware and, consequently, amazed at how much tipping fees had inflated.

Money and its ramifications never concerned him. He had no personal responsibilities. He had seen to it that his mother was taken care of financially, and then she died. So there was no one, and no problems. Money therefore was simply something to spend— and there appeared to be no limit to how much money could be spent, no bottom to the pot of gold. When you have the millions he had (some people estimate his estate at $12 million, but I personally believe $20 million is more accurate), what's to worry? Even if the lower figure is the correct one, he had no concern about the future. He could buy a candy bar or a new car with the same ease.

Perhaps it was that feeling of total security that made him so at ease with the world around him and with the people in it. He made so few enemies that even his biographers could never find anybody who would say an unkind thing about him. The more a person worked with Rock the more he or she liked him. And he, in turn, liked everyone—with one or two exceptions. By and large, however, he was one of those rare people who found good in everyone, and that feeling was reciprocated.

About the only thing that disgruntled him was his name. Even though almost everyone came to call him Rock—even his mother called him Rock—he never liked the name. When he was doing a promo for one of his television shows, for example, and the script called for him to say "Hello, I'm Rock Hudson and I hope you'll watch my show this coming Sunday evening at eight o'clock," he couldn't bring himself to say it. Instead, he'd say "Hello, I hope you'll watch my show this coming Sunday evening at eight o'clock," and they would superimpose his name beneath his face.

Most people called him Rock. I called him Rock, except when we were someplace where I didn't want people to notice him; then I called him Roy. He didn't mind it when people called him Rock, but he just couldn't bring himself to say the name. I think he always thought of himself as Roy.

My own theory is that the name Rock really hurt his life. He would have liked to have been thought of as a serious actor, but nobody would ever take a person named Rock seriously. I think he would have liked to have been taken seriously as a human being as well, but people named Rock are thought of as jokes. I know he desperately wanted to be a director, but I believe he was afraid to make that step, even though a lot of us urged him to do it, because I think he felt his name was too frivolous for such a serious calling as directing. Perhaps, had he remained Roy Scherer or Roy Fitzgerald, he might have led an entirely different life. But, perhaps he might not have achieved the fame that Rock Hudson did.

CHAPTER THREE
Early Years

When I met Rock, he was fully grown, so all I know about his childhood, teens and young manhood is what he told me. And he wasn't one to reminisce much. What I learned came in dribs and drabs, usually sparked by something we did together or something I said about my own beginnings.

My childhood had been the stuff of television sitcoms; his had been just the opposite. But there were some common areas in our histories. Both of us came from what can loosely be called the Midwest—Illinois in his case, Oklahoma in mine. Both of us grew up in the post-Depression, pre-World War II years. Both of us sprang from a WASP heritage. And, the most amazing of all the coincidences, we had both driven a small truck as our first job.

My trucking days, for Grey's Floral in Oklahoma City, were in the summer and during school holidays while I was going to college. I delivered flowers in my little truck all over Oklahoma City.

Oklahoma City was pretty large, certainly by Oklahoma standards, but it still had a lot of the small town about it. At least, it was small-townish in the part of the city in which I grew up. We had the wide streets and big old houses with gracious front porches that one associates with small-town living. Lots of flowers and friendships.

Those were difficult years for America, those years during and immediately after the Depression. And they were difficult years, I can see in retrospect, for our family. At the time, of course, they didn't seem difficult to me; children know only what they experience personally and, without a basis for comparison, I just thought that everything was fine, normal, and contented. I didn't know any better.

But things weren't fine. My father, who was in the insurance business, had some tough years. Then, to make matters worse, we were invaded by relatives.

My rich uncle went broke. He was determined to recoup his fortune and left for Mexico City (I still have no idea what he did there) leaving his family with us. So there was our immediate family— mother, father, and Judith, my younger sister—and now there was my aunt and her twins.

For a time, in order to support that whole gang, my father held down two jobs. Besides continuing with his insurance business, he also sold radios in a big downtown department store.

I grew up loving the movies. The Ritz, our neighborhood theater, had three different bills every week, each a double feature. One bill played Sunday, Monday, and Tuesday; then they changed and two more pictures played on Wednesday and Thursday and, finally, a third bill showed on Friday and Saturday. I would see them all, or as many of them as I could—the admission was a quarter, I think. Popcorn was a dime and a Coke was a nickel. Later, during high school, when I began dating, the Ritz was still the place to go and, afterward, we'd go to the malt shop next door for a hot dog and a Coke.

Sometimes, on Saturday, I would spend all day at the Ritz, until somebody from home would come and pull me out of the theater and drag me home.

I don't remember where I got the money for all those movies and all that popcorn and Coke. We were certainly not rich, but I imagine my father would slip me the change on Saturday mornings.

"You were so lucky to have had such a nice, normal, happy childhood," Rock always said to me after I told him anything about my early years. "Boy, how I wish I would have had your father!"

My father was great. Much later, when I was old enough to have formed some opinions, I learned that he was actually something of a bigot. After I grew up, I got into major disagreements with him about that part of his personality.

As a boy, I remember seeing very few blacks in my part of Oklahoma City. And the first time I became conscious of even knowing a Jewish person was when I was in high school. One of my good pals in school was a girl named Dorothy Roth. We had both been active in school plays and were in a lot of the same classes and the same activities.

One day, in the middle of December I asked her, casually, what she was doing for Christmas. That was, of course, a major holiday for our family, and as the great day approached we began making major and exciting plans.

"Nothing special," Dorothy said. "We don't celebrate Christmas."

I was stunned. Not celebrate Christmas? Unthinkable.

"Why not, for Heaven's sake?"

She looked at me as though I was pretty stupid, which I suppose I was. And then she said the reason they didn't celebrate Christmas was because they were Jews.

Now I was even more stunned. I was probably fifteen or sixteen and, while I must have heard of Jews, as far as I had known I had never seen one. But here, out of the clear blue Oklahoma sky, I suddenly learned that a good friend was a real, honest-to-God Jew. It was a shocker. But it was also a marvelous lesson, because I liked Dorothy and I learned in one powerful lesson that Jews are basically the same as everybody else.

To my father's credit, he never tried to infect me with his own bias or bigotry. A few years later, when the Depression slipped away and my rich uncle had recouped his fortune and he and his family had left, and my father's own financial status had improved, he hired a black woman to work in the house. May Ella was her name, and my father always treated her like one of the family.

When I told Rock about May Ella, he laughed.

"We never had any servants," he said. "In fact, my mother was kind of a servant."

He had grown up in Winnetka, a pretty wealthy town in Illinois, but his family wasn't one of the rich ones. He never told me how it was that the Scherers—his mother and father—happened to be in Winnetka in the first place, but they were. Rock was only three or four when his father abandoned them, and that's when Katherine, Rock's mother, had to do a lot of menial work to survive and support her son.

One of her jobs was playing a piano in a silent movie theater. Talkies didn't come to Winnetka until around 1930, when Rock was five. Katherine would take him to the theater with her, seat him on a stool beside her, and caution him not to make a sound. So Rock toddled his way to the theater often in those formative years, and he told me his first ambition was to be an actor.

"And except for a brief period when I wanted to drive a Greyhound bus," he told me, "I think I wanted to be an actor from then on."

Another of his mother's jobs was being a laundress, and one of Rock's earliest memories was going with her to the homes of ritzy people in Winnetka and having to stay in the kitchen while his mother did the washing. Because he was told to sit there and be a good little boy and be quiet, he sat quietly and watched while his mother dumped the clothes into the washing machine and, later, ironed the sheets and shirts and underwear of the rich people. Somehow, he realized it was demeaning.

But most of his childhood years were demeaning, and instinctively he knew that too.

The only stability in his life was Katherine, his mother, and she was a real rock in his pre-Rock days. She was a tall, strong, intelligent woman who had, however, a tendency toward bigotry. I remember how she merely tolerated Milton Bren, Claire Trevor's husband, because he was Jewish. And the Brens were probably Rock's and my closest friends, particularly after we got the New York apartment. Rock would always get angry whenever his mother evinced her bigotry.

Like most people in show business, Rock had no prejudices about race, color, or creed—or anything except, possibly, unprofessionalism.

Show business people are, generally, the most tolerant of any profession. I believe that is because there are people of assorted faiths, colors, and beliefs involved in the business, often in high places. If you have any sort of prejudice, you will almost certainly have a tough time getting ahead in show business, because inevitably one day you will find yourself working for, or with, a member of whatever group you hate.

Katherine's only other weakness was in her choice of men to marry. Rock's biological father, Roy Scherer, and his stepfather, Walter Fitzgerald, were the kind of young men mothers warn their daughters about. But Katherine Wood, warned though she was, married both and lived to regret both marriages.

Scherer just walked out the door one day and never came back. It isn't a new story, or one that is particularly unusual or dramatic. Merely a terribly sad story for the ones who are left behind.

As was perhaps only natural, the Scherer family blamed Katherine. Still, they helped her out somewhat; they were mostly farm families, and they would stop by with baskets of produce and eggs from time to time. During the summers, they would invite Roy, Junior (but never Katherine) to come out and spend a month or so with them down on the farm. So Rock's summers were healthy, although he missed his mother.

Later, when Rock had become a big movie star—and, again, this is also probably natural—they all came out and proclaimed their love for him and their admiration for Katherine. But that was much later, and it was no help to Katherine and her struggles when she was trying to raise her son single-handed.

The Scherers were never overtly unpleasant to her, merely cold. They assumed she must have done something to cause Roy, Senior, to walk out on her. After all, because he was their son, nephew, cousin, whatever, he could do no wrong. So, those baskets of food aside, she had no help from the Scherers. Her own family helped her, of course, but she wanted desperately to make her own way, and eventually she did. Doing laundry was her way of doing that.

Then along came Wally Fitzgerald, tall and handsome in his Marine uniform. Most of Katherine's friends warned her about him, too. He drank too much, they said, and was inclined to belligerence and got into a lot of brawls. But, because she thought her son needed a father and she was lonely, she ignored the warnings and married him. And he kept on drinking and he kept getting into fights, and he beat her and he beat the boy—who became Roy Fitzgerald—and proved to be a total louse.

One Christmas Katherine bought Rock a Flexible Flyer sled. It was something he had wanted desperately; all the other kids had them. She had saved up and bought it for him. It was his main, probably only, present that year, but it was enough. Now he'd be able to join his pals in belly-flopping down the streets and coasting down the hills. It was under the tree on Christmas morning with the mandatory big red bow attached.

What's more, it snowed that particular Christmas day, and Roy ran outside with his brand-new sled.

"Hey, look what I got!"

And he began running down the street, to get up speed, and then took off, belly-flopping with his beautiful new sled, and crashed right into a tree. He wasn't badly hurt—a few bumps and bruises—but the sled was totaled. Splinters and twisted iron runners.

When he finally got up enough nerve to go home, Walter Fitzgerald beat him badly.

"That's the last time you get a present, you little son of a bitch," he said. And, as long as Fitzgerald was his stepfather it was, indeed, the last present he ever got. Katherine might want to give her son a present, for his birthday or at Christmas or whenever, but Fitzgerald wouldn't allow it.

He had told that story to a few people he felt close to, among them Jack Scalia, who played his son on *The Devlin Connection*. When Rock was dying, Scalia brought a new, shiny Flexible Flyer sled as a gift. For a few moments Rock's eyes lit up as he contemplated the first sled he had had since that one he wrecked with such heavy consequences. That sled was still in his room when he died, and it could have been the last thing Rock ever saw.

Katherine eventually had enough of Walter Fitzgerald and his bullying behavior. This time, she was the one who did the walking out.

I had had a stepparent, too, but my story was completely different. When I was eleven or twelve, my mother found she had cancer and began a long, lingering, losing, and very painful struggle. Near the end, she was in such excruciating pain that she couldn't even bear the weight of a sheet across her frail body.

I would read to her. I remember reading *Gone With the Wind* to her in her last weeks. She had a wash cloth over her private parts because that was all she could tolerate. But she was enthralled by the story of Scarlett O'Hara and Rhett Butler, and I read every word of the book to her before she died. I was thirteen.

A couple of years later my father remarried, and I was fortunate again. My stepmother, Mary, a lady I now think of as my mother, came into my life, and she is a treasure. She and my father had a son, Harold, Junior, who was born when I was in high school. He and I have become very close.

My sister Judith is a typical old-fashioned girl. She married soon after she graduated from college and now has three grown daughters of her own. We always got along very well, although our interests and our personalities were totally dissimilar.

Rock had no siblings, and envied me mine. It was always just him and his mother against the world.

In 1979, when he was on the road with *On the Twentieth Century*, the company played Chicago, which is very close to Winnetka. Many of his old friends came to see him and, in fact, gave a big party for him. One Sunday, when the theater was dark, we drove to Winnetka and he took me on a tour. That was one of the few times when he opened up about his childhood. As we drove around, he pointed out to me the sights that were important to him as a boy.

"That house there," he said, pointing to a huge mansion set back from the street, "is where I had my first job as a kid."

He had been hired by the owner to put up the storm windows and take down the screens in the fall and reverse the procedure in the spring. He did that for a few years until the owner did something that made him angry—he couldn't remember what the offense had been—so he misnumbered all the screens and storm windows and walked out. He laughed as he told me about it, thinking of the way his replacement would have had to struggle to untangle the mess he had left.

"Served them right," he said. "And that house over there, on the corner, that's where my mother did the laundry and I used to have to sit in the kitchen and wait for her. Hours and hours I'd wait."

We came to another corner where there was a drugstore.

"It's still there," he said. "That's amazing that it's still there. That drugstore—see the windows on the second floor? That's where we lived for a couple of years while I was in high school. There's a little apartment there, and that was our home—just two rooms, but it was all Mom could afford."

His friends mostly lived in the mansions. Winnetka has a lot of mansions. His friends would invite him to their homes, but he couldn't reciprocate. After all, he couldn't very well invite those rich kids to visit him in those two rooms over the drugstore. He had grown up embarrassed by the disparity between what he had and what others had, and that embarrassment colored his entire adolescence.

He pointed out the park which the authorities flooded over in the winter, for the kids to ice skate. The malt shop where they hung out. And New Trier High School.

I think there is a misconception about the beautiful and handsome Hollywood stars. The public assumes that, because they are such incredibly attractive people as mature adults, that was always the case. It doesn't necessarily follow.

Rock, for example. As Roy Fitzgerald, practicing teenager, he was far from the most popular boy in his class. I believe that I was much more popular in Central High School in Oklahoma City than Rock was in New Trier High School in Winnetka. We used to talk about it often, comparing our relative positions in our high school pecking orders.

His problem was that he was gawky, awkward, ungainly. He was tall, already six foot-four, as a high school kid—but he only weighed maybe ninety pounds. A walking, talking beanpole.

That physical condition was, I suspect, attributable to several factors, not the least of which was a borderline case of malnutrition. Living in that tiny apartment over the drugstore (Rock had to sleep on the living room sofa) was bad enough, but Katherine made only survival wages. Macaroni and cheese was the staple of their diet. And, often, they did without the cheese.

Besides, he was a typical teenager—hyperactive, racing around, burning off the few calories he consumed.

So his physical appearance was not the commanding presence it later became. He had his raw good looks but didn't know how to capitalize on them. He was, therefore, only marginally accepted in that school, where the majority of students came from affluent, if not downright rich, families.

Not only couldn't he keep up with the Joneses, he had a hard time keeping up with the Smiths. He would be invited to parties but wouldn't go: he didn't have the proper clothes for those swanky affairs. He didn't have a car, of course. Because he couldn't afford to buy the latest hit records or go very often to the movies, he couldn't converse knowledgeably about the hot singing stars or the latest movie idols. He saw a few movies, mostly anything with either Lana Turner or Ava Gardner, but very few.

While his high school years were about midway between rotten and passable, I had a great time during mine.

Mostly I was into dramatics. I had the lead in both our junior class and senior class plays. The play we did in my junior year was a farce the name of which, mercifully, I have forgotten. But I did have one line which is forever etched in my throbbing brain:

"Resume your fancy checked trousers, Uncle. I have decided to live."

Try saying that fast a few hundred times. In my senior year, we did the lovely *January Thaw*. I won the Maskers Award, the top prize for acting in school, both years.

If that had happened to me today, I think I might have given serious thought to pursuing an acting career. But, in those days, in that place, the idea of becoming an actor seemed so far beyond me that I never even considered it. And, I suppose, I lacked the necessary drive. I have met enough actors by now to realize that most of them decided early on that they wanted to act, and nothing ever stood in the way of that ambition. They just went out and did it, and it is that total dedication that distinguishes those who succeed from those who only grasp wistfully at the glamorous straws.

While the acting was fun for me and I might have thought it would be marvelous to be an actor, what I really wanted to do was to write. I was one of those youths who grew up with the absolute conviction that one day I would write a novel that would sweep the world off its feet. The Great International Novel, never mind just American.

And so, when I went to the University of Oklahoma, I took all the creative writing courses I could cram into my schedule. But I never had a chance to write (the oldest excuse known to man). After college I went right into the Air Force. While I was in the service, I got married and had a child. And so, when I got out, I had to go to work to support my family.

I told myself that one day, when I had the time and a bit of financial independence, *THEN* I would write that important novel. I'm still waiting for that time to come.

Of course, it didn't take me long to recognize my own literary limitations. When I had to write press releases at MGM, I found that I was an adequate writer, but I soon realized there was not a major novelist lurking behind my press releases.

Rock and I, as we reminisced, found several areas of similarity. One was the fact that both our family trees had farmers dangling from their limbs, and as a consequence, we had both spent some summers down on the farm.

The Scherers, as I have said, would invite Rock to visit one of their farms for a month or so every summer while he was growing up. Katherine, never included in that invitation, was torn. She hated to be the poor relation and hated accepting charity from the family of the man who had walked out on her. And yet she knew that that time in the country, in the bracing fresh air with those heaping helpings of fresh-from-the-fields foods, was great for her son's health. So she swallowed her pride for his well-being.

With me it was a different story. The farmers were all on my mother's side, the Tiller side (which I always thought was a great name for a family of farmers). All of my mother's brothers had farms and her sisters had married farmers, all located in the country around Oklahoma City. So I was sent to one or another of my aunts and uncles each summer through my childhood.

It wasn't just play time; I became one of the hands and had to earn my keep. Mostly, since summer was threshing time on the wheatfields, I was the water boy, carrying buckets to the threshing machines so their thirsty crews could drink their fill.

It was a good life, because the Oklahoma farm people were a big-hearted, generous lot. They would all pitch in to help each other at harvest time. And the wives and daughters would set up long trestle tables, heaped with good food and plenty of it, at lunch time for all the hands—and that included me. Since I was a worker (water boy is a vital cog in the threshing machinery) I ate with the menfolk and sat next to them on the benches and partook of all that great food.

At college the fun continued. I became a member of the prestigious Sigma Chi fraternity and I guess I majored in having fun. I took courses that interested me—writing primarily—and those I enjoyed. But I ditched the others as much as was humanly possible and just managed to scrape through.

I had always worked, to give myself pocket money and to ease the burden on my family as much as possible. During my high school years, I had a part-time job in the Carnegie Library. I worked hard, but I also had plenty of time to read. So, by the time I entered college, I had read most of the books I would be assigned to read in my college courses. That left me a lot of time for collegiate fun and games.

Mine was the era of panty raids and all that lovely foolishness. It may have all been dumb, but, at the time it was a great deal of sport. And fraternity parties. We would go out at night and park ourselves in front of a sorority house and serenade the girls in our quaking but eager baritones, a can of beer in our hands and love in our souls. Since the girls were all from good families (and you know what they say about girls from good families) it often followed that our serenade bore fruit, or whatever it is that serenades bear, and we would be invited in to the sorority-house living room for milk and cookies, and so forth.

No such happy high jinks for Roy Fitzgerald, Rock-to-be. No college and no fraternities and no serenades. When he was in high school, there was a war on (he was sixteen at the time of Pearl Harbor) so he joined up as soon as he could. For young men like him, without much in the way of a promising future, the war was a great chance to escape from what threatened to be a heroically humdrum life.

He told me that he could hardly wait until he was eighteen so that he could enlist. And so, a few days after that milestone birthday, he took himself down to the Navy enlistment office and signed the papers. He was sent to the Great Lakes Naval Training Station and became a sailor.

By the time he had finished his training and was ready to go to sea, the war was virtually over. He did ship out and always remembered that thrilling moment when the transport on which he sailed steamed under the Golden Gate Bridge on its way out of San Francisco Harbor to the far, romantic, perilous Pacific.

Even though the war was fast winding down, there was still the danger of a kamikaze pilot slamming into a ship. The young boys on the ship, including Rock, were somewhat thrilled, somewhat scared, as their vessel made its just-at-dawn passage under the bridge. To give their spirits a boost, the ship's loudspeaker system played a hit record of the moment, "Sentimental Journey." The singer was Doris Day.

Rock says that many of the boys on the ship wept as Doris' clear, unmistakable voice sang those emotional words. Many years later, when he and Doris had become the hottest screen team, he told her that story.

"I told her how much that song and her voice had affected all of us," he said to me.

"What did she say?" I asked.

"She just looked at me and said 'Oh,' and walked off. For some reason, she wasn't impressed."

During the time he was in the Navy, I believe he had a romance (or maybe that's overdignifying the relationship, and it should be called simply an affair) with a woman. He was always a bit reluctant to tell me the details, but his mother knew about it, and I was able to piece the story together from the fragments he told me and the more substantial chunks she told me.

He had come home on leave to Winnetka and run into a girl he had known in high school. The affair wasn't with this old school chum, but with her mother. It was a quickie—a weekend thing, maybe no more than a one-nighter.

A few years later Katherine told me, after Rock had become a star or at least was on the verge of stardom, a letter came to Rock from Winnetka. Katherine was then still opening all his mail; later, when he became a superstar, the volume of mail was so enormous she couldn't handle it herself, and Rock retained one of the fan-mail services. But, fortunately, she was the one who intercepted this particular letter.

"Here came this letter," Katherine told me one evening, "and it was from this lady in Winnetka, and she was telling Rock that she was the lady he had had sex with when he was in the Navy and came home on a pass. And she went on to say that as a result of that sex she had had a baby—and the baby was definitely Rock's. What's more, she said it was a boy and looked just like Rock."

"Do you think she was telling the truth?" I asked. "Rock's never mentioned it to me."

"No, he wouldn't," she said. "It's not something he'd be proud of. But, I think that, yes, it could have happened."

"What did you do? Did you show him the letter?"

No, she hadn't. She had called the woman on the phone and, as we used to say in Oklahoma, she laid her to filth.

"I knew that that lady's reputation was pretty bad. So I told her that if she persisted with her story I'd see to it that everybody in Winnetka found out what kind of a lady she really was. And what I told her was the truth, because I knew all about her and knew she had slept with half the city."

That was the end of it, but later on Rock did mention to me a few times the possibility that he had a son back in Winnetka. Some of his old high school pals had come out to see him in California and had mentioned that there was this boy back there who looked just like him.

"He's the spittin' image of you, Rock," one of those old friends said.

Rock was intrigued. He always loved children, and one of his great disappointments was not having any of his own. So the possibility that he might have a son back in Winnetka was exciting to him. For a while he talked of going back and trying to find the boy, but he knew that would be opening up a can of worms that could easily turn into a keg of rattlesnakes. Both his mother and I advised against it. I am sorry now that I took that position, because it might have made his last years more pleasant.

He also said that he was concerned for the woman's image in Winnetka. He knew that she was married; it was probable that her husband was under the impression the boy was his son. It could have hurt the woman, the husband, and maybe the boy as well if he had gone back there and claimed that he was the father.

"Leave well enough alone," both his mother and I cautioned him, and he left it alone, although I have never been sure if what he left alone was really well enough.

Like me, Rock had dreams of being an actor while he was growing up. Also like me, he didn't believe a nobody from nowhere had a chance at an acting career.

His childhood ambition to act had been set aside when it seemed one of those impossible dreams. It wasn't until some years later, when he saw the movie *Hurricane*, with Jon Hall, that it surfaced again. He had always been a fine swimmer and swimming was about all Jon Hall did in that movie—swim and fight the winds. Rock told me he felt he could handle a part like that. Once again the idea of acting popped into the forefront of his mind. But it still seemed like too big a mountain to climb. (Later, when he started his film career, he met a stunt man who told him he had doubled most of Jon Hall's swimming scenes, and Rock was devastated.)

After he left, New Trier High became a leader with its theatrical program (Charlton Heston preceded him at the school; Ann-Margret followed him) but, at the time Rock was an undergraduate, there was only a very ordinary and very superficial drama course.

But, even then, the school was progressive. It had a system of no exams and classes only if the student felt like attending. Most of the time, Rock didn't feel like attending. If the weather was good, he would much rather go to the beach. That, plus the fact of the war, contributed to his lack of studying.

He matured somewhat during his Navy service. When he got out, he told his mother he wanted to go to college. She was pleased by the decision, but less pleased when he announced that the college he wanted to attend was in California. Actually, the reason for that choice was less the quality of California education than the chance to visit his real father.

He had learned that Roy Scherer, Senior, was living in the Los Angeles area and he was consumed by the desire to see his father. There had been, Rock told me, some communication between father and son—his mother never knew about that—and an invitation had been extended and accepted. So he packed his few meager possessions, cashed his Navy discharge bonus check, and took off for Los Angeles. He was quickly disillusioned.

Roy, Senior, had another family by the time he arrived in California, and suddenly being invaded by a down-and-out ex-sailor he hardly knew was not calculated to increase domestic tranquillity in the Scherer household. The rosy fantasy Rock had created about being welcomed eagerly by his father quickly evaporated.

He was also disillusioned about the prospects of higher education. He wanted to go to either USC or UCLA, probably because those were the two glamour institutions in southern California. Or maybe they were the only two he had ever heard of at the time. But he couldn't get in either, not with his poor high school academic record. Even though both schools were making allowances for war veterans at the time, they had to maintain certain standards. And Roy Scherer, Junior, by any standards, was not USC or UCLA caliber.

So he drove a truck, a delivery truck for a grocery-supply firm.

Rock did that for a year or so. He became a member of the Teamsters' Union and, long after it became necessary for him to do so, he
kept up his membership. He paid his dues regularly for many years.
In and around Hollywood studios, the Teamsters have a lot of clout.
Once, on location, he drove his car around the site where he was
filming, which is forbidden by the union—only Teamsters members
are permitted to drive on movie locations—and a union steward
rushed over to his car and stopped him.

"You should know better than that, Rock," the union man said.
"You know you can't drive your car here."

"I can't?" Rock said, pulled out his wallet and displayed his
Teamsters card to the steward, and drove off happily. He told me
that brief but gratifying incident was one of the highlights of his
life.

Rock never talked much about those early years in California. It
was not a happy time. Like so many young men of that generation,
he was at loose ends, drifting, not sure what (if anything) he wanted to do with his life.

Gradually the idea of becoming an actor fought its way out of his
deep subconscious mind, where it had been stewing from the time
of his high school fantasies, and penetrated his conscious mind.

What happened to cause that notion to surface?

From what he said, it was a combination of several factors. He
needed to make a living; that was the primary factor. And truck
driving, while it paid the bills, wasn't satisfying. He knew he didn't
want to drive a grocery supply truck forever.

Also, increasingly, it dawned on him that he was better-looking
than the average guy. Girls turned around and stared with more
and more frequency, more and more openness. He was filling out,
working into the spare six-foot-five frame nature had given him.
He became less and less the awkward klutz, more and more the
hunk.

Third, the movie business was all around him. Every day something would happen to make him realize he was in the center of the
film industry—he'd pass a studio or see a star or come across a
place where they were filming.

If you live or work in the Los Angeles area, you will inevitably see some movie stars at first hand. You probably won't dine with them or get to chat with them, but you will see them in person—in a car stopped next to you at a traffic light, in a department store, across a crowded supermarket, somewhere. And, if you have any sensitivity, you will quickly realize that they are just ordinary mortals. Not gods or goddesses, not superhumans or angels, they are life-sized men and women.

When that realization struck Roy Scherer, Junior, he put two and two together: he was as good-looking as the movie stars he saw, probably better-looking; and he was right there in Hollywood. And so he began thinking in terms of an acting career.

With me and my career, it was always (until I woke up to my limitations) a question of making some money to tide me over until I wrote my prize-winning, best-selling novel.

When I graduated from the University of Oklahoma, I went to work for the Union Oil Company in their Houston office as a rookie in the public relations department. A few years later the company transferred me to the West Coast, an event that was fine with me. I had often visited California—I had relatives there—and I loved it.

So I liked my new surroundings but I wasn't happy with my old job. Most of it was boring, and I didn't find writing about the octane content of gasoline particularly exciting. I determined to make a change in my life.

By a happy coincidence, I was then dating a girl who worked at MGM. By a further, even happier, coincidence, she was in the studio's personnel department. When I told her how disgruntled I was with my job, she said she would keep her eyes and ears open, and shortly she told me there was an opening in the publicity department.

"But you'll have to start out as the department's office boy," she said. I was twenty-seven at the time and I was making a good salary at Union Oil, but I didn't care.

"See if you can hold that job until I come in for an interview," I said, and she agreed to do her best. As soon as I could, I showed up at MGM and my girlfriend arranged for me to meet the department head, Howard Strickling.

He hired me—as office boy, but he said everybody in his department had started as office boy, even the girls—and I happily joined MGM. This was in 1957, as twilight approached for the big movie studios. As I observed in the first chapter, there were vestiges of the old glory around, but those vestiges were fast disappearing. The studio had a handful of players still under contract (primarily Robert Taylor) but not many, and, more and more, it was becoming what it eventually became and is today—a rental lot.

Still, the ghosts were everywhere—Gable, Tracy, and the others—and I honestly felt that I could see them and hear them. Of course, it was only my overripe imagination, but nevertheless it was a constant thrill for me to walk into the dressing room that Greta Garbo had used or sit at the table in the commissary where Lionel Barrymore had eaten.

I worked like a little beaver, and I am absolutely certain that I was the best office boy the studio—or any other organization—had ever seen. In three months Strickling recognized my genius and made me an apprentice publicist. A few months later I became a junior publicist. And shortly, after only a year at the studio, I became a senior publicist. I had arrived at the pinnacle.

My first permanent assignment as senior publicist was to handle a television series the studio was making. It was based on the old hit *Dr. Kildare* movies, and they had found a new actor, young, handsome, and talented, to play Kildare on TV. His name was Richard Chamberlain.

Mostly, though, I did movie work. I handled Robert Taylor's last two films at the studio but occasionally worked on television shows such as *Dr. Kildare*.

It was all great fun, and I had a marvelous time. It was exciting and I felt I was being productive, helping the studio turn out films and TV shows that were successful. The icing on my cake was that I was working with the stars, people I had hitherto only read about. Now I knew them.

The MGM publicity department was a huge and talented group of people, the model for the entire industry. There were publicists whose only job was to work with fan-magazine writers, for example. There were publicists assigned to wire services, to newspapers, to trade papers. There were publicists assigned to each of the two great competing gossip columnists, Hedda Hopper and Louella Parsons.

For some reason, Hedda took a shine to me and so, naturally, Strickling called me in one day.

"From now on, Clark," he said, "you are Hedda Hopper."

That meant that I was her private, personal studio contact. I think it was Hedda's previous studio contact, Esme Chandlee, who touted her onto me. I don't think Strickling wanted to give me that assignment, but he had no choice; whatever either of those ladies wanted, they got. In fact, they even dictated the Christmas gifts they wanted the studio to give them.

One year, early in December, Hedda took me aside.

"Now, Tom, dear heart," she said, "I know that Howard Strickling very soon will ask you what you think the studio should give me this Christmas. Well, I saw this lovely alligator bag at Bullock's Wilshire. So when Howard asks you for a suggestion, you tell him about this bag, and tell him that Sophie, in Bullock's pocketbook department, knows the one I want, so you just call her and she'll make sure you get the right one."

You couldn't believe Hedda's house at Christmastime, and I'm sure Louella's was the same. There were so many cartons and boxes of gifts that you literally could not get in the front door of the house.

But it wasn't all receiving and no giving. At Christmastime, regular as clockwork, Hedda would give me an inscribed photo of herself. I still have several of them.

Handling those ladies was probably the trickiest assignment in the history of public relations. Hedda assumed I was working for her, and I had to remind myself constantly—and occasionally mention the fact to her—that I was actually on the MGM payroll. She wasn't paying my salary; the studio was, so my allegiance was to them.

She might be on the trail of a story involving an MGM star and would call me to confirm some juicy rumor she had heard. I might know the facts or I might not, but the point was that I could not tell her, one way or the other.

"Now, Hedda," I would say, "you can't put me in this position. If it comes out, everybody will know that you got it from me, and my bottom will be in a sling. Get the story from somebody else, so I can honestly tell Strickling that you didn't get it from me."

And Hedda would understand. She was very fair that way and, with all her ego and other faults, I liked her.

Actually, I know for a fact that Hedda (and undoubtedly Louella as well) had several MGM employes in key departments on her payroll. So she had plenty of other sources for the gossip that was the raw material of her column.

As a publicist, I had a shaky tightrope to walk—a couple of them, actually. With Hedda it was the tightrope between what I knew she wanted from me and my loyalty to the studio, whose employee I was. With some of the stars I worked with, it was a rope between what they wanted and what we (the department and I) felt would be good for the studio and the particular film or series. And there was always that narrow, quivering line between what the public wanted to know about the stars and what we felt we should tell them.

One of the difficult stars at the time was Patricia Crowley, who was in the then-hit TV series, *Please Don't Eat the Daisies*. She became notorious around our department for causing the publicist assigned to her show to be booted off. Five or six publicists, mostly junior, got transferred away from her show because they offended her in one way or another. At the time, she had such clout that she could call Strickling and say "I want that person replaced," and it would be done.

Whenever a publicist was told to move on, Strickling would call me into his office.

"Clark," he would say, "Crowley did it again. You go down to the set and hold her hand a while, until I figure who will be the next sacrificial lamb."

Down to the *Please Don't Eat the Daisies* set I would go, and there would be beautiful Pat Crowley, all sweetness and innocence, and she would look at me with surprise.

"Why, Tom, darling," she would say. "What on earth are you doing here? Whatever in the world happened to Miss [insert the name of her latest victim]? Why isn't she here?"

"The last I saw her," I'd say, "she was in the infirmary, getting the knife pulled out of her back."

I liked Pat, even though she was a dragon lady as far as the junior publicists were concerned. Actually, I liked all the stars I worked closely with—Bob Taylor, Dick Chamberlain, Glenn Ford. I did a picture with Debbie Reynolds, too—*The Singing Nun.*

But my special favorite was Greer Garson. She came back for *The Singing Nun,* to the studio where she had reigned as queen for so long. She was now married to Buddy Fogelson, one of those legendary Texas oil barons. But Buddy was never in good health and very often would be unable to take her to any of the many affairs to which she was invited. So, as I was the unattached one in the department, I would be asked if I would be Greer's escort for the evening. It didn't take much arm-twisting.

I thoroughly enjoyed going places with the lovely Greer Garson on my arm. She was—still is—a total lady, charming, witty, and wise as well as beautiful. Her only fault might be her tendency to talk too much. All you had to do was ask her one question, or make one statement, and then sit back and listen to a steady stream of Garsoniana for the next few hours. Since her voice is one of the most lovely sounds known to man, her garrulousness was not too hard to take.

I got to know Elizabeth Taylor somewhat then, although I would come to know her much better in later years. I was one of several publicists who worked on a big production at the studio, *Sandpiper.* It was big because the co-stars were Miss Taylor and Richard Burton, and they were then at the apex of their front-page romance.

They had done some location shooting for that film at Big Sur, in northern California, then came down to the studio for interiors. But because at the time the Burtons were having some problems with the Internal Revenue Service, they were required to leave the country for a time. MGM bundled everybody off to Paris, to accommodate Elizabeth and Richard, where they recreated both the exterior Big Sur locations and the interiors on a Paris sound stage.

I had hoped to get the assignment to accompany them, but I didn't. My Paris experience was still some years in the future.

One of my tightrope stunts was to try and please some fan magazine writers the studio (particularly Strickling himself) simply did not like. Actually, Strickling despised the entire breed; all fan-magazine writers were, to him, contemptible. Among the group that were consequently barred from the studio was Rona Barrett. At the time, she was a little, pitiful nobody, eager and ambitious—but that's about all you could say for her. I felt sorry for her.

I knew the poor little thing was only trying to earn a living, only trying to get ahead in a tough business, and I knew that her hopes of earning a living and getting ahead would be seriously jeopardized if she couldn't write about MGM stars and MGM pictures. So I would sneak her into the studio and onto the sound stages where big films and TV shows were being shot. She still remembers.

One of the young stars I worked closely with was Chad Everett. The studio brass at first felt he was going to be a major star in features and put him in several big films. He starred opposite Ann-Margret in *Maid in Paris* and was with David Niven in *The Impossible Years*; he had a big role in a film with Robert Taylor, and he was with Debbie Reynolds and Greer Garson in *The Singing Nun*. The studio had thought he would catch fire, but he didn't even smolder. I still think it wasn't Chad's fault, but simply a case of all those pictures being duds. Nobody can catch fire in a movie that is all wet.

They had Chad do the pilot for a television show called *The Mayor of the City*, and that didn't sell either. So the brass at the studio decided they had given him enough chances and dropped his contract.

Then they sold another TV series to CBS. The network said they liked the concept of the series (it was called *Medical Center*) but they didn't like the actor in the leading role. Instead, they said, they wanted the actor who had been in *The Mayor Of the City*, Chad Everett.

So MGM was forced to renegotiate a new contract with the actor they had just recently dropped. I was so happy for Chad, who was now very definitely in the driver's seat. When he had been dropped, I had gone to his house to try and cheer him up; now I went there again, and we celebrated. If they had kept him under contract, he would have had to do *Medical Center* for $300 a week. Now he could just about dictate his terms, and he and his agent drove a hard bargain. He wound up not only getting a big salary, but also owning a percentage of the show that, since it ran for seven solid seasons on CBS, turned out to be a bonanza, gold mine, and El Dorado all rolled into one.

MGM's attitude toward Everett typifies the Hollywood attitude toward actors in general. As Alfred Hitchcock is supposed to have said, "Actors are like cattle." In the MGM publicity department we, always knew that our first priority was the studio, next the particular project we were working on, and—last and least—the actor.

Rock and I used to talk about that attitude a great deal. As an actor, he naturally found it reprehensible. He felt, in common with most actors, that without actors there would be no drama. And, in the Hollywood of that era, without the star system there would have been no Hollywood.

"Actors are the foundation of Hollywood and the whole movie business," he would say, or sentiments to that effect.

"But without the studios," I would argue, "the actors would have no place to work."

It was a senseless, pointless, endless argument, roughly on a par with the one about which is more important to a song, the melody or the lyrics. But when someone is emotionally involved with one side or the other—as Rock was and as I was, although to a lesser extent—the argument goes on. And on.

Rock's experiences as an actor, early in his career, were such that he knew whereof he griped. Until he came under the control of the diabolical agent Henry Willson, he was bandied around, forced to wait in outer offices for auditions that were superficial, his ego was trampled and his self-confidence—at that point in his life practically nonexistent—dragged through a lot of muck and considerable mire.

Willson was the man who recognized that Roy Fitzgerald had something. To give him his due, he did have an eye for talent. And a gift for names. He was the one who invented Tab Hunter and Rip Torn and Troy Donahue and Chad Everett and all those odd, but effective, names. And it was Willson who changed Roy Fitzgerald to Rock Hudson.

No one will ever know, of course, if Roy Fitzgerald could have made it just as big without the name change. Willson went to his well-deserved grave convinced that the name change was solely responsible for the eventual stardom of Rock Hudson. But Willson was a man of a vast, cruel ego.

Like many people, he enjoyed the creation of a product more than the marketing of that product. His genius was in turning raw material into a marketable entity. He turned the rough, raw, unprocessed Roy Fitzgerald into the polished, urbane, handsome Rock Hudson.

And then he practically ignored him.

He was not a go-getter as an agent. Once Rock had achieved some success, Willson just sat back and waited for offers to come to him. A true agent is always out there, hustling. A true agent may become a pain in the butt, but his clients get the good parts. A true agent earns every decimal point of his percentage.

Whenever Henry Willson's name came up in conversation when I was around, Rock's knee-jerk reaction was to shake his head sadly and laugh a mournful laugh.

"That louse," he would say. "I used to see all the actors getting good parts and I was stuck in second-rate material. So I would say, 'Henry, you have to get out and beat the bushes.' And he would say, 'He who beats bushes gets bit by snake,' or some such nonsense."

Eventually, when Rock couldn't take it any more, he fired Henry Willson. He did it reluctantly, because he knew that he owed Willson a lot—not as much as Willson thought, but still a lot.

I was with Rock that day. I wasn't there at the exact moment the axe fell on Willson's neck, but that evening Rock was a guest on Jim Nabors' television show. I had been supposed to take Rock's mother to the taping.

"Let's all go together," Rock said. That was unusual, because ordinarily, when he did a show like that, he preferred going very early. So I asked him why.

"Well," he said, "I fired Henry Willson today and you know how he's threatened me."

Willson had made ugly threats, which Rock had repeated to me.

Willson had told Rock that, if he ever left him for another agent, he would throw acid in his face so he would be so scarred he could never work again. Rock took those threats seriously, because he felt that Henry Willson was just crazy enough to carry them out.

We went to the taping in a group, and there was Henry, but he hardly seemed upset at all. Katherine and I huddled protectively around Rock, but the object of our fear was as cheerful and friendly as a puppy. Not only was there no acid, not even an unkind word was spoken.

Some years later a weak, flabby old man named Henry Willson came to see Rock. He was broke, he said.

"Things are really bad for me, Rock," he said. "Would you take a second mortgage on my house? It would be a big help to me."

Rock agreed and signed the papers, assuming a second mortgage on the Willson property. He handed over a check for many thousands to the man, who almost licked his boots in abject thanks. A little later, Rock learned that the house already had a second mortgage on it. And a third. "Oh, well," Rock said. "Now I can sleep better at night."

He was kidding, of course, because his conscience, in the Willson relationship, was clear. And it had always been clear. But, with that act, he finally got Henry Willson off his back. And his mind.

What was ironic about Willson coming to Rock for money was that, years earlier, he had worked a deal with Universal, calling for Rock to make seven pictures at the studio. A company was formed called Seven Pictures Company, which Rock and Willson owned jointly. One of the pictures it made was the very profitable *Lover Come Back*.

Although Seven Pictures Company only made four pictures, it was still a very rewarding venture for the partners. And Rock was able to say to Henry at the time that that deal was his annuity.

"I said to Henry," Rock told me, 'Henry, take care of the money you're making from Seven Pictures and you'll be set for life.' But you know Henry and money."

I certainly did. Willson was the kind of man who would charter a plane, fly fifty people to Las Vegas, put them up in suites at the best hotels, take over a whole restaurant for a night, and feed everybody and his brother. It wasn't so much that his was a generous nature, but simply that money meant nothing to him.

Rock took good care of the money he made from that Seven Pictures deal; it was the foundation of his fortune. Henry Willson could have been just as well off but spent it all and died broke in the Motion Picture Country Home.

Willson undeniably helped Rock get started in the movie business. If nothing else, the agent got him invitations to big parties early in his career—and, in those days, it was vital to a young career to be seen around at those affairs.

Rock was so raw at first that he was constantly making gaffes. He once told me this story, about one of his very first big parties, to illustrate his total naiveté.

He drove up to the house where the party was being held and parked his own car on the street. He had to walk a block or so, because the streets were lined with cars. He had never heard of valet parking. The parking boys looked askance at this man walking into the house, but, by then, poor Rock couldn't do anything about it.

"As I walked in," he told me, "I heard one of my favorite records, a Judy Garland number, and I thought, 'Gee, that's nice, and what a great sound system! Judy's voice sounds so real.' Then when I got into the living room, I found that it was really Judy singing."

He looked around the room for a familiar face. Not much chance of that, since he knew very few people in town. But, surprise! He saw Van Johnson and his wife Evie, whom he had met before, and so he rushed over to the table where they were sitting and asked if he could join them. They were talking away when Lana Turner bounced over and sat down next to Rock. He had been mad about her, from a respectable distance, for years—as I had been and as I imagine every right-thinking boy was in those days.

So Rock was thrilled when Lana sat next to him. He thought she was something very special.

"But the first words out of her mouth when she sat down," Rock told me, "were 'Shit, shit, shit.' Something had ticked her off and she was swearing a blue streak. I don't know what I expected, but it wasn't that. I was devastated, A great big bubble had burst."

That night he had a car, so he must have been on his way. In his truck-driver days, he had had to take the bus to work every day. In fact, with Los Angeles sprawling over such a wide area and with the city's bus service notoriously poor, he had to take several buses and travel for an hour to reach the place where he worked.

One of the buses passed the 20th Century-Fox studio and, on several mornings, he noticed men and women in formal attire streaming in through the Fox main gate.

"I remember thinking," he told me, "that these movie people are really wild, because they must have stayed up all night partying, and now they were going to work, still in their party clothes. It wasn't until I was in movies myself that I realized those people were just dress extras, reporting to the set to film some party scene."

In his innocence, he leaped to many erroneous assumptions about Hollywood and the movie business. He thought, as so many outsiders still do, that it was a place of glamorous people, doing glamorous things, a place of continual fun and games. He learned, soon enough, that most of the glamour is superficial and that making movies is more hard work than fun and games.

He always loved the business, but he quickly learned the reality of it, and the reality is that Hollywood's glamour is a veneer, and beneath that skin-thin veneer is a solid substructure made up of very hard, tough work.

Rock fit in well, because he was a hard worker. He was a party person, yes, but he was, first and foremost, a professional.

He had grown up seeing his mother work hard, and he had worked hard at odd jobs through most of his teen years. So the work ethic was ingrained in his soul.

"Nobody is going to help you," his mother had said bitterly. She had learned that lesson the hard way. "You have to help yourself, that's all, and the only way to do that is to work your tail off."

Early in his life, Rock had believed that he had a friend and ally in the church. As a small boy, he had been taught to rely on the church and he had been dutiful in his attendance. But in what was probably the single most traumatic experience of his boyhood, he was disabused of that notion.

He was born a Roman Catholic, and Katherine dutifully took him to church every Sunday. For a time he even attended a parochial elementary school. And he served as an altar boy for a while, too, when he was seven or eight.

But then one day, at Mass, he committed some minor misdeed. It was so minor that he had forgotten just what it was when he told me about it. He had botched his job as altar boy in some small way, and the priest hit him.

When he came home, trying desperately not to cry, Katherine immediately sensed that something had happened.

"What's wrong, Roy?"

"N-n-nothing."

"Tell me now, son. What happened?"

"Well——" And then the whole story poured out, the little misdeed he had committed and the reaction of the priest. The boy pointed to the spot on his cheek where he had been struck and his mother could see that it was turning a bright red.

"You stay here," she said, put on her hat and coat, marched herself down to the church, and confronted the priest and told him off in her characteristically blunt way.

That was the end of their association with the church, and it was traumatic for Rock because, until then, he had been taught that the church was sacrosanct and should be a major force in his life, forever and ever amen. But now, suddenly, he was told just the opposite, that he didn't have to go to church, or Sunday school, that he was no longer a Roman Catholic, that religion no longer mattered.

And religion never mattered to him again.

All through his adult life he refused to become a member of any organized religion and did not consider himself a member of any particular sect or faith. Of course, when his mother died, Rock insisted that the memorial service be Roman Catholic. He said it might not help her, but it couldn't hurt.

I remembered that when Rock lay dying; I had a priest come in and gave him the last rites of the church. I am sure he was aware that that was happening, and I think he was pleased.

I don't know if it helped him, but it couldn't hurt.

CHAPTER FOUR
Family

I believe that when Rock died he had only two regrets.

First, he would have loved to have acted on Broadway.

And second (probably the one thing he regretted most in his entire life), he would have loved to have had a family.

The thought of that son he probably had, back in Winnetka, nagged at him through most of his later years. I believe if I, or any of his true friends, had encouraged him to hop on a plane and go back there and try to find him, he would have. But none of us felt it was a wise thing to do, so we never said "Rock, go." And he never went. But I am convinced he thought about it a lot.

As everyone knows, Rock Hudson did have a wife for a time. It has become fashionable lately to dismiss that marriage as something that was arranged by Henry Willson to quiet the rumors that Rock was homosexual.

What made that interpretation of the marriage sound reasonable was the fact that Rock's wife, Phyllis Gates, had worked for Willson as a secretary. So everyone figured, ah ha!, that sly old fox

Henry Willson arranged for his secretary and his top client to get married so those nasty rumors would stop.

But that simply was not the case.

What makes me positive is that, first, Rock told me he had loved Phyllis a great deal. And, second, he and Phyllis lived together for a year—a year of cohabitation that even Henry Willson was unaware of—before they got married.

Nobody lives with a woman for a year simply to prepare for an arranged marriage later on. The only reason the two lived together is simply that they had fallen in love and were consumed with passion. Rock had seen her in Willson's office and had asked her out on a date, and one thing had inexorably led to another.

Rock talked about Phyllis a lot to me those late evenings when we sat around, listening to music, drinking, talking, reminiscing.

"That year we lived together," he said on more than one occasion, "was the best year of my life."

He said the two had been passionately in love, they had shared their lives, they had laughed together, loved together, discovered intimate things about each other.

"But the minute we got married," Rock would say, "and she became Mrs. Rock Hudson, everything changed. Like that, it changed. She did a complete about-face."

How did she change?

"Well, she was very impressed by things like my stardom, by the money, by all the trappings of my name and all the glamour nonsense. You know that I don't give a single damn for all that stuff, but she did. And she would become very jealous when I went to work."

And, of course, he had to work. He went to Africa, then, to do *Something of Value*. Phyllis came to the African location for an extended visit and stayed with him until the shooting finished. Then they went to Rome on what Rock had hoped would be a second honeymoon. But they had a big falling-out in Rome ("It was the culmination of everything," Rock said) and when they got back to California, it was over.

Two curious things about the end of that marriage. First, even though they both lived in Beverly Hills, close to each other, their paths somehow never crossed, and Rock never saw Phyllis again. She did not come to the house when he was dying.

And, second, Rock was always curious why Phyllis, who had reveled in being Mrs. Rock Hudson, immediately took back her own name when they were divorced. Many women in similar situations continue to use their ex-husband's name; she didn't.

"She had loved being called Phyllis Hudson," Rock said, "but she went back to Gates as soon as she could. I always found that curious."

I think Rock came very close to getting married one other time, years before I knew him, with Marilyn Maxwell as the party of the second part.

Marilyn Maxwell was a lovely person. I never knew Phyllis, but I did know Marilyn, and I could certainly understand why Rock fell for her. But I think he loved Marilyn's son, Matthew Davis, even more than he loved Marilyn.

Matthew was the son of Marilyn and her ex-husband Jerry Davis, but she had custody. And he and Rock had a great relationship: Matthew was the son Rock had always wanted.

Once Rock and I went to visit Marilyn and Matthew. At the time things weren't going so well for her. While Rock and the boy tossed a football back and forth outside, Marilyn told me of her problems. She was no longer young enough to play ingenue roles and yet not old enough for character parts. She was in that awkward age for a woman, and parts were just not coming.

"It's tough," she said. "I've got the alimony, of course, so Matthew and I aren't going to starve. But we've got to watch our nickels and dimes."

A few days later, she called. Rock was out, so I talked to her and she was very excited and happy.

"Oh, Tom, such good news!" she said. "I've got a job. How about them apples? I'm going to work next week."

She told me she had a gig in a nightclub—she could sing as pretty as she looked, which was very pretty, indeed. I had seen her act, and it was a good act. She sang well and she looked dynamite.

Rock and I were very happy for her.

The next day, as she prepared to leave for that job, which was, I think, in San Francisco, she was in her closet, getting her clothes out, when she apparently had a stroke. When Matthew came home from school he found his mother in the closet, lying on the floor, dead.

The poor little boy—eight or nine at the time—ran next door, tears streaming down his cheeks. And the neighbor, who was a good friend and knew of her closeness to Rock, found his number in Marilyn's address book, and called. Fortunately, we were home; we were at Marilyn's house within ten minutes.

Matthew, who was hysterical, almost leaped into Rock's arms. Rock carried Matthew to the car and took him home with him without another word. I called the authorities and the press and stayed in the house until the undertaker took Marilyn's body away. Marilyn's own public relations man came, but he dissolved into a hysterical puddle, so I handled all the details—my old MGM take-charge training coming to the fore. I was there for several hours.

We tried to locate Matthew's father Jerry, but it took us a few days before we could find him. He was in Mexico on a vacation trip. In the meantime, Rock kept Matthew with him constantly, talking to him, trying to get him to laugh or at least smile and eventually succeeding.

As soon as we reached Jerry Davis he came back to Los Angeles immediately, scooped up his son, and took him to live with him. Rock and I had meanwhile made the arrangements for Marilyn's funeral, which turned out to be a dreadful experience for Rock. It developed into one of those Hollywood circuses, complete with shoving photographers and screaming fans and all that hysterical nonsense.

When we got home after the funeral, Rock and I sat down in the living room. I believe he was thinking that, if he had married Marilyn, as I am sure he had wanted to do, he could have adopted Matthew and the boy would still be there.

"What a lousy life," he said to me that evening. It was the only time I can remember him saying that his life was anything less than terrific.

Then he leaned across and tapped me on the knee.

"You have to promise me one thing, my friend," he said. And

when he said "my friend," I knew this was something heavy. "I want you to make me a solemn promise that if anything happens to me, if I die, don't ever let them turn my funeral into a circus like poor Marilyn's."

"OK, I promise," I said, "but you have to make me the same promise."

"It's a deal," he said. But neither of us thought there was any danger ahead. We were both in top condition, especially Rock, and we both fully expected to live forever, or at least another fifty years or so.

In addition to Matthew Davis and that possible son back in Winnetka, there was one other child Rock felt close to, and this one he actually thought about adopting.

When he was making *Darling Lili* in Paris, there was a lengthy scene involving a bunch of children—tykes and waifs and gamins or whatever. Rock fell madly in love with one little girl in that group.

She was a tiny French lass, with one of those dark and magical French faces, big and bright blue eyes and jet-black hair and a way about her that totally captivated him. And she was an orphan. He made inquires about the technicalities of an American adopting a French orphan and was about to begin the necessary paper work when he had second thoughts.

It wasn't that he loved the child any less. On the contrary, it was because he loved her so much that he reconsidered.

"I said to myself, 'Now, just suppose I bring her back to Beverly Hills with me,' " he told me. "Here she is, in this huge house, practically all alone. I'm off at work, and often work until well after her bedtime. She'd be here with only the servants. So I thought, well, it wouldn't be fair to the child.

"She needs to be with people who love her, not with servants. She needs companionship, not a bunch of old people. At least, at the orphanage in Paris, she has friends her own age. Here, with me, she might have more luxuries, but a lot less friendship. If I was married, it would be a different thing, but I'm not."

So he tore up the adoption papers. He had never told the girl about his plan, so he didn't have any disappointment to contend with. She just gave him a big hug when he said goodbye, and turned around and went back with the others, back on the bus and back to the orphanage. And Rock came home, still childless and unhappy because of it. He did donate a great deal of money to that orphanage and hoped that that enchanting little girl had something of a better life because of his largesse.

The only family Rock had, with any consistency, was his mother. He was her only child, she his only caring relative. So they spoiled each other.

Even when Rock went into the Navy, Katherine stayed as close to him as she could. She took a job, for the duration, as a switchboard operator at the naval base in Chicago.

The Scherer family continued virtually to ignore her.

"Katherine never forgave them," Rock would say. "She hated the whole lot of them."

Of course, as soon as Rock became a star, they all came out of the woodwork, professing their eternal love and undying admiration, parading the banner of Family Forever and expecting favors in return.

In 1974, when Rock was touring with *I Do! I Do!* with Carol Burnett, they had a week between when they closed in Washington and the opening in St. Louis. So Rock and I rented a car and went for a week of what Rock called "relative-viewing."

First we viewed some of my relatives, although they weren't real blood relatives. They were just exceptionally good friends from Houston who had been a kind of surrogate family to me. They had a marvelous farm, complete with a pre-Revolutionary War farmhouse near Harrisburg, Pennsylvania. Glenn Smith was my friend's name, and his parents, Col. Clyde Smith and his wife Toni, sent a plane to Washington to pick us up and take us to their farm. Glenn and his ladyfriend flew up from Houston to be with us, and we all spent three or four great days there. Glenn and I had been friends since my days working in Houston; at that time, he even baby sat for my wife and me. Later, I introduced him to Rock, and he and Rock became good friends, too. As a matter of fact, Rock sort of took over that friendship, and Glenn would often visit us in California. He flew out to attend the memorial service after Rock died.

Then we decided to rent a car to drive on to St. Louis. We decided that we wanted to rent a convertible (Rock always loved to drive with the top down) and drive along the Blue Ridge Mountain Trail on our way. But there was absolutely no convertible available at the time in Harrisburg.

Clyde Smith spread the word among his friends—all very rich folks—that a convertible was required. And, of course, there was a brand-new Eldorado convertible lying dormant in somebody's eight-car garage.

"Take it, we're not using it," the people who owned the car said. "We have—let's see—ten others."

So Rock and I borrowed the car and set out for St. Louis, Missouri, with a planned stopover in the Olney, Illinois, area, where most of the Scherer family was concentrated, for further relative-viewing.

They had a huge family reunion, with Rock as the centerpiece. They paraded their "beloved cousin," as they called him, for all their friends and neighbors to see, and the reflected glory was so bright sunglasses were required. The affair was actually held in St. Louis, which is not far from Olney, and it was held during the run of the show.

Katherine flew in from California for the reunion, and she cheerfully wore her most expensive dress and, even though it was mid-August, the mink stole Rock had given her. She put on all the best and brightest jewelry Rock had given her, too. Rock loved shopping for her, and had bought expensive necklaces and bracelets and earrings at the Bulgari store in Rome and other fine jewelry stores in Paris and London and wherever his travels took him.

Katherine flaunted it all.

"I love it!" Rock said. "Look at her, isn't she terrific? She is being so grand for all those bastards who gave her the shaft back when my father left her." It was a great moment for lovers of poetic justice.

At one point during the reunion, Rock's Uncle Luther Scherer sat down next to me. He was such a dedicated farmer that, even at that reunion, he was wearing his overalls. He leaned over to me and said, in a conspiratorial whisper, "Mr. Clark, let me tell you something. Now, I'm just a plain, simple farmer. Nothing fancy about me, as you can plainly see. But, let me ask you something, Mr. Clark. Do you find me a worthy man?"

"Please call me Tom, Uncle Luther."

"OK, Tom, thank you. Now, then, I'm asking you, man to man, do you find me a worthy man?"

"Why, yes, sir. I certainly believe you are a most worthy man."

"Well, that's good. You know, I'm just a plain man, a very plain man. I've spent a lifetime working the soil, feeding the people. Do you consider that a worthy life?"

"Indeed I do, Uncle Luther," I said, wondering where this conversation was taking me. "Very worthy indeed."

"I'm certainly gratified that you do, Tom. Farming isn't an easy life, you know. Up at dawn, in bed at dusk, subject to nature's whims. But I have found it to be a satisfying life, raising crops to feed the hungry people in the big cities. Do you think I have led a worthy life?"

"I certainly do, Uncle Luther. I certainly do. Hard to think of anything more worthy."

"That is sure nice to hear. Now then, Tom, since you believe I am a worthy man, do you think you could get me on *Let's Make a Deal?*"

When I told Rock about that conversation, the two of us dissolved into a lengthy outbreak of laughter.

There were perhaps sixty people at the reunion. And, before we sat down to eat, we all joined hands in a huge circle while Uncle Jerome, the family patriarch, said a prayer, a grace for the family. It was a nice grace, and at one point Uncle Jerome said these words:

"And, dear Jesus, we want to thank you for the fact that we decided to relinquish our beloved son, Rock, to his mother, Katherine."

Across the room from Katherine, I could see her lips tighten and feel her whole body stiffen at those words. But she didn't say anything. All the rest of the day, however, her eyes were flinty and her mouth a grim slash across her face. In the car later, as we drove back to our hotel, she sat in the back seat, still seething. She was very quiet, ominously quiet.

Then suddenly she barked out that one word: *"Relinquish!"*

Nobody said anything. Rock and I just looked at each other, trying to keep a straight face.

"Relinquish!" she said again, with even more bitterness.

We got to the hotel and were sitting in the living room of the suite, drinks in hand.

"Relinquish! Those damn hicks!"

She never got over their use of that word. Forever after, all we had to do was say to her "Katherine, have you relinquished anything lately?" and she would get red in the face and start muttering under her breath.

Katherine had had a tough life. After Roy Scherer had walked out on her and she had walked out on Wally Fitzgerald, she had quite a few years of loneliness.

Long after Rock had left, she finally got lucky and married a very nice man named Joe Olson. So Rock was just very happy that, until Olson passed away, Katherine had at last found some happiness.

One day she got a call from a lawyer telling her that Walter Fitzgerald had died.

"Mrs. Olson," the lawyer said, "I understand that you were formerly married to Walter Fitzgerald."

"Yes, I was."

"Well, I was his attorney, and I must tell you that he has left his entire estate to your son, Roy Fitzgerald, a.k.a. Rock Hudson. But, before we discuss that, Mrs. Olson, I have to ascertain your wishes as to the disposal of your ex-husband's remains. What shall we do with the body?"

"Don't ask me that again," Katherine said, "or I will be forced to tell you what you can do with it."

The caller quickly changed the subject and got down to the nitty-gritty. Not that Rock needed any money, but Katherine felt it would only be fair if, after all the grief Wally Fitzgerald had caused her son, he would be generous in death.

"What is the value of the estate?" Katherine asked.

"Mr. Fitzgerald left an estate consisting of one racehorse and several hundred dollars." Rock never saw any of it, not the race horse and certainly not the several hundred dollars. He might have liked the racehorse.

Katherine thoroughly enjoyed being the mother of a superstar. She played the role brilliantly. She was tall and handsome and, when she could afford it, she dressed very well. Rock made it possible for her to afford it because he loved giving her anything she wanted.

Once he gave her a round-the-world cruise. It began in Miami, sailed pleasantly through the Panama Canal, came up the Mexican coast, and stopped in Los Angeles before continuing on across the Pacific. Katherine decided to have a party on the ship while it was docked in Los Angeles. She mailed invitations from Miami to dozens of her friends and then, on the ship, she made more friends and invited them, too.

The invitations had read the party would be in her cabin. So Rock and I went down to the pier, boarded the ship and went down to her cabin. On the cabin door was a neat little card, with these words:

MRS. OLSON'S PARTY HAS BEEN MOVED TO THE NEPTUNE LOUNGE.

It had gotten so large it had outgrown the cabin, and she had to hire one of the ship's lounges for a few hours to squeeze all her guests in. There were not only many of her Los Angeles friends and new cruise friends, but she had also invited many of the ship's personnel. One of those was the cruise director who, it developed, had not been too friendly toward her. He had probably dismissed her as just another widow on the prowl for a man.

When we got to the lounge, there was Katherine in a jaunty yachting cap playing the elegant hostess. Of course, the sudden appearance of Rock Hudson caused a sensation, the sensation Katherine had been waiting for. She had not told anyone that she was Rock Hudson's mother and had been savoring the surprise she would cause. As soon as he walked in, she took great delight in introducing "my son, Rock Hudson."

The unfriendly cruise director got a particularly flowery introduction. His jaw dropped. Katherine turned to me and said, as the cruise director listened, "Tom, you know it's really so sad. We're going to stop in Alexandria and there is an excursion to Cairo and the Pyramids, but it's all booked, and my friend here, the cruise director, can't get me on it."

"Oh, Mrs. Hudson—I mean, Mrs. Olson," he blabbered, staring at Rock in awe, "don't you worry your pretty little head. When we get to Alexandria, you'll be on that excursion if I have to carry you on the camel myself."

Katherine gave me a big wink. This was a moment of triumph for her. She had waited for it all across the Gulf of Mexico, through the Panama Canal, and all up the coast of Mexico. It was worth the wait.

When she returned from the cruise, she told us that, after the stop in Los Angeles and the secret of her identity was out, she was the star of the ship. The cruise director couldn't do enough for her from then on.

Uncle Jerome, the head Scherer, was the spokesman for that large and boisterous family. Every year he sent out his annual letter at Christmastime, summarizing the events of the preceding twelve months in the family—births, deaths and other notable occurrences. There was always a paragraph or two devoted to Rock's activities, of course.

Rock would call the family back in Olney, once in a while. Usually it would be Uncle Jerome. Rock felt he had something of an obligation, even though they had been cold to his mother and himself when they could have used warmth. But he was a family-oriented person and believed in keeping up a semblance of family solidarity. The concept of family meant much to him, possibly because he had never really known what it was like to be part of a real family like the ones he saw in the movies or on TV. He envied me my warm and loving family very much.

I believe, as I said earlier, one of the main reasons he came to California after his Navy service was a desperate attempt to find a family he could become part of. His father had been only marginally glad to see him and his stepmother was a harridan; Rock and the woman developed a mutual dislike immediately. His short time in the bosom of that family was unpleasant for all concerned.

Later I learned that, all through his years as a star, Rock regularly sent his father a monthly check.

"Why are you doing that?" I asked him. "The bastard walked out on you and your mother and wasn't very nice to you when you came to see him after the Navy. You certainly don't owe him anything, so why are you sending him money every month?"

He shrugged.

"Oh, I don't know," he said. He was always uncomfortable discussing his big-hearted gestures, of which there were many. "I guess it's because, after all, the man is my father. I feel an obligation."

And he kept sending that monthly check until he heard that Roy Scherer, Senior, had passed away.

Even though Rock had no real, solid family life such as the one I had, the trappings of family life meant a great deal to him. All the holidays, for example, were terribly important to him.

Thanksgiving was a big day in his life. While she was alive, his mother was always the Thanksgiving hostess. Early in his career, when he had been part of the Hollywood boating crowd, he had a house on Lido Isle, where he kept his boat moored. Then, the studio had asked (*demanded* is perhaps a more accurate word) that he move closer to the studio, so he had given that house to his mother.

She only lived on Lido Isle a few years, because she decided she didn't like it there, no matter how ritzy the neighborhood was. Lido Isle homes are jammed together—the land is very valuable—and she said she was getting claustrophobia. The houses are built so close together, with high walls on either side, that you see nothing from the side windows but wall. She said she felt like she was living in a coffin. So Rock, loving son that he was, bought her a place with more room, sitting high up on the bluffs in Back Bay. No claustrophobia there.

And it was in that comfortable home that she was the hostess every Thanksgiving. She really was an incredibly accomplished hostess, too. She would cook this magnificent dinner, yet she never seemed to be in the kitchen. She was out in the living room with her guests, playing bridge (a fixture at virtually every affair Rock was a part of) and talking and laughing and then, like magic, she served this huge, elegant, delicious Thanksgiving dinner.

The guests were pretty much the same, year after year. Rock

and me, of course. Claire Trevor and Milton Bren lived only four doors away and were probably Rock's best friends, and mine, so they would be there. Katherine's own best friend, a woman named Marge, was a regular, as was another couple of old friends who drove up every year from San Diego. So there were usually eight of us, just enough for two tables of bridge and one table of turkey.

But Christmas was even more important to Rock. He was the host for the Christmas dinner, at the house, and it was a very large deal to him. He went all out at Christmas.

As the holiday approached, he grew as excited as a small boy waiting for Santa Claus. His eyes sparkled and he made up lists and he drew up menus and became very secretive about what he'd bought for whom.

He did all his own shopping for Christmas gifts, and all his own wrapping, too. He wrapped with great care and finesse. His packages were all adorned with handsome bows and slashes of bright ribbons. The gifts themselves were usually chosen with care, and were also usually very costly.

But he was very conscious of the need to be charitable at the holiday season, as well. Every year he got a great many empty bushel baskets and filled them, like cornucopias, with foods he had bought himself at the supermarket. We would pile those baskets in the station wagon and drive downtown to a mission and ask the people there to distribute them to the neediest families they could find. It always gave Rock a great feeling of satisfaction to do that, but he never allowed me or any of his other publicity people to mention that to the press.

We generally had a larger crowd at Christmas than Katherine did at Thanksgiving, primarily because the house was bigger and could accommodate more. We would have Milton and Claire, of course, and Katherine and whoever she cared to invite; the others would vary from year to year. But it was usually a joyous crowd of about fifteen or twenty, and it was always a happy time.

When Katherine died, all the holidays lost much of their luster for Rock. We never again had the big Christmas dinner party. The first year after her death, Rock simply could not bear the idea of being in the house on the holiday. Christmas could not have been joyous that year. So we took ourselves to Hawaii for Christmas, and the year after that we were in New York. Anything, and anyplace, as long as it was away from the house and the memories that lived there.

We did have a big party that year we were in the New York apartment for Christmas. But because the guests were all new friends from New York, they brought no memories with them. We had so many of the important theatrical people there that somebody said if the building had collapsed, it would have been the end of the New York theatrical scene for twenty years; all the movers and shakers of the Broadway stage were in our apartment that day.

I admired Katherine as much for what she wasn't as for what she was. While she certainly enjoyed her status as the mother of a figure everybody in the world knew, she didn't become the nouveau-riche bitch she could easily have become. She could flaunt with the best of them, putting on her furs and jewels and being very regal, but she only went in for flaunting to get back at those who had snubbed her in the past.

Mostly, she lived a quiet, unostentatious life. I remember that she needed a new refrigerator just after she had moved into her new house in Back Bay. She asked me if I would give her a hand in shopping for that appliance. She insisted on going to the discount stores. I would have gone to the better stores, but she said that would be silly, that a refrigerator is a refrigerator, so why not get one at a place where it will be cheaper?

She had nice clothes, lovely jewels, a few fine furs, and she drove a big, luxurious car. But Rock had given her most of that; she herself seldom went overboard and never went hog-wild.

Rock cared about few of his relatives other than Katherine. There was one of the Scherer girls who had married a nice young man named Tom. He often had business in the Los Angeles area, and would visit us. Rock liked Tom and his wife and their visits were always welcome. But that was it. Most of the Scherers were not particularly sophisticated, and Rock, who had sophistication thrust upon him, had totally outgrown them.

One aunt was typical. Rock used to tell me about his Aunt Evelyn. He never called her just Aunt Evelyn, however; he always used her full name: "Aunt Evelyn Who Picks Her Nose and Eats It."

He would talk about Aunt Evelyn Who Picks Her Nose and Eats It to all his friends, too. Whenever anybody else told a story about a relative, he would always top them by telling them about Aunt Evelyn Who Picks Her Nose and Eats It.

When there was that family reunion in St. Louis, all the Scherer clan came to see the show, Rock and Carol in *I Do! I Do!* And when after the show they all came backstage to say hello to their famous relative and to meet his co-star, Rock introduced them all, one by one, to Carol, as they crowded into the little dressing room.

"And this," he said to Carol triumphantly, "is my Aunt Evelyn."

"Nice to know you," Carol said politely, holding out her hand.

"Carol," Rock said, a little more insistently, "this is my Aunt Evelyn. You know, my Aunt Evelyn Who—."

"Oh!" said Carol, finally getting it. "*THAT* Aunt Evelyn."

She quickly withdrew her hand.

CHAPTER FIVE
Entertaining Royally

I have seen and met royalty of all kinds, and I honestly believe Rock and I lived a lot better than many of them.

Actually, I truly believe that, in today's society, the stars of show business are the real royalty, the true chosen people. Nowadays, of course, the biggest stars of show business are rock singers and they, as a class, have very little class. But there are still some acting royalty around—movie and television stars—who, like Rock and others of his era, live regular royal lives.

It wasn't only Rock's money—of which he had a seemingly bottomless pit, a bank account without limits—but the combination of the fiscal and the glamorous that made it all so wonderful.

You have to try and understand what it meant to be Rock Hudson.

It meant getting first-class treatment anywhere and everywhere without having to demand it or even ask for it.

It meant having people fawn over you—for them that likes to be fawned over—simply when they saw you coming.

It meant being able to have the best of everything without having to think about whether or not you could afford it. When you can buy a new car without asking—or caring about—the price, that is being loaded in the first degree.

But above all, I think, it meant being automatically loved and respected and envied by anybody and everybody you came in contact with. The love was almost tangible. When I was with Rock, I could feel it emanating from the people he met. It reached out and enveloped him, and some of it spilled over and got me, too.

Rock was not to the manor born. All the good taste he had, all the sophistication, was acquired after he became an adult. He was a quick study in that and other things, and was quick to adapt to the good life. By the time I met him, he was a man of good taste—when he chose to exercise it. On occasion, he could revert back to the original Roy Scherer and have no taste at all.

When we became good friends, he knew good wines, good books, good clothes, good food. He was urbane and classy. He may have enjoyed dressing like a slob around the house, but he could, when the occasion demanded, look like the most elegant man in the world. Many times, however, he would pick out a tie that was absolutely wrong for the suit and shirt he was wearing, and I would have to tell him to change it. Frequently I'd have to go with him to his tie rack and find a proper tie for him to wear. His taste in things like that left a lot to be desired.

But, because of his height and his carriage and his incredibly handsome face, he wore clothes magnificently. He could be the ultimate in masculine elegance.

And the house was elegant, too. Yet at the same time it was very comfortable. In her book about Rock, Sara Davidson says it was known as The Castle. I never in my life heard anyone call it by that name, and there really was nothing about it to create a castlelike image. It was a large house, yes, but not austere, not ostentatious.

About the only thing in its layout that might be considered extreme was the two living rooms, separated by the central entrance hall. At first thought, two living rooms might be considered one two many, but it turned out to be a very useful feature. One could be used for one purpose by one of us, while the second could be used for something else by the other. It gave us flexibility.

The second floor was pretty traditional—two bedroom suites, two bathrooms, all very ordinary in their arrangement. We did have a lot of closet space but, of course, Rock's profession demanded that. He had to maintain a large and varied wardrobe for the many and varied functions he was required to attend.

Rock always had in his contract that any clothing the studio furnished him would revert to him after the filming was over. So, if the script demanded certain items Rock did not own, the studio would supply them and, after the shooting, those items would become his property. His closets bulged with all kinds of odd clothing: safari outfits, strange sweaters, odd suits and jackets, many sets of tails.

Much of this excess baggage was stored in the basement. I suggested, on many occasions, that we throw it all out or give it to a charity or burn it. But Rock could not bear to part with anything. Once I found an old pair of some kind of trousers, moldy and smelly; I was about to throw them in the trash when he stopped me.

"Hey, you can't throw those out," he said.

"Why not? They're no good to anybody. Even the Salvation Army would throw them back."

"Hell, Tom," he said. "Those are my foul-weather sailing pants. I might need them."

So they went back into the basement while Rock waited for some foul-weather sailing. For all I know, those pants are still in the basement today.

There was a staff at the house, but only what was really necessary to run the place—nothing in excess.

Originally there was Joy, who had been Rock's housekeeper for many years. She was a wonderful woman, and very efficient, but then she began drinking a bit too much for her own good. Days would go by when we wouldn't even see her. She would go into her room and simply never come out for days on end. When she finally did emerge, royally hung over, she would be contrite and apologetic.

Even when she was present, she grew sloppy in her work; beds wouldn't be made, ashtrays wouldn't be emptied, dishes wouldn't be washed. Rock and I were both working full-time or more, and we felt we had a right to expect those details to be tended to automatically.

"We really have to get rid of her," I said to Rock one evening when we came home to find the house in a state of particular shambles. And where was Joy? Out in her room, sleeping it off.

"I can't do that," said old tender-hearted Rock. He might not have thought to give her a raise, but neither could he think of firing her. "She's been with me so long. She'll come around."

"Oh, come off it. We've given her chance after chance, and she's getting worse, not better."

"I know, but I just can't fire her."

The final straw came when Rock said to her, one morning, that he was expecting guests for dinner. There would be nine people, he said, and he went over a suggested menu with her. She said that she would have everything ready for cocktails at eight and dinner at nine.

At nine o'clock that evening, Joy sauntered into the living room, sat down, and began laughing it up with the guests. Rock asked her if dinner was ready. She shrugged and said she hadn't started it yet, so she guessed it wasn't quite ready. We wound up taking all our guests down the hill and into Beverly Hills for dinner.

I knew Rock would never fire her. So I did.

After Joy was gone we went through a long series of employees—some couples, some individuals. I did the hiring and the firing when none of them proved satisfactory. And then James came along.

James was entirely British, a well-trained and experienced butler/houseman. James stayed with us until Rock died. He was, of course, not a maid—as he kept reminding us—and so we had to get a helper to do the cleaning and all that. But James ran the household.

He was the sort you could rely on. I might say to him "James, we will be ten for dinner tonight. Fancy. Let's put on the dog," and James would really put on the dog. Everything would be the finest—the best crystal and china and silver, and a really uptown menu.

But, on the other hand, I might say "James, there's a bunch of people dropping by after shooting tonight so, you know, keep it nice and informal." And James would set out platters of cold cuts and salads and the second-best china and glassware, and it would be just right.

James took care of the laundry and watched over everything for us. Some of our friends felt he was a bit too imperious and dictatorial, but that was a small price to pay for his reliability. We were traveling so much that we didn't want to have to concern ourselves with the day-to-day operational details of running the house. We knew those details were in capable hands with James on the job.

And, what was most important, James loved the dogs—and they loved him. Rock and I were both very fond of dogs and kept accumulating them. At the peak, our dog population numbered seven. A lot of servants would have objected to having to care for seven restless dogs, but James took it all in stride.

While James didn't clean, he did make the beds, which was not as easy as it sounded. I must admit I was fussy about how I wanted my bed made, and so was Rock. We both wanted our beds made a certain way, or else we had difficulty falling asleep. Rock was tall—six foot five—and I am only two inches shorter, so we both had oversized beds with specially made oversized sheets. James quickly got the hang of the way we wanted our beds made.

We never saw James in the afternoon, after lunch. He would reappear at dinnertime. He spent those hours in his room, alone. I never found out what he did in that time; it really was none of my business, and I didn't pry. We respected his privacy, and he kept his private life to himself.

If Rock and I were going to be home alone, I often asked James to fix dinner and then leave it.

"Just leave it out on the stove," I would say, "and we'll hot it up when we want it."

That was because we ate at very irregular hours. Sometimes, if we were involved in watching a sporting event on TV or were showing a movie, we might not want to eat until ten or eleven. So we wouldn't see James at all; when we felt hungry, we'd go into the kitchen, turn on the burners under whatever it was he'd prepared, warm it up, and have a happy dinner without muss or fuss. At times we didn't eat dinner until midnight.

We could be very informal on those nights. But if we felt like it, we could be very formal in that house. It lent itself equally well to either attitude. By converting both living rooms into dining rooms and utilizing the patio, we could accommodate two hundred people at a sit-down dinner, which we did on several occasions. But we could also have a few people over for a barbecue and a game of bridge. We did that hundreds of times.

Rock loved to entertain, and he was good at it. He was a wonderful, gracious host. He had a great gift for putting everybody at his or her ease, of making people feel comfortable and at home. When we had those large parties he circulated constantly, mingling to make sure all his guests were happy, that there were no wallflowers or loners.

I think our one concession to genuine luxury was our outside staff. We had two gardeners to do the heavy work so that Rock and I, when we puttered in the garden, wouldn't have to waste our time weeding and feeding, but could do the pruning and transplanting and those things we considered fun.

But even more than the gardeners, on the luxury front, was the man we had to take care of our cars. He wasn't a chauffeur; we both enjoyed driving, and having a chauffeur wasn't our style. This man did nothing but see that our cars were always gassed up and ready to go, cleaned and polished, up to snuff mechanically. Whatever car we chose to drive would be ready the moment we wanted it.

Both of us loved cars. Between us we often had four or five, plus the house car for James or whoever to use.

The only time we didn't drive ourselves was on New Year's Eve or such other occasions when we didn't want to worry about having to stay sober. For those times, we would hire a driver and usually go out in the big, extended-wheel-base Rolls Royce we had just for show. Sometimes, if we couldn't get a driver we liked for those times, we would hire a limo. One thing Rock insisted on was that nobody drive after drinking.

That stemmed from a combination of things—his realization that too many tragedies are caused by drunken drivers, plus the knowledge that a driving-while-under-the-influence arrest could hurt his career badly. So he was scrupulous about that.

And, I must confess, I found having that man around to take care of our cars was a lovely thing. It is nice to know that, when you go outside to get into your car, you don't have to think about it, but you know it will always be clean, full of gas, and mechanically sound. There is never the nasty surprise of going out to the garage and finding your car has a flat tire.

Rock wasn't the type to want, need, or countenance the services of a valet. If anybody would have suggested to him that he have somebody dress him, he would have laughed. Even so, he did permit James to pack for him.

Whenever we traveled, James would pack. Rock would tell him where we were going and whether or not there would be a need for formal wear, and that was it. James would always pick just the right clothing. Sometimes I would help him, because I knew the type of affairs we would be attending and what was needed, but then James would put it all into the suitcases. He was a whiz at packing, and when we unpacked, the suits and shirts would rarely need to be pressed.

All in all, life in that house was as close to perfection as you can get. We had all our toys—movie projecting equipment, music sound system, games, cards, books, gardening material—and we had people to take care of our basic needs and wants. Whatever we wanted was there, good and plenty. Even peace and solitude were available.

No royalty ever lived more royally than we did.

CHAPTER SIX

His Friendships

With a few exceptions, Rock got along well with everybody, and everybody got along well with Rock.

First, the bad news.

The fact that he was badly treated by Blake Edwards and Julie Andrews while he was making *Darling Lili* with them has been widely reported. No point in going into too many details of that event here, but he did resent it and never had a kind word to say about them from then on. Although he didn't have an unkind word to say about them, either. He simply forgot that they existed.

For the benefit of anyone who never read or heard about what happened in England, Ireland, and France during the filming of that picture, I will provide a few of the horrible details.

The whole project began auspiciously and, for Rock, with a tremendous amount of anticipation. He had met both Edwards and his wife Julie, at a few Hollywood affairs, and they had seemed very pleasant. And, of course, like millions of other movie fans, he had admired Edwards as a director and writer and, like even more millions, he thought Julie wonderfully talented and totally charming on the screen.

So he was pleased when, in 1969, they approached him to do a film with them. Like most Hollywood contacts, this was done through the good offices of agents: their agent called his agent. Nobody in Hollywood ever calls anybody directly; if they did, agents would be unnecessary and all agents would have to find honest work.

The word we got was that Blake Edwards was going to do a musical with Julie and wanted Rock as her co-star. Rock was thrilled; Julie was then at the height of her career and anything with her in it would (or so it seemed at the time) automatically be a box-office blockbuster. Besides, he had always had a secret yen to do a musical, so that was icing on the excitement cake.

Rock invited Blake and Julie to come to dinner (that was one of the nights I told James to put on the dog, and the dinner oozed elegance). Blake and Julie pitched the story they had in mind. No script had been written, Blake confessed, but he had it all in his head. It sounded good to Rock.

Rock said yes. Blake went back and started writing the script, and Rock was walking on air.

When shooting began, they did some of the interiors in Hollywood, on the Paramount lot. The first day of shooting Rock got his call and, professional that he was, reported for work precisely on time. The assistant directors said he should go to his dressing room and would call him when they were ready for him.

It was a lovely dressing room: large, comfortable, furnished with such conveniences as television, a fine stereo system, chairs and couches upholstered in leather. But Rock just sat there, all day. Nobody came to see him or talk to him. And he wasn't called to do any work. At four in the afternoon, he was dismissed.

The next day the same thing happened.

And the next.

Not once in those three days did he hear a word from either Blake or Julie. The only contact he had with anybody was with a second- or third-assistant director who would come by regularly at four o'clock to say he could go home.

He was fuming, but he was never the type to fume in public, so he just poured out his frustration and anger to me. I agreed that it was no way for a star to be treated—no way, actually, for anybody to be treated, star or not.

"Look, Rock." I said. "Here's what you should do. Tomorrow, call in sick. Tell them that you'll be here, at home, and, if they really need you, you'll be able to come in, but since you don't feel very well, you'll stay home until they actually need you."

That is exactly what he did the next morning. In fact, I made the call, telling one of the assistants that Rock was slightly under the weather but could come in if he was really needed.

Within twenty minutes, Blake was on the phone.

"Hi, Rock," he said. "How're you feeling? Look, I think we will start shooting your scene this afternoon. Do you think you can make it?"

Rock said he'd be there. That afternoon, when he reported to the set, he was put to work immediately. But Blake and Julie didn't take the hint. They treated him like dirt throughout the entire shooting schedule.

When they filmed in Ireland, at a remote location, Blake and Julie traveled to and from the set in a helicopter. They would arrive in a grand manner, alighting from the chopper just in time to go to work. Rock and the others had to travel between the hotel and the set in cars, a long and jouncy trip over abysmal roads that took more than an hour each way.

Rock and all the rest of the cast and crew were put up in an average hotel—certainly nothing fancy—while the Edwards were staying in a very lovely villa.

Throughout the filming, it was more of the same. The Edwards never talked to Rock, or gave him any special treatment—and, after all, he was a star equal at least in magnitude to Andrews.

Later, the company moved to France, and some scenes were shot at the estate of the Duke and Duchess of Windsor. Rock told me that the Duke doddered out and was friendly with everyone and enjoyed looking through the camera to see what the shot would look like.

The Duke and Duchess invited the principals into the chateau, after the filming was completed, for cocktails. Rock was standing with the semiroyal couple when Her Grace turned to him, as Blake and Julie listened, and said:

"And what is it that you do with the company, young man?"

Rock realized that this had to be a planned insult, because Wallis, being an American to begin with and reputedly a big movie fan, would certainly have had to know who Rock Hudson was and what it was that he did.

"I'm sorry, Your Grace," he said. "I thought you knew. I'm Mr. and Mrs. Edwards' chauffeur."

Julie Andrews, whose on-screen image was made up of equal parts of sugar and treacle, was actually something else in what passes for real life.

Rock growled one day when he told me of something that had happened at Paramount after they got back. The studio was then in a bullish period, and, by coincidence, many really top-quality stars were on the lot simultaneously: Rock, Julie, John Wayne, Barbra Streisand, Lee Marvin, and some others. So the studio publicity department decided to capitalize on the presence of so many high-powered names.

They asked them all to report at a particular time to pose for a group picture. They wanted it for ads and for the Hollywood trade papers. They had a headline—PARAMOUNT IS WHERE IT'S HAPPENING—all planned. The picture would be taken in front of the big, famous Paramount gate, and was scheduled to be shot at noon, which they felt was a convenient hour for everyone.

And, as the clock struck twelve, the stars were all there—except Julie Andrews. Rock, Duke, Lee, and even Barbra, who has been known to be difficult, were on hand. Everybody, but no Julie. They waited twenty minutes and then called her dressing room.

"Oh, we're sorry," said her maid, "but Miss Andrews is lying down and cannot be disturbed."

She never showed. They took the picture without her. And that uncooperative attitude did a lot to cause her career to fall from its peak to place where it ultimately landed.

Rod McKuen was another of the handful who incurred Rock

Hudson's displeasure. I was partly responsible for the Hudson-McKuen falling out. At the time, I was representing McKuen for publicity purposes, and I had gotten to know him very well.

He was riding at his highest then, in the early seventies, with his own recording company and his own publishing company, and his books of poetry and recordings of songs were greeted with occasional praise. He even had a hit record, "Jean, Jean," a song he had written for the movie *The Prime of Miss Jean Brodie* and that had been nominated for an Academy award.

Rod called Rock—I don't know how he managed to get his private number, but he did—and asked for a meeting.

"I have a great idea for you, Rock," McKuen said, and Rock, ever polite, agreed to meet with him. At that meeting, McKuen suggested that Rock record an album for Stanyan, Rod's company. While it would be a Stanyan record, McKuen explained, it would be distributed by Warner Brothers, which was then releasing McKuen's products.

"What sort of an album?" Rock asked.

"Some of my songs," Rod said.

"I'm really not a singer," Rock said.

"But you have a very nice speaking voice. Just leave the rest to me and my people. We'll make you sound great."

One thing Rock always wanted to do, of course, was sing. It was that yen to do a musical that got him into that fine mess with Blake Edwards and Julie Andrews, and the same yen was about to propel him into another mess, equally fine.

He agreed to do the album for McKuen.

McKuen spared no expense in the recording process. He had a marvelous arranger/conductor, Arthur Greenstreet, who took a group of McKuen songs and made them sound very lovely. They recorded in London (recording costs were cheaper there) and they assembled fine musicians and technicians.

Rock was thrilled with the experience, and with the result. He brought the tapes home and we played them over and over, and he smiled appreciatively. Actually, the poor guy simply couldn't sing. He did have a nice voice—full, rich, resonant—but that's not all a singer needs. He had problems with such niceties as pitch and key and things like that. Still, it was an entirely acceptable album, and we thought it would have entirely acceptable sales.

Rock was under the impression that Rod had told him, definitely, the album would be distributed widely by Warner Bros. Records, and be offered for sale in record stores all over the country. Warner Bros., however, never did so. Instead, McKuen simply added it to the Stanyan catalogue of records he sold through mail order.

In the record industry, records that are marketed via the mails are considered definitely second- or third-rate, a sort of cut-rate merchandise. Rock was furious when he learned of the McKuen plan.

In the first place, his album would be sold for a low price. Rock's proceeds from record sales would be small, even given a big sale. But, even more than the money, there was the matter of prestige. Rock had made an album he was proud of, even though that pride was somewhat misplaced. Still, his name and reputation would be damaged by the fact that his first (and, as it turned out, only) album would be sold by mail.

There's a little record store in Century City that sells that kind of album. We went in one day and bought a stack of them for a dollar apiece. The album hadn't been promoted. No copies were ever sent to disc jockeys. There was no air play. It was simply added to the already bulging McKuen catalogue, and the sales were slim to none.

Rock was about the angriest I ever saw him. He immediately cut Rod McKuen out of his life.

"If he'd told me from the beginning that that was how he was going to distribute the album," Rock said to me, "I wouldn't have minded. I would have done it anyhow. But the fact that he was so devious about it is what really ticks me off. I'm just not about to forgive him."

The next Christmas the usual festivities were going on at the house. There were thirty or forty people there, laughing it up, opening presents, drinking champagne. Dinner was just about to be served when James came over to me.

"Mr. Clark," he said, "there's a person in the kitchen who would like to see you." So I went into the kitchen and there, standing abjectly just inside the back door, was Rod McKuen.

"I just came by," he said, in a voice made huskier by emotion than his already-husky normal voice, "to wish you guys a merry Christmas."

"Come on in, Rod."

It was raining, and Rod came into the kitchen, dripping water all over the floor.

"Do you think I could see Rock for a moment?" he asked.

I went and told Rock that Rod was there, very humble.

"Oh, Jesus, not him," Rock said, but he shrugged and went into the kitchen where Rod was waiting, soggy but patient. Rock was back with us in five minutes.

"What happened?" I asked him.

"Not much. He said, 'Merry Christmas,' and I said, 'Merry Christmas,' " Rock said. "I guess he just felt guilty."

Rock never saw Rod again.

Those were the only two cases where Rock was so angry that he dropped the objects of his scorn out of his life, totally and irrevocably. There were a few other people he didn't particularly like, but not to the point of taking any action about it.

One of that latter group was Tony Randall. Tony was just kind of an annoyance, nothing overt.

Once, Tony asked both Rock and Doris Day (they had all worked together in *Pillow Talk, Lover Come Back,* and *Send Me No Flowers*) to meet him for lunch at the Polo Lounge in the Beverly Hills Hotel.

"I've got a great idea for another movie for the three of us," he said. Rock's reaction was to roll his eyes up, but, ever polite, he agreed to the meeting. I imagine Doris' reaction was virtually identical. Anyhow, they all met for lunch.

Rock came home laughing hysterically.

"You won't believe," he told me, "the idea that that guy had. Listen to this. His idea was that Doris and I are married and then she decides to become a swinger, and for the whole middle of the picture, I'm not in it at all. And, meanwhile, Doris is supposed to be out, carrying on with Tony."

"What did Doris have to say about that?" I asked.

"Well," Rock said, "Tony was telling the story and when he got to the part where her character left me and started swinging with him, she stopped him in the middle of a sentence.

" 'Wait just a second, Tony,' Doris said. 'Do you mean to tell me you expect an audience to believe that I'm going to leave him'—and she pointed to me—'for you?'—and she pointed to Tony.

" 'Well, yes, I guess so,' Tony said. 'That's the whole plot.'

"Doris laughed and said, 'Forget it, Sonny Boy. It could never happen.' "

And that, apparently, was the end of that meeting.

While they were working together, Rock and Tony got along OK. Tony, like Rock, was a pro, and Rock respected that. He got along with everybody who had a professional approach to work.

Early in his career, when he was one of a flock of contract players at Universal, Rock had to play the political game. It was one he didn't enjoy and was not particularly good at. He resented it, as a matter of fact, feeling that an actor shouldn't have to indulge in such grubby tactics.

But it was, unfortunately, part of the accepted way of life in Hollywood then, especially among the lower echelon of actors under contract to the studios. To get the better parts, to maneuver and wriggle and squirm and fight and battle for the good ones, took a lot of effort. As well as a lot of innate nastiness which Rock simply did not possess. If it hadn't been for the fact that he was so extraordinarily handsome, he undoubtedly would have been shunted aside by others who played the political game far better than he.

Among those other, more politically oriented, actors at Universal at the time was Tony Curtis. He and Rock, being young and good-looking and romantic, competed for the best parts the studio then had to offer. And, where Rock was not a born scrambler and conniver, Tony was.

"He tried to sabotage me a lot in those days," Rock told me on more than one occasion. "He would do things like going to a producer who was considering both of us for the same part and telling him bad things about me—how I drank too much and caused trouble on the set, things like that."

But Rock got the best parts, despite all that. Either Tony's behind-the-hand badmouthing backfired and turned the producers off or else they just felt that Rock was right for the part and they would take their chances.

Because of those early experiences, Rock was never particularly fond of Tony Curtis. They had both scrambled up the Hollywood ladder and so, of course, their paths crossed even after their Universal sentences were up. Whenever they met (and I was present on several of those occasions) the smiles were polite, the handshakes brief, the exchanges cool and perfunctory.

Rock was one of those people who do not forgive. He did make a tenuous peace with Rod McKuen, and his relationship with Tony Randall never reached the point where there was anything to forgive, but the others were on his list permanently. He never forgave Blake Edwards or Julie Andrews. To my knowledge, he never even sent them Christmas cards—and his Christmas-card list encompassed most of the civilized world.

There was one other person with whom he had a falling out. That was the producer Ross Hunter, and that bout of incompatibility was particularly distressing to me because I was independently fond of both men. Besides, Rock and Ross had been great friends and had so much in common that I felt it was a tragedy that they had that falling out.

I had represented Ross when I was working for Rupert Allen and Ross was producing *Lost Horizon*, with Liv Ullmann and Peter Finch. I got to know Ross very well during that period. He is one of the funniest, nicest persons I had met in Hollywood. He was always pleasant to be with, and I had always enjoyed his company.

I found out, from things he said and things Rock said, that they had been good friends some years before, but something had happened and the friendship ended abruptly.

That split had existed for so long that I know for a fact that neither Rock nor Ross could remember exactly how it had started. I felt the two should heal the breach; they were, in my view, two people destined to be good friends. But it was more than a decade before I accomplished that goal.

Their mutual lack of memory about what had caused them to disagree was almost funny. I first asked Ross about it.

"Oh, Tom," he said, with a wry little smile, "I think I did something on one of my pictures that Rock thought was unfair. But for the life of me I can't remember what it was."

And then I asked Rock what had started it.

"Hell, I don't remember," Rock said. "I think it was something I said about one of his pictures that he didn't like, but I'm really not sure any more."

So I told Rock what Ross had said and I told Ross what Rock had said, and that was the end of it. The feud that had lasted for some dozen years was finally over. From then on, until the end of Rock's life, the two were back as close friends. I felt good about that.

Rock was the kind of person who valued old friends and old friendships. Just as he had nurtured the old grudge against Tony Curtis from his Universal days, in the same way he treasured the old friendships he maintained with others from that same era.

Julie Adams was one of several of his fellow Universal contract players Rock remained close to. He and she would get together often and reminisce, and when they laughed about things (Tony Curtis was one of their pet objects of mutual derision) it seemed to me like when I got together with some of my old college friends.

In fact, I believe those seventeen years at Universal corresponded, in Rock's life, to the collegiate experience he never had.

"You know," he said to me one evening after Julie Adams had been over for a visit, "I think the first few years I was at Universal were the happiest time of my life. No money, but, boy, was that a fun time for me!"

It was the time of his romance with Phyllis Gates, a time of discovery, a time of dreams coming true (or at least, becoming possible); a time of the first glimmer of recognition, a time of realizing that all those distant and glorious thoughts of fame and fortune were attainable.

"We were all kids together," he went on. "Julie and Piper and even Tony."

Piper was Piper Laurie who, like Rock, had had to struggle because of the name she had been saddled with. And, like Rock, she was (and still is) a fine actress, but people tended to write both of them off as silly twerps with silly twerpish names, and whoever heard of a silly twerp with a silly twerpish name who could really act?

Many years later, when Rock and I were in New York, we were out for a stroll on Columbus Avenue, which was then becoming a fashionable street. Rock and I had developed a sixth sense as we saw fans approaching; we could tell the ones who were going to stop and try to talk to us. When we saw them coming, we would always speed up and look the other way.

We were walking along leisurely and here came a couple of ladies, and Rock and I looked at each other. We just knew that these two approaching ladies were going to stop and talk, so we went into our act, walking faster and avoiding them. But they refused to be avoided. They stepped right in front of us and we had to stop.

"Boy, you sure are getting uppity in your old age," one of the ladies said, and then Rock and I had to start laughing. The two ladies we thought were fans coming to ask for autographs were Piper Laurie and Maureen Stapleton.

Rock and Piper fell into each other's arms, and it was another of those college reunions: Universal U., Class of '54.

Rock really liked everybody—99 per cent of everybody—and it was almost embarrassing how much they all liked him.

Judy Garland, for example. Rock and Judy were crazy about each other—platonically, of course. The affection was deep and lasting. But we knew even then that Judy had her problems, which kept getting worse and worse.

Rock was the one she would call most often when she was high on pills or sauce or whatever. The calls could come at any hour, day or night.

"Oh, Rock," she would say in her slurry voice.

"OK, Judy. It's OK. What's the problem now?"

"What? Oh, nothing. No problem. It's just that I am—well, the thing is I don't know where I am, or what I am, and I'm not even sure who I am."

It was pitiful for anyone to be like that, particularly someone as vital and alive and talented as Judy Garland. Rock would try to comfort her, and usually he succeeded. Sometimes, he would go to wherever it was she was and take her in his arms and console her until the demons had passed, at least temporarily.

Another good friend was Tyrone Power. Rock served as godfather to Ty Power's son, born after the actor died of a heart attack in Spain. For years after Power's death, Rock was frequently in touch with his widow, Debbie. She called once to tell us that Ty's boy, Rock's godson, was appearing in a play at his college.

"I know he would like very much if you came to see him," Debbie said, "but he's too embarrassed to ask you. But you know how it is with a mother—where her son is concerned, nothing is too embarrassing. Will you come?"

Rock could never deny an appeal like that (to him, motherhood was almost sacred) so he and I drove out to Pomona or some equally remote place, where we proceeded to spend what we both came to call "the worst night of our lives."

Debbie had neglected to tell us what play young Ty was doing. Of all things, it was *Macbeth*. Now Shakespeare is marvelous stuff—done by people who know what they are doing. In the wrong hands it becomes poisonous. And that night the hands were not merely wrong, they were inhuman. This was Amateur Night. Besides, we were sitting on folding wooden chairs, and there is nothing more uncomfortable after the fourth or fifth hour than a folding wooden chair.

Still, when Tyrone Power IV walked on stage, you could tell he had it. I still think he is going to make it, because there is some of the old Power power present in him. Heredity exists.

Taryn Power, Ty's daughter, lived in the same apartment building as Pat Fitzgerald, the woman who introduced Rock and me. And, often, when we played bridge there with Pat, Taryn would come in. She would take Rock aside when he was dummy.

"Tell me about my father," she would say. "Please, Mr. Hudson, tell me anything you can."

And Rock would tell her about Tyrone Power, the Ty Power he had known and liked. It got so he told Taryn the same stories over and over again. She never tired of listening to them.

The friendship between Rock and Elizabeth Taylor is well known. Some people have tried to read more into that friendship than there was. They were, simply, two people who liked each other enormously and respected each other even more. Today, Elizabeth Taylor is in the forefront in the fight against AIDS primarily because she was so affected by Rock's death.

Their friendship began when they did the marvelous film, *Giant*, together, in 1956. It continued, even though there were long stretches when they hardly saw each other. It blossomed again when the two were among the star-strewn cast of *The Mirror Crack'd*, with Angela Lansbury as Miss Marple in the adaptation of an Agatha Christie mystery. It was filmed in London, and Elizabeth and Rock each had suites at the Savoy and would have dinner with each other every night, alternating suites.

We were in New York when Elizabeth (who hates, incidentally, to be called Liz) had her triumph on the Broadway stage in *The Little Foxes*. The evening of the company's first rehearsal, Florence Klotz, the costume designer, gave a very intimate dinner party for Elizabeth in the private dining room at McMullen's, on Third Avenue. Only her closest friends and associates from the play were invited, and Rock and I were proud to be in that select group. We were perhaps twenty in all.

Among the guests were Lillian Hellman, who had, of course, written the play, and Maureen Stapleton, who was also one of the mainstays of the production. Both of those estimable ladies have well-recorded faults—Miss Hellman was inclined to be imperious and Miss Stapleton is inclined to drink a bit.

Apparently, at the rehearsal that day, Miss Hellman had commented, in loud and stirring terms, on some of the things about the proceedings she found objectionable. She was not a word-mincer, and she continued her frank commentary during the dinner. And Miss Stapleton glowered into her scotch as the others toasted everything from the play to the way penguins look on a summer's evening.

As toast after toast was proposed and drunk, and as all of the guests—Rock and me included—made speeches in praise of Elizabeth Taylor, and while Miss Hellman in her whisky contralto kept making her acid observations, Miss Stapleton said nothing. She just belted them down.

Finally she stood up.

"May I say a word here?" she said. Of course, we all listened attentively because Maureen Stapleton is known for her wit, which can be so caustic it makes lye seem like maple syrup.

She turned to Lillian Hellman, lifted her glass in the playwright's direction, and said, "I just want to say to you, Miss Hellman, get the fuck out of our lives."

That ended the party, quickly and permanently. But it was fun while it lasted.

Rock and Doris Day remained great friends long after they had stopped working together. They had private nicknames for each other: he always called her Eunice, and she called him Ernie.

"I just think she looks like a Eunice," he explained to me when I asked him about those names, "and she thinks I look like an Ernie."

He and Lauren Bacall also had a private little code between them, left over from the time they co-starred in a movie called *Written On the Wind.*

Whenever they met, this was invariably their first bit of conversation:

ROCK HUDSON: "What a man sees in a woman. . . "

BETTY BACALL: ". . . and what a woman sees in a man. . . "

BOTH TOGETHER: ". . . is written on the wind."

Then they would laugh hysterically and fall into each other's arms. That exchange wasn't dialogue from the film, it was the catch phrase used in the ads for it.

When that movie was being made, Betty's husband, Humphrey Bogart, was dying. Every night, after filming wrapped, Rock would take Betty home and visit with Bogie for a few minutes. He admired both of them.

Dinah Shore was another old and good friend. When she had her very successful talk show, Rock would never appear on it—except on her Christmas show. Somehow she persuaded him to be her Santa Claus one year, in beard and false tummy and all that, and it became a tradition for as long as her show lasted. Every year Rock was Dinah's Santa Claus. It helped him get into the Christmas spirit.

Rock, who had grown up with absolutely no knowledge of how the upper crust lives and acts, taught himself to be as urbane and polished as he looked. It was an acquired veneer. From the time of that gaffe at Gina Lollobrigida's villa, he studied, observed, noted, copied, learned. And he became as suave as silk.

Rock rubbed elbows and, occasionally, knees with royalty. So did I, because where Rock went, I went. I was not however, there when he was presented to Queen Elizabeth, but both Rock and I became very chummy with Princess Margaret.

It was Roddy McDowall, who knows everybody in the world except perhaps Muammar Qaddafi, who introduced us to Margaret. There have been a great many unfavorable and unkind words written about her but, I can only judge her from my (and Rock's) personal experience. We both liked the lady. In fact, we found her a fun person to be with.

In the first place, you might not expect it of a regular royal princess, but she is a great dialectician. In fact, I think she can handle more dialects than anybody I have ever been around, and I've been around a great many masterful storytellers.

She also knows the lyrics to every song ever written, just about. And likes nothing better than an evening around a piano, with people calling out song titles and the pianist whipping into the accompaniment and she leading the group in singing the song.

We saw her in London several times and, once, when we were both in San Francisco, we all went out to a dinner party together. She was the guest of honor at the affair, given at the impressive Getty home.

At first we had a small problem with what to call her. We were not the type to drop "Your Highness" into every conversation, yet she was obviously not the Maggie or Peggy sort of gal. So we did what we found her other friends did—we said "Ma'am," and, as we got to know her better, we called her "P.M," for Princess Margaret.

Rock was able to meet people like that—royalty and presidents, such as John Kennedy—very smoothly. If he stood in awe of anybody, it was the Hollywood legends.

Ingrid Bergman, for example. In common with the rest of mankind, he thought she was probably the finest actress in the movies, at the time, and the owner/operator of one of the great faces in the history of the known world.

Inevitably they met. It was at some party, and Rock stood there, jaw dropped, as that beautiful woman made her entrance. And, in due time, they stood together, and were introduced, and it was up to Rock to say something.

To his eternal chagrin, the only thing he could think of to say to Ingrid Bergman was "You sure are tall."

When he told that story to Carol Burnett, she said it reminded her of the time she was at a party like that and among the guests was her secret crush, Cary Grant.

Carol's husband at the time, Joe Hamilton, knowing of her infatuation for Grant, tried to persuade her to go over and be introduced, but in the presence of this man she had admired so long and so ardently, she was simply too shy.

As they were leaving, she felt a tap on her shoulder, and turned to find herself face-to-face with Cary Grant.

"Excuse me, Miss Burnett," he said. I just wanted to tell you how much I enjoy you on television and to thank you for all the hours of wonderful entertainment you've given me."

She stood there a moment, trying to grasp the enormity of the event that was happening to her. Then she realized it was now her turn to say something.

"Oh, thank you so much, Mr. Grant," she finally blurted out. "And I want you to know that I feel you are a credit to your profession."

Then she ran out of the house, in tears.

"And, forever after," she told Rock and me, "I have been angry at myself. Imagine—I told Cary Grant that he was a credit to his profession!"

So Rock would tease Carol by saying she was "a credit to your profession" and she would counter by saying "You sure are tall."

CHAPTER SEVEN

Travel

There's a great big world out there, and the only point in having that great big world is to see it. Rock and I, among other shared pleasures, both found travel the most pleasurable of all.

Whenever either of us read anything—in a book or a magazine or newspaper—about some exciting place in some distant land, we both itched to get up and go and see that place for ourselves.

Often, as a consequence, our trips would be planned on the spur of the moment. We both kept our passports scrupulously up to date, and it didn't take us long to pack (with James' able assistance, needless to say), so that if Rock might say "Hey, we don't have anything to do for the next few weeks, let's go to London. I'm hungry for some real fish and chips!" We just took off and went to London. We could call and make our reservations—people were always happy to accommodate Rock Hudson—and get packed and be off in a couple of hours.

Our first trip together was to Australia in 1972, when Rock was invited by the Australian film people. He had won Australia's equivalent of our Oscar, the Logi, so they had asked him to come to Sydney to accept it.

"Want to go to Australia?" he asked suddenly.

"Well, of course. I'll go anywhere."

"Maybe we could stop in Tahiti or Fiji or somewhere like that on the way," he said. "See if you can work it out."

So I worked it out. Tahiti had always intrigued me—the name is one of those automatic calls to adventure—so we made our plans.

Rock had been to the South Pacific in his days as a sailor in World War II, and he had always said to me, "Tom, you have never really seen a sunset until you've seen a South Pacific sunset." And he said he was looking forward to showing me my first South Pacific sunset, when we got to Tahiti. I was all primed for something spectacular.

Our plane was scheduled to leave Los Angeles late at night. The scheduled time of departure was after eleven o'clock. In those days, people dressed up to fly on an airplane, which was very silly, so we were in our suits and ties. Today common sense dictates casual and comfortable dress for those long and often miserable flights.

"I tell you what," Rock said as we were getting ready. "Why don't we leave now and go over to Trader Vic's and get ourselves in the proper South Pacific mood?"

I was game, so we went to Trader Vic's in Beverly Hills and drank mai tais and munched on egg rolls and spare ribs and figured we were getting a primer in South Pacific-style food and drink. (Of course, it was about as authentic there as it would be to open a fortune cookie and think you are in China, but we didn't really care.)

So we lurched onto the plane and as soon as we were airborne, we promptly fell asleep. We arrived in Papeete about five in the morning, slightly hung over, looking pretty disheveled and feeling likewise. We had to wait in the Papeete airport—a grim and uncomfortable place in the best of times—for three or four hours until our plane left for Moorea, a short flight to an idyllic island. Moorea and Bora-Bora are Tahiti's satellites, like moons around a planet, and the island of Tahiti itself is not particularly lovely. But Moorea and Bora-Bora are thoroughly enchanting.

We got to Moorea about nine or so in the morning and, as we had feared, our room was not yet available. So we sat in the lobby, drinking some wild Moorean concoction with eighty-three different kinds of rum and a blue paper umbrella floating serenely on top.

Most hotels on the South Pacific islands have their rooms in the form of small individual structures built on stilts out over the lagoon. So when we finally got to our room, it was worth the wait. We could sit on the deck and watch tropical fish of all kinds, in all sorts of wild colors and all manner of wacky shapes, cavorting in the crystal-clear water. And we dove in and swam among them.

We had lunch and took a long nap and then, after another swim with an entirely different cast of fish, we saw that the sun was beginning to call it a day. Rock became very excited.

"And now, my friend," he said, "it is time for your first South Pacific sunset. Rock Hudson Productions, in cooperation with God and Mother Nature, is proud to present for your approval—a wild and wonderful sunset! But we have to do this right. I believe a moment of this importance in your life calls for martinis on the deck to start with. Why don't you call room service and have them send up a handful of martinis?"

"With what do you suggest I make that call?" I said. There was no phone in the room and, ergo, no room service.

So Rock went up to the main hotel and asked the bartender for a dozen martinis to go. The best he could come up with was a wine carafe, which he filled with what he said were martinis, and he plopped the carafe in a plastic dishpan and surrounded it with a few weary ice cubes. The martinis were the worst either of us had ever tasted. But, gamely, we drank them, sitting on the deck and toasting the setting sun. And we waited for the gaudy sunset to make its appearance.

"You just wait a few minutes," Rock said. "You will see colors you have never seen before in your entire lifetime on this planet."

"What's that big black cloud doing there?" I asked.

And that stinker of a cloud sailed across the western horizon, totally obliterating the sun. There was no sunset that night, at least not in the part of the world where we were waiting so patiently.

"Oh, well," Rock said. "Foiled again. But I promise you a

smashing sunset tomorrow night. That cloud would not dare to come back. OK—now it's beauty hour.'

To Rock, "beauty hour" meant it was time for both of us to get spiffed up for dinner. That was always the expression he used to suggest that we both shower and change. In Moorea, we dressed in white pants and colorful shirts and went to the dining room in the main hotel.

The next night, we were back on Tahiti itself, at a swanky highrise hotel hanging off a cliff in Papeete. And this night, he vowed, he would produce a sunset to remember. Things looked promising, because our penthouse suite faced the western sea, and there was an island offshore to give the sunset a bit of contrast and dimension. Besides, the martinis were delicious—chilled to perfection, served immaculately in frosted glasses with olives and all the fixin's.

We had a very private balcony, so Rock suggested we go out on the balcony and watch the sunset from there, martinis in hand and hopes high. We were just about to get dressed for dinner—the call for beauty hour had gone out—and so, in preparation for the ritual beauty-hour shower we had no clothes on. We just had some towels wrapped around our bodies.

It was a warm tropical evening, and we sat there, in our towels, happily drinking martinis and watching what turned out to be one of the most glorious sunsets the South Pacific had ever seen. The western sky was painted in reds and oranges, pinks and purples, of a vividness I had never seen before. With the palm trees and that little offshore island silhouetted against that vibrant sky, it was a sight to remember. Rock was vindicated.

When it was over, and night had fallen, Rock turned to me and said "Well, now, how was that?"

"Boy, when you make a sunset, you sure make a sunset!" I said. "Really, Rock, it was breathtaking."

"OK. Now our interrupted beauty hour continues."

And we got up, started to go back into our room—and found that the door had shut and locked behind us. We could not get back into our room and were marooned out on the balcony, with only our skimpy towels between us and total indecency.

We managed to squirm our way across to the adjoining balcony. We rapped on the sliding glass door. You can imagine what our neighbors thought—they were presumably having a predinner nap and suddenly heard a rapping from their balcony and there was Rock Hudson and some other guy, with only towels on, smiling and waving.

That evening set the tone for our future travels. Having fun was the goal. Rock loved life and lived it to the fullest, and that, to him, primarily meant experiencing everything he could possibly experience, seeing everything he could possibly see.

And, because of who he was, we were always welcomed with open arms, and often other parts of the anatomy as well. On that first trip, for example, we were greeted exuberantly in the two Australian cities we visited, Sydney and Melbourne.

One of Rock's quirks surfaced on that trip. As you may imagine, whenever a star visits a city where Hollywood stars are rarities, he or she gets dozens, often hundreds, of invitations. People drop notes off at the star's hotel, which has generally been mentioned in the press, inviting him to all kinds of functions and parties and affairs. Most stars automatically toss them into the wastebasket, but not Rock.

He would read them all carefully and, occasionally, accept one or two.

It all depended on the invitation, of course, and how it was worded and whether Rock felt the people were sincere and honest. In Sydney, on that first trip, there was a very nicely written letter from a woman who simply said she was a fan and would be honored to have Rock as a guest for dinner at her home so she could show him how a typical Australian family lived.

That piqued Rock's curiosity.

"It might be interesting," Rock said, showing me the neatly written letter. "Feel like going?"

"Sure. We're free Tuesday night. Why not?"

So we stunned the lady by accepting her invitation, and she and her husband picked us up at our hotel on that evening, and we had dinner at their house, with all the family around. She was, it turned out, a very sweet middle-aged housewife who had had a crush on

Rock Hudson for years. The family was pleasant, comfortably middle-class, and the dinner she served was good, plain, home cooking, which was nice after all those restaurant meals. It was a very enjoyable evening, and one that would be repeated in many different countries over the next dozen or so years. It was a good way, Rock felt, to get to know the real people, not just the high society folk we met as a matter of course on those trips.

Often, we were able to accept an invitation from some foreign source and combine it with promotion for a coming movie. That way the expenses could be divvied up and nobody got hurt too badly. Rock was, for example, invited to go to Buenos Aires in 1973 by an Argentinian television producer. He wanted to do a program about Rock's life and thought the capper would be if Rock appeared live for a short interview. But he couldn't afford to bring Rock and me down in the style to which we were accustomed.

At the time, Rock had just finished shooting *Showdown* for Universal and, besides, his television show, *McMillan & Wife*, was a big hit in Argentina. So I got Universal and NBC to join the Argentinian producer; the cost of the trip was split three ways, we went and had a great time, the producer got his interview, and both Universal and NBC got their promotion. Everybody was happy—especially Rock and me.

Before we left California for that trip, Stefanie Powers told us we had to look for antiques in B.A. (as us travel experts call Buenos Aires).

"Antiques in B.A.?" Rock said. "What have they got, old bolos and guitars?"

"No, no," said Stefanie. "Don't forget, a lot of Nazis went to Argentina after the war. And they schlepped all their old furniture with them. There are some great buys, if you like that heavy old German furniture."

So, when we were in B.A., we tried to get to the street she had mentioned to us, a street supposedly full of what Stefanie called "the greatest antique stores in the whole wide world." Rock loved that kind of furniture, and his mouth was watering, figuring he was going to get some fabulous buys.

But we literally could not reach that street. We started out several times but were stopped by hordes of smiling, cheering, yelling, kissing, hugging fans. We finally had to give that idea up.

The studio and the network asked that we extend our trip and go to Rio de Janeiro and do more promotional work there. They didn't have to ask twice, because it was carnival time in Rio. You just haven't seen crowds or witnessed wholesale jollity until you've been in Rio at carnival time.

All barriers come down—social, moral, whatever. Anything and everything goes. You check your inhibitions at the airport, like they used to check their guns at the door in the Old West.

While we were in Rio, we made the obligatory sightseeing tour up to Corcovado, the mountain that has the gigantic Christ figure standing atop it with arms outstretched. That day, a heavy cloud sat on top of the mountain, obscuring the statue. We climbed the steps until we were at the base of the figure and then—a miracle!—the cloud lifted and there stood two friends from Hollywood, Valerie Harper and Ruth Buzzi. Valerie always took credit for that particular miracle, claiming some sort of divine power, which she very well may have.

They loved Rock in Rio but, with all the hoopla and the carrying-on, they didn't bother him. They were too busy to be bothered bothering people. So in Rio we could go anywhere—except that, with the carnival crowds, you couldn't get there from here.

At the time we were in Argentina, the head man of the ruling junta was, like the rest of his countrymen, a wildly enthusiastic Rock Hudson fan. We were told that he wanted Rock's autograph and would be pleased if we would come to his office, for the purpose of writing Rock's name on a photograph.

Of course we obliged. Who knows what can happen to anybody, particularly a norteamericano, who doesn't accept the invitation of the head man of a military junta? We showed up at his office, signed the picture, and exchanged pleasantries.

"How are you enjoying Argentina?" His Nibs asked us through the interpreter.

"Very well, Your Excellency," Rock said. But the disappointment of trying to reach that street of antique shops still rankled. "Our only problem is that your people are so friendly and so enthusiastic that we find it difficult to get around the city. We wish we could see more of your beautiful country, but it is impossible."

The general frowned. He talked, in Spanish, with his aides for a minute or two, then turned back to us.

"It is solved," he said. "Tomorrow you will be flown to Mar del Plata where, I assure you, no one will bother you."

So the next day we went to Mar del Plata, a rip-snorting little city, Argentina's equivalent of Las Vegas. There they are used to seeing celebrities (mostly Argentinian, but also from all over South America and Europe too) and are therefore less impressed and less intrusive in their adulation. We were able to move around easily, without our every step being an occasion for a miniriot.

One evening we went to a little club late at night, because we had heard that there was one of South America's top singing groups performing. They were called Las Chacharillas, a gaucho group, and they were terrific. But the crowd got a little boisterous when they spotted Rock—they were all stewed to the gills—and we had to leave. As we were leaving, one of the singers came over to me.

"Señor," he said, in fractured but willing English, "after the show, we usually go to a little bar (he gave me the name) and if you come, we will sing for you."

So, later that evening, we went to the little bar and it was like a gaucho jam session, with many singers and vocal groups and instrumentalists getting up and having an impromptu songfest. The patrons were all fans of that kind of music, very appreciative and knowledgeable, and called out song requests. They couldn't have cared less about Rock Hudson being in their midst, as long as Las Chacharillas sang "Adios, Macushla," or whatever it was they wanted.

So the drinks flowed and the songs warbled and when we left the place, we were amazed to see the sun shining brightly. It was seven in the morning, and we had been there all night.

Some years later we got a letter from Las Chacharillas, telling us they were coming to Los Angeles. So we invited them over to the house one night, and had everybody we knew in the music business there to hear them. Even Doris Day came, and Ricardo Montalban

*R*ock's mother, Katherine Fitzgerald.

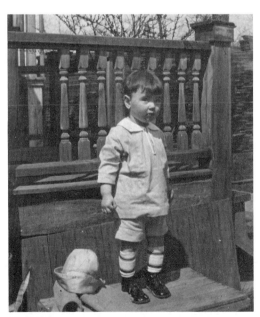

*B*orn Roy Harold Scherer, Jr., Rock grew up in Winnetka, Illinois.

*A*bove: Rock, also on a German postcard.

*R*ock, in an early publicity photo.

*L*eft: Rock, as pictured on a German postcard. He was extremely popular in that country where he won eight Bambi awards, the German Oscar.

*A*bove: Rock with Miss Wee Wee.

*R*ock, with his wife, Phyllis Gates.

*A*bove: Rock with co-star Jane Wyman on the set of *All Heaven Allows* (1956).

*T*op left: Rock, in a publicity still from *Bengal Brigade*, made in 1954.

*B*ottom left: Rock is having some fun on the set of *Giant*, seen here with Elizabeth Taylor and director George Stevens.

*T*his is the photo that got Rock the leading role in *Pretty Maids All in a Row* (1971) because the producer's wife saw it and thought he was perfect for it.

*R*ock with Dorothy Malone and Kirk Douglas on the set of *The Last Sunset* (1961).

*R*ock and Doris Day starred in three hit comedies, but the first, *Pillow Talk* (1959), was the most popular.

*A*t Amanahashidate in Japan, Rock (left) and Tom looking through their legs at the lake, which gives a mirrored reflection showing what you would see if you were looking at it straight on.

*I*n 1980 Tom and Rock sailed to Cherbourg, France on the *Queen Elizabeth II.*

*T*his page top: Nancy Walker, who appeared with Rock in "McMillan and Wife," and her husband David Craig, joined Rock and Tom in Italy on the 1980 European trip. That's Rock behind Nancy.

*A*bove: Having just completed the daily mile around the deck, Rock, Claire Trevor, and Ross Hunter pretend to be utterly exhausted, on the 1982 Christmas cruise on the *Stella Solaris*.

*L*eft: A candid shot of Rock on vacation in Italy.

*A*bove: Rock from "McMillan and Wife."

*T*op Right: Rock with Elizabeth Taylor and Liza Minelli at the Golden Globe Awards in the last year of his life.

*B*ottom right: Rock and Linda Evans, with whom he appeared on "Dynasty."

*R*ock from the last formal photo session taken before he died.

got up and sang with them. They presented us with their records, which went into our joint record collection—the collection that disappeared about the time Marc Christian left.

While we were still in Mar del Plata, the Argentine version of the Screen Actors Guild, their union of performers, held a luncheon to honor Rock and made him an honorary member. I think Rock eventually had more honorary memberships in more organizations than anybody since J. Edgar Hoover.

Incidentally, at that luncheon, and wherever and whenever I traveled with Rock, he always introduced me, simply, as "Tom Clark." He never prefaced or followed my name with any explanation—it was not "my publicist, Tom Clark" or "Tom Clark, who is my business associate," or even "my friend, Tom Clark"—and I appreciated that. So I was always treated as an equal by the people we met, never in any way condescending or snide.

I was never excluded from anything, either. If Rock was invited to anything—a reception, a luncheon, a dinner, whatever—he always assumed the invitation was for both of us, and I would accompany him, and I assumed the same. To my knowledge, no one ever attempted to invite him by himself or to keep me away for any reason. I know that if such an attempt had been made Rock would not have allowed it to happen. He would not have gone if I had not been included and accepted.

We usually traveled light. We became such experienced travelers that we knew what clothing we would need—and James always anticipated our needs—and took along only what was absolutely needed, nothing more.

Of course, if the trip was going to be a long one, that was a different matter. When Rock went to London to do *I Do! I Do!*, we knew we would be there for four months. And we knew that those four months would spread out over two seasons—winter and spring. So we each took a steamer trunk full of clothing, and bought considerably more on Bond Street.

In fact, as it turned out, we went from London to Canada, as Rock was going to do the show there for three weeks after the London run closed. So he had Mark Miller fly to London just to pick up our clothes and take them back to California. He didn't want to have to worry about all that luggage during the Canada trip. And so we went to Canada with a minimum of personal luggage.

Another memorable trip we took was to Japan, in the spring of 1978, when the cherry blossoms were in gorgeous bloom. The occasion was Japan's first movie award ceremony. The Japanese film industry had decided to set up an Academy Award system modeled after ours and asked Rock to be their guest at the first big bash.

We decided to use that invitation as an excuse to see that part of the world—not only Japan, but, if we could swing it, Red China. This was before China had really opened up to American tourists, when the first crack was appearing in what previously had been a closed society.

We stopped off in Hawaii en route. Any excuse to go to the Mauna Kea Hotel on the Big Island we immediately seized. I think that was our favorite resort, our favorite place to unwind completely. We made it a point to go there every three or four months for a few days, at least, and it became something of a second home to us. We knew the maids and waiters by name, and they always gave us a warm welcome.

This time we only stopped for a day or two, then flew on to Tokyo. And there we were, as usual, given the royal treatment (except instead of being wined and dined we were saked and sushied) and we had a delightful few days.

Our only problems were the same ones encountered by many Americans, particularly tall ones. Japan is a world built for the Japanese, naturally, and they are by and large short people. So the doorways are low, and both Rock and I were continually bumping our heads as we entered and left rooms and buildings. And every time we did it and said "Ouch!" all the little Japanese girls would giggle, a sound something like a gurgling, happy-go-lucky brook. They thought it was a lot of fun to see a big, gawky American clunk his head on a doorway.

In Japan, when you enter a home or a shrine, you take your shoes off. In many places, they give you clogs to put on your feet in exchange. Here again our largeness caused a bit of a problem. Both Rock and I wore size 13 shoes, and the tiny Japanese had never figured on anybody coming along with feet that big. Size 13 clogs didn't exist. So we would have to slip and slide along in our stocking feet.

After the award ceremony, we were invited to visit a remote inn in a tiny resort, Amanahashidate, far up in the mountains. It was still exactly as it had been for many centuries, with not a sign of a modern convenience. The toilet facility was a hole in the floor. The beds were mats spread on the floor. Still, for a couple of days, it was a wonderful experience.

That rustic quality contrasted markedly with our stay in Tokyo itself, where the film industry had put us up at the Imperial Hotel in what must have been the largest hotel suite in the world. It was so big that I don't think we every fully explored it. We were afraid of getting lost and never finding our way out.

The Japanese authorities generously gave us a guide and arranged for us to visit Kyoto—entirely at their expense—and they even tried to arrange an audience for us with the emperor. But he was ill at the time, and so, unfortunately, that never came to pass.

And then it was on to Hong Kong, where we stayed at the glorious old Peninsula Hotel in their Marco Polo Suite, which was almost as large as the one in Tokyo. This suite came equipped with a live-in butler and maid; because they actually have their rooms in the suite, they are on call twenty-four hours a day and jump when you ring for them.

Friends had arranged for us to have a guide in Hong Kong who showed us things the average tourist doesn't see. (We saw the average touristy things, too, because they are fun, but we also went over, beyond, and behind those normal sights.) He took us to a store the Red Chinese had set up, because we had gotten permission to go on to Red China and this was a way of indoctrinating us as to what we might expect, a sort of introductory course into the Red Chinese way of life.

"Here, Mr. Hudson," the guide said, holding up a large green bottle, "is a very popular Chinese wine."

"What's that floating in it?" Rock asked.

"Oh, traditional unborn mice," the guide said. "You will find it very tasty."

Rock turned to me and we both gagged a little. Drinking wine with unborn anything floating around in it was not our idea of a jolly time. We didn't even like born mice in our wine.

Then we were contacted by the Red Chinese authorities. As another step in our previsit indoctrination we were asked to move into a Red Chinese hotel for two days prior to our trip. It wasn't exactly a request; it was more of a demand. That didn't sit too well with Rock, either.

"I don't like the idea of them telling me what I must do," he said. "You know how I hate it when people tell me what to do without giving me an explanation."

I certainly did know that. If people carefully told Rock what they wanted him to do and why they wanted him to do it, he was usually very cooperative. But he did not like it when he was ordered to do something without the accompanying explanation.

"I don't think I'm going to move into their hotel," he said. "I like it right where we are."

"Well, let's wait a bit," I said. "Maybe somebody will come over and explain it all to us."

So we waited. But that night, as we had dinner in the Peninsula's grand old dining room, we noticed a group of actors come into the room. They were all New York people, and among them was the television game show host, Gene Rayburn. Rock had met Rayburn at some point in New York.

Rayburn and a couple of his friends spotted Rock and came over to our table to say hello. Actors are like that: always game for a conversation, especially if it involves the performing business.

"What brings you to Hong Kong?" Rayburn asked.

"Well, we were in Tokyo and decided to come over here, and now we're planning to go on to China," Rock said.

The entire group started talking at once, telling us not to go, and began citing chapter and verse as to why it was a dumb thing to do and how difficult it was for tourists in China at the moment.

"You have to carry a flashlight with you at all times because the electric power goes off at seven o'clock."

"You have to eat where they tell you to eat, when they tell you to eat, and what they tell you to eat—and it's all only marginally digestible."

"You can't go anywhere by yourself."

"You have no idea what you're going to see and no choice in what you're going to see. You may be taken to see the Great Wall or you may not, depending."

"They make you stay there for a minimum of eight days. And it doesn't matter if you get sick or not, you can't leave the country before those eight days are up."

"It's all one great big mess."

Later, when the group had left, Rock shook his head.

"That tears it," he said. "I'm not going. It doesn't sound like fun—and I still don't think I want to go anywhere where they put unborn mice in the wine."

"It could be very exciting," I said. I still would have liked to have gone.

"No, that's it. We're not going."

So we didn't go. Instead of seeing Red China in the raw, we went back to the Mauna Kea in Hawaii, and spent a week in the large, lush lap of luxury.

And, sadly, neither of us ever did get to China. Rock, of course, will never go, but I still hope to make it some day. It was something like our glorious dream of going to the Greek isles.

That had long been one of our better-quality fantasies. Rock had a wonderful plan for a Greek-isles excursion. We were going to charter a yacht and take a group of friends—naturally, they would all be bridge players—and cruise the Greek isles leisurely for a month or so.

"I want to have a lot of men in white coats on the yacht," Rock said, "to serve drinks and empty ashtrays. This is going to be the best trip we ever had."

So we made serious inquiries about yacht chartering and we began putting down lists of people we would invite along. But whenever we set a date, something came along and we would have to postpone the trip. It got to be a sort of sad joke in our lives, that Greek-isles trip that somehow never happened.

I kept urging him to forget everything else and make that trip, even if it meant forgoing a part.

"Come on, Rock," I'd say. "Let's do it. The hell with this not being the right time or with all your other excuses. Let's just screw everything else, and just take off and go."

But he couldn't do that. He would always have some good, legitimate reason—good and legitimate in his mind—why we couldn't go. At least not right then.

When Rock was dying, one of the steady stream of visitors mentioned that he had recently returned from a trip to the Greek isles. Rock and I exchanged glances.

"That's one I still owe you, Tom," he said, but he never was able to pay off that debt. So we never did get to the Greek isles together, and I've always regretted that I wasn't firmer in my urging him to go while he still could. It would have been a trip to remember, the way Rock had envisioned it.

On Christmas 1974, among Rock's presents to me was a series of French lessons at the Berlitz School. These were private lessons and very intensive—four times a week. I went to two of them, but I could tell it wasn't going to work. I simply do not have a good head for languages. When I worked in Mexico as a unit publicist on a series of MGM pictures I had picked up just enough Spanish to make my basic wants understood, but that was the extent of my mastery of any foreign tongue except Texan.

"Look, Rock," I said, after the second lesson, "why don't you come with me? That way we can study and practice together, and maybe we'll both learn to get by in French."

Rock had always said that if a person can speak French and English, he can be comfortable in any country in the world. That was why he had given me those French lessons. Moreover, we were at that time thinking about a trip to France and probably other countries where French was spoken, so it would be valuable to be fluent in that language.

Rock wasn't working at that particular time, so he said he would go with me to the lessons. (I was working then, for Rupert Allen, but a lot of my work was at night, covering various functions, so

Allen said it would be OK with him if I took off an hour or so a couple of afternoons a week for the lessons).

So we began taking the French lessons together, and Rock really worked hard at it. He had much more of a natural gift for languages than I have. And, besides, he had his nights free, while I often had to cover some affair in the evening. So he was able to devote considerably more time to his practicing in the evening than I could. Result: He was way ahead of me, and gloated about it. I didn't mind that so much, but he did a lot of his gloating in French, and I couldn't understand a word he gloated.

Perhaps because of that situation, Rock asked me to come and work for him and his own production company, Mammoth Productions.

"I really need you," he said. "You know a lot more about the business end of this business than I do, and you are much better at dealing with people than I am."

So I told Rupert Allen I was resigning, and went to work as the vice-president of Mammoth Productions.

By a happy coincidence, Rock was invited to Madrid. Some people in Spain were planning a retrospective of Rock Hudson films and asked him if he would attend.

"How about if we go to Madrid for that retrospective," he said, "and then we buy a car—I've always wanted a Peugeot—and drive to France. We hole up there for a month or so and speak nothing but French. We'll really get the language down pat by then."

It sounded like a terrific idea and, as it turned out, it was the best vacation either of us had ever had.

He really threw himself into his French lessons at Berlitz then, in preparation for the trip. And he signed up for one day of what they call "total immersion"—he stayed at the school from eight in the morning for the entire day. He was closeted with four instructors during that day, and they spoke not a word of English to him all day long: *rien* but French. He had to order his lunch in French and ask to leave the room in French. That night his eyeballs were glazed.

"Mon dieu!" he said. "Quel travail!"

We were scheduled to leave on a Thursday, as I remember it. But the Saturday before our departure date, he suddenly had one of his typical brainstorms.

"You know," he said, "I've never been to Portugal. Have you?"

I hadn't either.

"Well, then, let's go there first. We can go to Portugal for a few days before we have to be in Madrid. *JAMES!*"

And James rushed in and started packing, and I called and made the arrangements, and the next evening we were off to Portugal, to Lisbon and Estoril. And then Madrid. We were in those two countries for about a week.

"How about we go to Rome for a while?" he said. "Milton and Claire (Milton Bren and his wife, Claire Trevor) are there. I'd like to show you Rome."

I had no quarrel with that, so we went to Rome. This was long after his debacle at Gina Lollobrigida's and, by now, he was reasonably fluent in Italian. And we had his usual driver, Mario, and the Brens were great fun to be with and we had a delightful week in Rome.

By this time, with typical Hudson fickleness, he had switched from wanting a Peugeot to needing a Porsche. We decided to go to Munich to pick one up from a dealer there. But, of course, we went the long way—we took a train from Rome to Venice, spent a few days absorbing gondolas and canals, then flew from Venice to Munich.

As we stepped off the plane at the Munich Airport we were suddenly surrounded by a cheering crowd, and there were several beaming security people.

"It is marvelous that you came here for it, Herr Hudson," one of them said. We hadn't a clue what he was talking about. "Your presence will truly make this a night we will always remember."

The security men whisked us into a limousine. We drove into the city and were proudly escorted to a lovely suite in a grand old hotel on the ancient city square. As we drove in and talked to our escorts, we were able to piece together what it was all about. We were the beneficiaries of a gigantic coincidence.

Our visit happened to coincide with the night of the first national television broadcast ever scheduled in Germany. The people of that city had been looking forward to the broadcast excitedly, and had invited a lot of international celebrities to attend. Not one of them had showed up. (Rock hadn't been invited—at least neither of us had been aware of any such invitation.)

When we stepped off the plane, they naturally jumped to the conclusion that that was why we were there. We did not disabuse them of that notion and consequently had a great time as their guests.

What made the coincidence even more confounding was the fact that the first movie to be shown that night was *Lover Come Back*, starring Rock Hudson, Doris Day, and Tony Randall. So, when we were relaxing in our suite later that evening we switched on that first German national telecast, and there was Herr Hudson talking German to Fraulein Day.

We watched for twenty minutes or so and then decided it was time for dinner. After all, Rock had seen the picture before. So we asked the concierge to recommend a good restaurant, and we walked to it, and went in—but it was completely empty. Nothing is as disconcerting as being the only patrons in a huge restaurant. We started to eat and then, about an hour later, suddenly there was a flood of customers. They had all been home, watching Rock Hudson make love to Doris Day. And, when they came into the restaurant, there sat Rock Hudson. I have never seen so many shocked people at one time in my life.

For some reason, Rock had always been tremendously popular in Germany. Like most American stars, he was very well liked in all of Europe, but he was particularly appreciated by the Germans. He won eight Bambis (the German popularity award) and I believe that is still a world Bambi record. And so his appearance at that restaurant that night was a cause for what seemed almost a national holiday. It continued for the duration of our stay in Germany. Wherever we went there were cheering crowds and blown kisses and big smiles, and I even detected some heel-clicking. It was a terribly moving experience for Rock. Like anybody, he liked being liked.

The next day, the Porsche dealership delivered Rock's new car to the hotel. It wasn't the fanciest or most expensive model they had, but it was still a Porsche, and we both hungered to drive it. We took turns, but Rock got to go first, which I suppose was only fair. After all, it was his money that bought it.

We just tossed our bags in the car and set off, with no destination in mind. We knew that eventually we would wind up in Paris but, en route, we simply went where the road looked most inviting. Every night we would call home, to check in and see if there were any emergencies or interesting job offers for Rock. But, otherwise, we just meandered idly around western Europe.

Our first stop was Switzerland where, on the spur of the whim, we visited Deborah Kerr and her husband, Peter Viertel. Their home, in Klosters, was a marvel, with their own private alp out the big living-room window. When we told them of our aimless gadding about, Deborah wondered why we didn't visit the Italian lake country. Rock had shot *A Farewell to Arms* there, and Deborah's prompting made him remember how beautiful it is.

"Great idea," he said. "I've always wanted to show that country to Tom, so this is the perfect time."

So we went down into Italy for a few days, then we drifted around some more. And that's the way it went for the next several weeks. Just aimless wandering, following the road that seemed to offer the most romance and the most adventure, taking every seductive detour.

There came a point, however, when it seemed to me that Rock had abandoned our plan (which was having no plan at all) and had succumbed to that terrible American curse—needing a destination.

We were in northern Italy, heading vaguely in a southwesterly direction, and I saw signs pointing to Milano. I mentioned that I had never seen the Milano opera house, La Scala, and it was supposed to be so beautiful.

"Let's take a look," I said.

"No, we don't want to do that," he said. "I know where I'm going."

He was driving at the time and he just stepped down on the accelerator and barreled ahead. I muttered something about La Scala Milano and he muttered back that he had already seen it once and then he said, again, "I know where I'm going."

I was getting a bit pissed off, but I didn't say anything more. And he kept on going until we pulled into the little city of Portofino. When we arrived there, I understood. This was Rock's gift to me. He had called ahead without my knowledge and made reservations for us at the Hotel Splendido. He had been there before, knew it, and felt it was the most exquisite hotel in Europe. He had wanted to surprise me with Portofino and the Splendido, which was why he had been so brusque and so determined to get there.

As soon as we checked in, I could sympathize with his admiration for the place. If you think you've died and gone to Heaven, you haven't—you have merely gone to the Splendido Hotel in Portofino, Italy. It sits up on a bluff, the blue Mediterranean spread out in front of you, and the hotel's service and food and furnishings and everything are truly the finest anywhere.

"Is this better than Milano?" Rock asked, as we sat on our balcony, aperitifs in hand, nibbling on a tray of scrumptious hors d'oeuvres a smiling waiter had brought.

"Much better," I said. "Sorry if I was gruff."

"OK," he said. "And I'm sorry I couldn't tell you, but I wanted all this to be a surprise."

And then it was, finally, on to France. After Portugal, Spain, Italy, Germany, Switzerland, and Italy again, we would finally get the chance to try out the French we had studied so diligently back at Berlitz in Beverly Hills.

We drove west along the coast from Portofino, and crossed the border into France during a torrential downpour. We really had no idea where we were and, of course, no idea of where we were going. When the rain stopped, we found ourselves in a little Riviera town named Eze. So we decided to stop for lunch. We were both hungry and Rock suddenly realized the area looked familiar.

"I know where there is a place to eat," he said. "If I remember, there's a restaurant in a castle in Eze that hangs over the Corniche, and that's just ahead. Let's go there."

So we went—Rock had a remarkable memory for things like restaurants, bars and hotels—and it was a very special place. This was, we decided, the place we would premiére our knowledge of the French language. We would speak only French and nothing else.

It was hot, after the summer storm, and we were thirsty, so the first words Rock uttered in French were a request for ice water.

"Je desire l'eau avec. . . " he began. But he couldn't think of the word for ice. So we began playing charades, trying to pantomime "ice"—shivering, making cubelike gestures with our hands, drinking with chattering teeth.

The waiter finally nodded that he understood, and went away, and returned with water with lemon. Then water with a tea bag. Then water in very small, cube-shaped glasses. Everything but water with ice cubes in it.

"We spent hundreds of dollars," Rock said, "and all those hours of slavery, and we can't even get a glass of ice water."

We plunged ahead with ordering the rest of our lunch. I think I had decided on an omelet—*oeufs*—and got some kind of pasta dish. Rock had wanted a sandwich with ham—*jambon*—and got some very tasty boiled cucumbers.

From then on we abandoned our attempts to speak French, spoke English, and were better understood.

We moved on to Cap Ferrat, where we stayed at the lovely old Colombe d'Or and where we ran into Otto Preminger who was there with his son, Erik.

"What good fortune to run into you here!" Preminger said, beaming his crocodilian beam. The once-great director had fallen on hard times after a string of flops, and nobody wanted him or his pictures. "I have a great film in the works, with a truly remarkable part for you. We are both very fortunate today!"

Rock smiled. He knew, as I did, that Preminger was persona non grata in Hollywood at the time and that the chance of him making another film were slim to anorexic. He told Preminger that he had a full schedule, and simply had no time for anything else. He wanted to let the director down softly because, after all, he had done some fine motion pictures and, besides, Rock didn't have it in him to be unkind.

But Preminger wouldn't be let down softly, or any way. He kept pestering Rock, waylaying him at breakfast every morning, buttonholing him at lunch, cornering him at dinner. Finally Rock had had enough. Still, he couldn't bring himself to say anything cruel to Preminger. Instead, he told me it was time for us to leave.

Besides, the weather had turned sour and we couldn't sit on the beach. We were stuck in the hotel, which afforded Preminger more opportunities to pitch his futile plans. Our agenda had been to drive on to Barcelona and put the Porsche on a ship there, for shipment to Los Angeles. But Rock suggested we ship it from Nice, just around the corner from Cap Ferrat, and fly up to Paris. And that's what we did.

Neither of us had been particularly fond of Paris in the past. There was no denying the physical beauty of the city, but Parisians are generally rude and unfriendly. Perhaps one of the reasons Rock had never liked Paris very much was that, of all the European countries, France was the one in which he was least popular. The French liked him, but they didn't love him as effusively as the Germans, the Italians, or the Spaniards did. It would have been only natural for Rock to reciprocate that feeling—or, rather, that lack of feeling.

But things changed for both of us on that trip. We checked into the Plaza Athenée Hotel on a Saturday afternoon. On Sunday morning, Rock suggested that we go to the Thieves' Market.

That was a kind of outing he enjoyed immensely—flea markets, garage sales, rummage sales, auctions. And the Thieves' Market in Paris is the world's greatest garage sale. We spent hours there that day, in joyous browsing. A few people recognized Rock, but just enough to give his ego a little pat, not enough to be annoying.

We had lunch at a little restaurant on a side street—one wonderful thing about Paris then was that you could be assured of good food in even the meanest-looking, off-the-*rue* establishment—and it was a thoroughly enjoyable day. By the time we got back to the hotel late that afternoon, our attitude toward Paris had totally changed. For the better.

The only problem we had was getting back to the hotel. Since we had been having so much fun and getting along so well, we decided to spurn the taxis that were waiting for fares at the Thieves' Market and take the subway—or, as they call it in Paris, the Metro.

We found the station and a long line of people waiting to buy tickets. I got in line and Rock stood off to one side, trying to be as unobtrusive as possible, which is not easy for someone who is six-five and wears one of the most recognizable faces in the world.

I finally reached the ticket window. I knew enough about the

Paris Metro to know that there was a first class and a second class and that smoking was permitted only in first class. We were both smokers, so I asked, in slow but accurate French, for two first-class tickets.

I'm sure the ticket seller understood exactly what I wanted but, being a typical rude Parisian, he chose to pretend that he didn't. He gave me one of those Gallic shrugs. I tried again. Another shrug, this time accompanied by an eloquent shaking of the head and rolling of the eyes. I tried a third time.

Now the people in the line behind me were getting restless. They had trains to catch, so I can't blame them. The ticket-seller motioned that I should step aside, and I'm sure there was a slight triumphant gleam in his beady little eyes.

I went to Rock and said, "I'm sorry. I just couldn't get that damn fool to understand what I wanted."

"Let me try," he said.

So he got on the line and slowly worked his way up to the ticket seller, who again went through his whole act and made believe he couldn't understand what Rock wanted. Rock tried three times, as I had, but all he got for his trouble was the whole repertoire—the shrugs, the head-shakes, the eye-rolls. We were about to give up and take a taxi to the hotel when we heard a welcome American voice calling out "Hey, Rock, can we help you?"

An American couple came over to us and quickly got us our tickets, and we rode with them on the Metro. The man, it turned out, was a winegrower from the Napa Valley, in northern California, who had been the technical adviser on Rock's picture *This Earth Is Mine.*

"I was the fellow who taught you how to pick grapes, remember?" he said, and Rock truly did remember.

So we shook our heads over our futility with the language—all that time, money, and effort and we couldn't even order a glass of ice water or buy tickets on the subway. We had to have help from a California grape-grower to find our way home!

Rock liked to steal a few days here and there, when he was making a film on location, to explore. Some stars show up when shooting begins and spend all their nonworking hours in their hotel room or the hotel bar. Not our Rock. If he was due to start a film on, say, a Wednesday, he would leave four or five days earlier than necessary so he'd have those days to look around the city. And, on any day off, he'd always be out exploring.

The Martian Chronicles was set to film in 1979 on the island of Malta. We knew we would be there a few months and we would certainly have plenty of time to see everything Malta had to offer in that time. But we looked at the map—and, as we had some time, we decided to go first to Sicily, another Mediterranean island neither of us had visited.

We should have known we were headed for trouble as soon as we took the flight to Sicily. The first part of the trip—we had been in London—was great, a marvelous flight from London to Milano. First class, of course, but this particular first-class service was even first-classier than usual. It was a dinner flight, and they set up a table between us, with beautiful china and crystal and linens, and the food was as exquisite as the service.

But our flight from Milano to Palermo, the Sicilian port of entry, was delayed by, as it turned out, seven hours.

We went to the Alitalia Club in the Milano airport, but it had closed: it closed promptly at nine o'clock, no matter how many people were waiting for delayed flights. They apologized profusely— very sorry, *signori*, but it is closing time, *si?*

"Let's get a cab or a car or something and go into Milano," Rock said. "No point in staying out here when there's a city to go see." Fine with me. But when I made a last check at the ticket counter to see about the estimated time of departure, the clerk said it could be any time now.

"Better you don't go to the city," he said. "The plane, she could be going up *un momento.*"

So we stayed in the airport, which was a mob scene. We had to sit on our suitcases and, of course, *un momento* turned out to be six more hours. There was no bar or restaurant open in the airport, so we just sat on our suitcases and waited. And fumed. And waited some more. Then it was fuming time again. Getting there is not always half the fun.

We finally reached Palermo around four in the morning. The Savoy Hotel in London had made reservations for us in Palermo at what, they assured us, was the finest hotel that Sicilian city had to offer. The concierge at the Savoy had received a confirmation of our reservation, and I had that confirmation safely stowed in my wallet.

When we got to the hotel, at that ungodly hour, the cab dumped us on the sidewalk and sped away.

The hotel's front door was locked, but we pounded on the door and finally the night man, yawning and scratching, came and let us in.

"Reservations for Mr. Rock Hudson and Mr. Tom Clark," I said.

He rubbed his eyes, put on a pair of wire-rimmed spectacles, and slowly ran a stubby finger down the register book.

"Sorry, *signori*," he said. "No reservations."

"But I have a confirmation," I said, and pulled it out of my wallet and thrust it at him.

He examined it carefully, then went back to the book. Again, he went down the list of names on a couple of pages.

"*Si*, you have a confirmation," he said, "but, no, you don't have reservation."

"Well, what can we do?" I asked. "It's four o'clock in the morning and we've been up all night. We have to have someplace to sleep. Where can we go?"

"Oh," he said, "we have plenty of rooms. I have nice room for you. But you don't have a reservation."

That was our quaint welcome to Sicily.

Rock had, as usual, read up on the island and, also as usual, wanted to see many of the places he had read about. He particularly wanted to see the spot where the Allied invasion had landed in the dark days of World War II. We spent the better part of a day wandering about as Rock, guidebook in hand, tried to match the descriptions he was reading with the terrain itself.

Then we rented a brand-new Fiat and drove around the island, exploring in our usual style: no specific destination, just going where the most inviting road led. We did spend a day or two at a lovely resort we found, and we saw the city of Catania and several herds of ruins. As far as we were concerned, ruins had never been particularly exciting. Probably a gap in our personality, but we always felt ruins looked too shoddy.

We were zipping along a Sicilian autostrada, bound from somewhere to someplace, when suddenly the car exploded. Or so it seemed. It turned out it was just the air-conditioning unit that had blown up, but it seemed at first as though it was the entire vehicle.

Rock was driving at the time—we generally took turns—and there were black clouds of acrid smoke and little spurts of flame coming from the engine. He pulled over immediately and we jumped out, expecting the gas tank to explode and wanting to be as far away from that event as possible.

Rock ran along the highway, waving the other cars out of the way in case of that expected blast. The drivers recognized him and thought, gee, that's nice of the big American cinema star to wave at us. Wait 'til I tell Mama about that! OK, we'll wave back. So car after car slowed down, with drivers and passengers waving cheerfully as they floated by our burning car without a care in the world.

But one of the passing motorists must have understood the problem and stopped at a highway phone and called the police. They arrived, sirens blaring, lights flashing. Rock, in his controlled Italian, explained that the car had gone boom. *Boom* is boom in any language.

They looked puzzled, however, yet they did call a tow truck and the mechanic extinguished the fire. He hooked his hook up to our car and began towing it away.

"Hey, what about us?" I yelled, and Rock yelled the same yell in Italian.

"Oh, you want to come along, too?" the mechanic said, and we smiled that we did, and climbed into the tow truck with him and the blackened shell of our brand-new Fiat.

He deposited us at a toll station where he explained in broad pantomime that we should be able to call for help.

The toll-taker recognized Rock, and embraced him and said he would make a call in his behalf. He called for a taxi. As we waited for the cab, seated in the toll-taker's booth, he would say, to every driver who came by, "Hey, look who's in my booth—Rock Hudson!"

And Rock would smile and, occasionally, sign an autograph, as we waited for the cab to take us back into Catania. It got so bad Rock couldn't take being on display any more, so we walked across the highway and sat down in a clump of bushes where nobody could see us.

The taxi finally arrived and we got in gratefully. It was a beat-up old Chevvy and it moved in fits and starts, and the springs stuck out of the seats, but at least it wasn't burning. The driver was an elderly gentleman who kept staring at Rock in his rear-view mirror.

"Hey, you Rock Hudson?" he asked finally. Rock confessed that that was who he was.

"Hey, Rock Hudson! I've got a terrific script for you!"

We were planning to leave for Malta the next day, and we were not too unhappy about saying goodbye to Sicily. It is a beautiful island, but we were delighted to anticipate a change of scenery.

We got to the Catania Airport, for the flight to Valetta, Malta, in ample time. That airport was crazy. Apparently the Sicilians fly a lot within the island, carrying such odds and ends as pigs and chickens with them. So the airport was crammed with people carrying squawking chickens and oinking pigs, and burlap bags containing unidentifiable creatures making unfathomable sounds.

We checked the Arrivals/Departures board and saw this notice: TODAY'S VALETTA FLIGHT HAS BEEN CANCELLED.

Here we go again. (Or here we don't go again). Now it was desperate, because Rock had to report on the set the next morning. We checked with the ticket-counter people and they suggested we might be able to get to Malta if we flew from Sicily back to Naples, on the Italian mainland. We might be able to catch a flight from Naples to Malta. No guarantee, of course, and no way of checking.

"But no other way," he said with a helpful smile.

Rock was always so professional, and the thought of perhaps not reporting for work on schedule threw him into a terrible state of pure panic.

"Do something, Tom," he said. So I wound up chartering a plane, and flying to Malta directly. Some others, who were stranded too, chipped in and joined us. It actually cost us no more than a regular flight.

That was probably the most nervous and frantic I ever saw Rock, because of his almost pathological fear of not getting to work on time. On another trip, I saw the Hudson temper in all its glory.

He and Princess Grace—Grace Kelly of Philadelphia, Hollywood, and Monaco—had been great pals for a long time. They were on the same wavelength and, although Her Serene Highness exuded that aura of ultrasophistication and pompy circumstance, she was actually a pretty down-home sort of gal. She liked nothing better than to kick off her shoes, tell jokes, and roar with very unregal laughter.

Whenever she visited Hollywood, her good friend and my former boss, Rupert Allen, always gave a party for her, and we were always there and, usually, Grace and Rock would wind up in a corner, laughing it up over who knows what silliness. They loved each other's company.

Once they were having such a private ball they forgot the time and when they looked up, the party was over. They had both had a few too many drinks and were laughing so hard they could hardly think straight. Grace was staying, on that trip, with the director Mervyn LeRoy and his wife Kitty, and the LeRoys wanted to go home.

"I think I'll stay a while longer," Grace said. "Rock will bring me home, won't you, Rock?"

"Absorootootedly," Rock said, and he and Grace collapsed in a puddle of laughter again.

So they stayed and stayed and finally everybody had left, so Rock and Grace had to go too. But, as so often happens, their time together had been so much fun they didn't want it to end.

"You hungry?" he asked.

"Starved," Grace said.

By now it was probably two in the morning. Los Angeles is really a small town, and the sidewalks are carefully rolled up and stored around ten o'clock or so. There are only a few all-night places to eat, and Rock knew one of them—Ollie Hammond's on La Cienega Boulevard. Not the classiest of dining spots, but at that hour and in their advanced state of hilarity, who cared? Greasy spoon, here we come.

So they went to Ollie Hammond's, all dolled up in their fancy Hollywood party finery, looking about as out of place as a jar of steak sauce at a vegetarian banquet.

They sat down, ordered their eggs or chicken-fried steak or whatever, and laughed their way through the meal. Then the check came, and Rock sobered up immediately. He never carried any money with him. He never carried any credit cards. That was one of my duties, to pay for things, but I wasn't there.

So he went to the cashier with his check.

"Good evening, madam," he said. "My name is Rock Hudson."

"I certainly know who you are," said the cashier, a large blonde lady who had seen better days. And nights.

"That makes what I am about to say to you a bit easier," Rock continued. "You see, I have this check for the food my companion and I consumed, but, alas, I have no money with me. I assure you I am good for the seven dollars and fifty-nine cents. I will leave my watch with you as security, and someone will be over in the morning to pay the check and reclaim the watch. Will that be satisfactory?"

"It won't be necessary for you to leave your watch, Rock honey," the cashier said. "You just bring the money back when you can. We trust you."

I went over the next day and paid the check.

On another of Princess Grace's Hollywood visits, Rock threw a huge and elegant party for her. This party became famous in Hollywood circles because the Los Angeles *Times'* gossip columnist at the time, Joyce Haber, first used the expression A List to describe the quality of the guests at that affair. Ever since that night, A List and B List have become part of the Hollywood language—for better or, probably, worse.

But that was how thick Rock and Grace were, which is why, when Rock and I traveled to Monaco a few years later, we had no hesitation about calling the palace. I placed the call myself and spoke to Grace's secretary, who was very pleasant and polite.

"Oh, what a shame," she said. "Her Highness is in the United States at the moment, visiting her family in Philadelphia. She'll be devastated that she missed you. But I know His Highness will want to see you. Let me switch you over to his secretary and he will make an appointment for you to visit."

And then this uppity character got on the phone.

"Yes?" he said, ice and authority exuding from his very upper-class voice. I explained who we were and said that Mr. Hudson merely wanted to say hello to the prince—they had met a few times on Rainier's visits to Hollywood—and I was calling at the suggestion of Princess Grace's secretary.

"You are a motion picture star?" the secretary asked.

"No, not me," I said, "but Rock Hudson, with whom I am traveling, is a very important motion picture star, yes. But mostly he is an old and good friend of the princess."

"We don't care about motion picture stars," the snippy voice said. "His Highness, Prince Rainier, has better things to do with his time than entertaining. . . motion picture stars." He said those last three words as though they were a bad taste in his mouth.

Now I was mad.

"Wait just one darn minute," I said. "It wasn't our idea to call you, it was the suggestion of Princess Grace's secretary."

"I really couldn't care less why you are calling," he said. "I am just informing you that the prince doesn't wish to be bothered by every Tom, Dick and—what did you say your companion's name was? Now if you will excuse me, I am very busy."

And he hung up, without even hoping that I would have a nice day. I stood there, the phone in my hand and fury boiling up in my chest. I repeated the conversation to Rock, who promptly boiled over.

We immediately placed a call to Rupert Allen back in Hollywood. Besides being Grace's and Rainier's friend, Allen represented Monaco for public relations in the United States. Rupert immediately called Rainier, who immediately tracked us down at our hotel and called to apologize for his secretary's rudeness. He invited us to visit him, but by then we were just about to leave, so we never did. We later learned that that officious secretary was fired or decapitated or whatever it is they do with offenders in Monaco.

Of course, not all of our travels were overseas. We did a great deal of traveling throughout the United States, too. And we even occasionally liked to visit such real tourist meccas, as Disneyland, which was virtually in our backyard.

As a matter of fact, Rock loved Disneyland. He was like a big kid, enjoying the rides and the atmosphere and eating tubs of popcorn and several hot dogs. He had one diabolical trick he enjoyed pulling at Disneyland.

He would spot a family taking pictures. Most often it would be the father posing his wife and children then carefully lining up the shot and clicking the shutter. Rock would wait until the father was just about to snap the picture, then he would leap into the background, behind the wife and kids. Being tall, he could do that very easily. Then he'd leap out again. They never would notice him, but he would take great delight in imagining how it would be when they got their pictures back from the developer. And, in that shot of the family in front of the Disneyland Castle, there would be Rock Hudson, the movie star, smiling and waving. Thinking of their surprise tickled him no end.

Since many of our trips were the result of having been invited by governments or agencies of governments, more often than not we stepped off the plane and would be met by a limousine, parked on the runway, waiting for us. No annoying waits at customs or on immigration lines for us—we whizzed through those formalities on the wings of official sanction.

But there were times when all the glitzy welcoming ceremonies and forced smiles and hearty handshakes became a bore. So, very often, Rock decided we would just go, without telling anybody we were coming. Of course, the minute he was spotted, it all began anyhow. He was just too big and too recognizable to escape detection, and disguises were useless. He might put on a pair of heavy, horn-rimmed glasses and wear a cap pulled down over his face, but it never helped much. We simply perfected our technique of walking fast and not looking either right or left and not stopping as the best way to avoid confrontations.

The great thing about being as well known as Rock was that wherever we went we were introduced to the greats and near-greats. The desire to meet a major movie star infects kings and queens, generals, the leading people of the world. And Rock was one of the majorest of major movie stars, so everyone everywhere wanted to meet him.

We met them all. In every country where we went, particularly on a visit where we were the invited guests, we would always be guests of honor at some arranged luncheon or dinner with the head of state or some comparably exalted personage.

Wherever we went, Rock had friends in high places. When we went to London, as we did frequently, we would always have dinner with his English cronies, and they were distinguished people. For me, one of my all-time thrills came at one of those dinners. One evening Rock and I escorted Elizabeth Taylor and Ava Gardner to a posh restaurant for dinner. As I sat there, the object of stares from around the room, I thought how fortunate I was, this kid from Oklahoma City, having dinner with Rock Hudson and two of the most beautiful women in the world.

I couldn't help thinking about that old joke about the Pope and the little Jewish man who managed to sneak onto the Vatican balcony next to the Pope, and his friends in the crowd below spotted him up there and said "Who's that on the balcony with Abe Glickstein?"

I wondered if anybody in that restaurant that evening said "Who's that having dinner with Tom Clark?"

Rock had been to the White House on several occasions. Just before Rock's final illness, President Reagan invited him to a state dinner. He had never worked with Ronald Reagan, but he had worked with Jane Wyman when she was Mrs. Reagan, and they had become fairly close friends at that time.

But he was more of a Jack Kennedy fan. Rock was invited to a dinner for President Kennedy at the Beverly Hills Hotel, and his date that evening had been Marilyn Maxwell. It was a relatively small affair and Rock noticed that there was an empty chair at each table, obviously being saved for the President. Presumably he would circulate, sitting at each table for one course.

At Rock's table, the empty chair was next to the place that had Rock's name on it. So Rock began to worry—what will I talk to him about when he sits next to me?

Then he thought, well, my name was Fitzgerald once and Kennedy's mother was Rose Fitzgerald before she married Joseph Kennedy, so I'll just talk to him about the history of the Fitzgeralds. Who knows, maybe we're related?

And so, when President Kennedy came over to his table and sat down, Rock was ready.

"Good evening, Mr. President," he said.

"Good evening, Rock," John Kennedy said. "Say, I'm glad to have this chance to talk to you. I know you are really Roy Fitzgerald and that means we're both Irish, being as we are both Fitzgeralds. You know all us Fitzgeralds are related, right?"

"That's right, sir," said Rock. "And I'm sure Ella will be happy to hear about it, too."

CHAPTER EIGHT
Making Movies

R ock liked nothing better than making movies. But, toward the end of his career, after he had discovered the stage and the stage had discovered him, I think he preferred acting in front of a live audience to acting in front of a camera. But maybe not. Maybe it was just that the stage was a new toy and so, for the moment, the old toy was forgotten. Perhaps he still, given a choice, would have opted for making movies. One thing for certain: he preferred both to television work.

His agent for many years, after Henry Willson, was a lady named Flo Allen. I was very fond of Flo, as was Rock, but sometimes I felt she might have been more forceful in what she did for Rock.

Very often I would see his contemporaries—who didn't have his box-office value—getting big parts, and I would question her about them.

"That would have been a great part for Rock," I'd say. "Did you try to get it for him?"

She would equivocate, never really answering me, and once she even said, "Rock's film career is over—I can't get him a job at all."

I simply didn't believe that.

He was hotter than ever at the time she made that statement to me. His TV shows had made him popular with a whole new generation as well as solidified his popularity with his old fans.

I remember a particular film role Rock should have gotten. They were casting a movie to be called *Lucky Lady* and someone (I forget now who it was) was set for the lead. Then something happened and that actor either bowed out or was dropped, and the part was open. I heard about it through my contacts and called Flo and said she should get that part for Rock.

"No," she said, "they'll never consider Rock for that part."

"Look, Flo," I said. "We'll never know if they will consider him for the part or not unless we give it a shot, will we?"

But she never gave it a shot, and they cast Burt Reynolds. The picture turned out to be a catastrophe, but that's not the point; she missed a chance. And she missed other chances, too. I remember reading Herman Wouk's *The Winds Of War* when it first came out and, later, the second part, *War and Remembrance,* and thinking that Rock would be ideal for the leading role.

After a few false starts, the two books were sold for a miniseries. I called Flo. Rock was then virtually the uncrowned king of the miniseries, because of the sensation he had caused with *Wheels.* I said that she should get to work and get Rock that part of Pug Henry.

She called me back a few days later and told me she had spoken to Dan Curtis, producer-director on the project, and that he was, she said, "mildly interested" in Rock for the part.

"But he wants Rock to fly in and audition," she said. We were in New York at the time, and Curtis was in California. I was stunned; actors of Rock Hudson's stature are not asked to audition. It is just not done.

"I hope you told him what he could do with his audition," I said.

"Well, no. He seemed adamant on the point."

"There is no way on God's green earth that Rock is going to audition for Dan Curtis."

And he didn't, and the part went to Robert Mitchum, who was

much too old for the romantic scenes that were part of the script. Rock would have been ideal, but Flo let the idea sink without a fight.

Rock liked making movies because he had fun in the process. His professionalism on the set didn't preclude his being part of the joking and kidding around that is the hallmark of every happy movie set.

He was making a movie on location once in Suriname, in South America, when the opportunity for a practical joke suggested itself. Rock enjoyed a good practical joke.

"We were shooting on a jungle road," he told me. "It was very hot, very steamy. I was supposed to walk down this path in the jungle, with the camera tracking me, and then veer off into the jungle at a certain point. Before the scene, I checked the area carefully—I didn't want to fall into any pits or meet any large snakes. I noticed a small patch of quicksand. Aha!

"I figured it would be fun to pull a joke on the crew, so I did the scene and then stepped into that quicksand. I was up to my waist in a few seconds, and then up to my chest. I held on to a branch so I wouldn't go in any further. By now, the director was looking for me.

" 'Hey, Rock, come on,' he yelled.

" 'I'm sorry, I can't come,' I said.

" 'Why not?'

" 'Because I'm in some quicksand and getting sucked down,' I said, very nonchalantly.

"They came running and pulled me out. It was fun—I never was really in danger, and we all had a good laugh."

He loved to lighten up the sets when he was working with stunts like that. His problem in movie-making was never on the set, it was before the picture began—it was his difficulty in picking the right project for himself.

After Rock and I became associated professionally, I read the scripts that were offered to him. He seemed to value my opinion, and he knew that he was a poor judge of material for himself. Flo read scripts, too, and she and I would speak on the phone almost every day, comparing views on the various projects Rock had been offered.

Rock would occasionally override both of us. That generally happened when he was stroked by a producer who knew his weakness: he could be flattered by an appeal to his desire to be creative.

Both Flo and I might have said a particular script was bad, but if the producer went directly to Rock and said, "Rock, whatever is wrong with the script, you and I will work out—we'll have an artistic meeting, you and I, and fix everything."

That phrase *artistic meeting* was what got to Rock every time. The idea of being in with the creative people was catnip to him; he fell for it hook, line, and sinker every time. They would just be stringing him along, but he'd leap at that juicy bait and sign on the dotted line. He did some bad films because of that.

A lot of lousy movies get made in Hollywood, but a lot of even lousier ones don't get made. If you could read some of the incredibly bad scripts that are circulated by recognized agents you would be absolutely stunned. Your pet iguana could write better scripts.

Because of that, there is the tendency to leap out of your socks and jump for joy when a halfway decent script comes along. Those halfway decent scripts get made frequently as a result, and that's why we have so many halfway decent movies. Not totally decent, just partly decent, semigood.

Like anybody, I made my share of mistakes. I put Rock into *Embryo*, in 1976; it turned out to be terrible. He got back at me, the next year, by doing *Avalanche*, over my advice that he run as far away from it as possible.

The idea had been submitted to him directly (I think it was one of those "artistic meeting" ploys) by Roger Corman. There had been no script for me to reject. Instead, Rock came to me and told me about how he was going to do it.

"Roger Corman wants me for this movie he's going to produce and direct," he said. "It's all about an avalanche at a ski resort and the people who are trapped there."

"Sounds awful," I said.

"Sounds good to me. I heard all about it at the artistic meeting. You know, I've always wanted to do one of those big disaster movies. It should be fun."

"OK, but you know Corman. Mr. Cheap himself. You know that

kind of film depends on how good the special effects are, and with Corman involved, the avalanche will probably look like it was shot in the kitchen sink."

But Rock wanted to do it, so he did it. And the avalanche sequences were worse than if they had been shot in Corman's kitchen sink. He had gotten hold of some new French electronic system that created special effects by computer, and the avalanche looked like it was shot through tapioca pudding.

But, anyhow, Rock did his disaster film—and it was a true disaster. Fortunately, it opened in New York during a newspaper strike, so it was never reviewed. He was, at least, spared that part of the disaster.

One script I rejected for him was called *The Ambassador*. Then, a few years later, after Rock and I had split up and I was living in New York, he called me.

"Tom, do me a favor?"

"Of course."

"I agreed to do a movie," he said, "and I'd appreciate it if you would read over the contract they've given me and see if it's OK." When we were together, that had been one of my duties—to read the contracts and make sure Rock was being treated fairly.

"Be happy to," I said. "What's the picture?"

"It's called *The Ambassador*," he said.

"Oh, Rock, I read that and it's a dreadful script. I rejected it for you a couple of years ago; that script has been knocking around Hollywood a long time. I'm sure you can find something better than that to do. Don't do that one. It's a bomb waiting to go off."

But he did it. They rewrote the script for him—after another "artistic meeting"—but it didn't help. It was so bad that it never was released theatrically. I think it was shown a few times on some second-string cable networks at three o'clock in the morning.

Rock was actually a rather difficult actor to cast, especially later in his career. Earlier, of course, he was the handsome young romantic leading man, a role he handled admirably. But as he matured and his face became more interesting, he defied easy categorization.

He could always do the romantic things, of course, but there was much more to him than that. And he wanted more. He wanted the good, mature roles to go with his good, mature appearance. He wanted serious parts, but I believe the Rock name worked against him. That and his past history of doing lightweight material combined to militate against his being cast in those serious roles he craved.

He did a few. One was probably his favorite film of all—*Seconds,* which he made in 1965.

When Paramount held its first screening of that movie, I was invited and I stopped, at the door, to talk to Bob Goodfried, who was Paramount's publicity boss and a very knowledgeable movie man. He shook his head sadly when I asked him about *Seconds* and its prospects.

"We just don't know what to do with it," he said. "It's a very interesting movie—you'll see—but the Rock Hudson in this movie isn't the Rock Hudson the public is used to seeing, or wants to see. We really haven't a clue as to how to sell it."

So they took the easy way out and didn't sell it at all. They had another picture— *Alfie*—which came out at about the same time. I know the studio mentality, and if they have two pictures, they will push the one they think has the biggest potential. So they pushed *Alfie* and, because they didn't know what to do with *Seconds*, they did next to nothing. They didn't even give it a gentle nudge. They let it wither and die.

Rock was bitterly disappointed, because he felt it was his best work up to then. Time has proved him right about that, incidentally. *Seconds* has achieved, over the years, the success and renown it never got when it was initially released. It has become a cult favorite. It is shown in almost every college cinema course, and Rock frequently was invited to come to those classes and talk to the students about *Seconds.* He was so gung-ho about the film that, if he could possibly work them in, he would accept those invitations.

But, when it was first released, Paramount was right. Nobody at the time wanted to see a serious Rock Hudson. Even he came to realize that, the hard way.

He told me that he was in New York, soon after *Seconds* came out, with a group of friends. They had tickets to see Gwen Verdon in *Sweet Charity*, but when they reached the theater they were told Verdon wouldn't be appearing that night, for some reason. They all decided they didn't want to see the show without her, turned their tickets in, and wandered around Times Square.

"We came to the theater where *Seconds* was showing," Rock told me. "I was the only one in the group who had seen it. Since the others hadn't, and they wanted to, they persuaded me to go in and see it. It didn't take too much persuasion. Well, anyhow, it was a Saturday night and we were just about the only people in the whole theater. It was a big theater, too, and there were just the six or eight of us. I felt awful."

Rock loved to work so much that he abhorred idleness. That meant he was always pressuring Flo Allen and me to let him do something, even if it wasn't any good. He often said he would rather be doing mediocre material than doing nothing.

Flo was an optimist who often went along with Rock when he swallowed that "artistic meeting" nonsense, and both of them would believe smooth-talking producers who promised to fix unfixable scripts.

Rock would try to convince me, the born skeptic, that he should do a script I had told him was vile. He would tell me how the producer had vowed to fix it, how it would be rewritten, how he was going to sit in on those "artistic meetings" and make sure it would be OK.

"Tell them to fix it first," I would say, "before you agree to do it. If it's fixed, fine and dandy. If not, have a nice day. Don't sign anything until they have fixed it. OK?"

But, very often, he would succumb to the producer's promises and Flo's optimism. Consequently, Rock Hudson appeared in a great many bad pictures.

I kept urging him to hold out, to wait for the big pictures. His only competition, I said, were actors such as Gregory Peck and Charlton Heston, and they waited for big, A-quality scripts. The pictures might flop, but at least they had a fighting chance.

"You're just as bankable as Peck or Heston," I told him, and that was absolutely true.

Besides, he was younger than they were and was aging in a very mellow way. He looked better than ever and he could easily handle any part that came along. But he took a lot of dumb parts in dumb movies—like *Avalanche*—just because he couldn't stand not working. And, to make matters worse, for some reason they often miscast his leading lady. In *Avalanche,* for example, he was cast opposite Mia Farrow. She is a fine actress, as her recent work with Woody Allen proves, but she and Rock as a team were about as right as Whoopi Goldberg and Charles Boyer.

"You have cast approval," I said to him. "Why don't you just say no to Mia Farrow? She's not right for you."

"Oh, well," he said. "Roger Corman thinks she's good for the box office." So he accepted her, and they were terrible together.

Like every actor, he had his hot streaks and his cold slumps, his periods of feverish activity and his spells of frigid inactivity.

After the disappointment of *Seconds,* he had done *Tobruk*—part of his Universal deal—and then took a year off to lick his wounds and sulk.

Then along came *Ice Station Zebra.* This was to be a big film at MGM, an A+ epic, and Rock was eager to do it. Marty Ransohoff was the producer and John Foreman, Rock's agent in those days, had contacted Ransohoff about Rock, but nothing had come of that contact.

I was at MGM then, and one day Rock came out to the studio to have lunch with me. Ransohoff walked by and nodded to both of us on his way out of the commissary.

"Boy, I would love to do *Ice Station Zebra,*" Rock said to me. "But Foreman says Ransohoff won't give me the time of day."

I couldn't believe that. I knew Ransohoff was, in fact, a big Rock Hudson fan.

"Rock," I said, "Marty probably doesn't even know you are interested in the part. Foreman must have spoken to one of his flunkys. Look, as soon as we're finished lunch, you go up to his office, knock on the door, and tell him you'd like to be in his picture."

And that is exactly what Rock did. He went to see Ransohoff and said, "Marty, I'd like to be in *Ice Station Zebra.*" Later John Foreman said—and I believed him—that he had been working on the deal all along. Anyhow, Rock got that part, which did so much for him, because he went into Ransohoff's office and asked for it. It was difficult for Rock to do that, but he did, and it paid off.

Ice Station Zebra revitalized Rock's career, and he followed it up with pictures that should have been just as big—*The Undefeated* with John Wayne and *Darling Lili* with Julie Andrews—but turned out poorly. The fact that they weren't successful was due to several factors, none of which was Rock's fault.

I leaped out of my chair when I read a script called *Pretty Maids All In a Row*. It was, I believe, the finest script I ever read in my entire life. And the auspices under which it was going to be made were the best: Roger Vadim was going to direct, Gene Roddenberry (the man who created *Star Trek*) was going to produce, and the cast would include Angie Dickinson, Roddy McDowall, and Keenan Wynn, all tops in their trade.

And it turned out brilliantly—at first. But it was a black comedy, destined for an X rating. MGM had never had an X-rated film and decided to recut it so it could qualify for an R rating. The recutting ruined it, and another great movie was sacrificed on the altar of studio politics and greed.

Then there was another fallow period for Rock, with nothing exciting coming his way. That's how it was that he was available to do *Murder By the Book,* the TV movie from which the *McMillan & Wife* series evolved. And, once again, Rock's career took off like a big bird.

But, through it all, he longed for more. We screened many movies at the house, and very often, when the lights came back on, Rock would shake his head sadly.

"That's another part I could have done," he'd say.

And he could have. But the sad, awful truth was that many producers had pigeonholed him, and it wasn't a very pretty pigeonhole to which he'd been assigned, either.

Much of that stemmed, as I have said, from his name. But I believe some of it was also the product of his early days at Universal, when he was thrown into a procession of silly, mindless films. Hollywood is a place where quick impressions are often lasting impressions, where a pigeonhole is as permanent as imprisonment on Devil's Island. Because of his name and all those weak kneed early films he was typed, in the rigid minds of many Hollywood executives, as a handsome face and that's all.

Given half a chance, he was a fine actor—but he rarely got even a quarter of a chance.

Until he was teamed with Doris Day he had never done comedy. At first, he was frightened by the prospect. He was, however, smart enough to realize the first thing when you tackle anything new is to consult the experts.

In his case, the expert was his co-star.

"I watched Doris very closely on our first film together," he told me. (*Pillow Talk* was their first, followed by *Lover Come Back* and *Send Me No Flowers*). "Her timing was incredible—and she was a very good teacher, too."

I still have his script from *Pillow Talk*, one of the few things of his I managed to hang on to. All through it are his notations in pencil, with his instructions to himself. And very often there are words like these:

"Doris says stress word 'maybe' in this speech."

I have talked about the slumps and fallow periods in Rock's career, but they were actually infrequent. Generally, he was almost always hot, almost always in demand. For some years, he was the Number One Box-Office star and, obviously, anybody in that category can have his pick of projects. The problem was that, during his hottest period, he was under contract to Universal and therefore seldom free to take the outside offers that flooded in.

One of his big disappointments was having to turn down MGM when they wanted him for the lead in *Ben Hur*. That sounded like it would be a real big one, which it was. Both MGM and Rock went to see the Universal brass, pleading with them to let him do *Ben Hur*.

"Why, sure, Rock," one executive told him. "By all means, go do *Ben Hur*. Would we stand in your way? But, in exchange, you have to do us a small favor: You have to sign a three-year extension of your contract with us."

In other words, for Rock to do that one film which would probably take a year to make, he would have had to agree to stay with Universal for an additional three years.

"There was no way under the sun I was going to do that," Rock told me. So he had to turn MGM down and missed being in *Ben Hur* as a consequence.

"You made a big mistake, Rock," I said to him. I explained that contracts are there to be gotten out of—all nicely, all legally. Nothing is irrevocable. But a picture like *Ben Hur* comes along very seldom.

Rock did learn one very important lesson from that *Ben Hur* experience, however. He learned that he needed the opportunity to do things over and above those Universal had for him. So, when his contract eventually did run out, before he re-signed he insisted on a clause that gave him the right to do one picture a year away from the studio. He used that clause often, too.

That was how he was able to do *A Farewell to Arms* for David Selznick, with Jennifer Jones. Actually, at the time he was offered that role, he was also offered another one, and had a difficult choice to make.

"I could have done *A Farewell to Arms*," he told me, "or I could have had the lead in *Sayonara*. Well, I made the wrong choice."

There were sensible reasons why he opted for *A Farewell to Arms* over *Sayonara* at the time. In retrospect, of course, it seems like a dumb move, but before either picture was made, *Farewell* seemed the better bet. It was from the classic Hemingway novel; it had Selznick, one of the legendary producers; Charles Vidor was directing; and Jennifer Jones was his co-star.

Sayonara, on the other hand, had Josh Logan as the director and, while he was a proven commodity on Broadway, he had only a few movie credits. And, as for co-stars, there was an unknown Japanese actress and Red Buttons. So Rock made what seemed to him, at the time, the only possible choice: *A Farewell to Arms*.

It was not a success. But *Sayonara* turned out to be a huge hit. That unknown Japanese actress, Miyoshi Umeki, got an Academy Award. So did Red Buttons. And Josh Logan and Marlon Brando, who took the part Rock would have had, got Oscar nominations.

Through all the years of his original Universal contract, Rock had many offers (which he could not even entertain) to do outside projects. With a few rare exceptions, he turned them all down reluctantly. Through all those years, outside producers and studio heads and directors would tell him that he had to get out of that Universal contract and promised him that, as soon as he did, they would have work for him.

"That contract is holding you back," they would tell him. "Get out of it. Do other things."

His Universal contract called for him to do a certain number of films at that studio. To expedite his freedom, he decided to work his way out of the contract by doing as many films as he could, as fast as he could. He told Universal to put him in anything and everything that was being shot. They obliged him. For a couple of years he made picture after picture, going from one to another. Damn the quality, full speed ahead.

He finally worked his way out of the contract. He had been with the studio for seventeen years. And there are those, familiar with the economics of Hollywood, who say that first Deanna Durbin, then Abbott and Costello, and later Rock Hudson were the ones who had kept Universal afloat. Yet, when he left the lot after his last day at the studio, not one Universal executive was there to say goodbye, to shake his hand, to thank him for all the good things he had done for them.

"It seems to me," Rock said to me frequently, "that the least they could have done was to send some third assistant vice-president down to wave at me as I left."

But Universal was that way. The studio had insisted he put the gates in front of the house—for security—and that he put in the steam room and gym—for fitness—and they had paid for those improvements. But a few days after he left the studio, he received a bill from Universal for both those items. Rock shrugged and paid, even though I told him he should let them sue him for it.

Of course, as soon as he was at liberty all those people who had promised him work the moment he got out of that contract were nowhere to be seen. He had expected to be inundated with offers; his phone didn't ring.

He had outsmarted himself. By doing everything he could do at Universal, he had been in a lot of junk. As a result, for a time his box-office bankability dropped off, too. He had been caught in a catch-22 that almost strangled him.

That period was hard on him. More than anything else, appearing in front of a motion picture camera was his greatest joy.

He ignored television, at first, in common with most big Hollywood names. As I have already noted, he wanted nothing to do with that upstart medium. But, inevitably, television became more and more important, and eventually the TV moguls came knocking at his door.

Insistently.

On Television

Rock, as I have said, was from the old school of Hollywood, the old movie star school. To them, and to him, television was an infant art form, and a rather squalling, squeaky infant, at that. It was, in their collective view, unworthy of serious consideration. Certainly, these people—Rock among them—would never deign to do any TV themselves. And they would rarely even stoop to watch it.

Remember, television was a New York creation. All the good things that were done came out of New York: the dramatic shows such as *The Philco Playhouse* and *The U.S. Steel Hour* and such series as *The Defenders*. Hollywood's studio heads wedded to the concept of exhibiting their product only in theaters, could have jumped in and cornered the TV market, but they didn't. They simply closed their eyes, buried their heads in the sand, and hoped TV would just go away.

They let the opportunity slip past them.

Their attitude affected Hollywood actors. With a few exceptions, the big stars just wouldn't do television at all. The idea of doing a drama live—and all the early dramatic shows were live—absolutely terrified them. And then, when some shows began to be filmed and/or taped, the quality was so shoddy, the corners were cut so obviously and so sharply, the scripts were so poor and the camera work so amateurish that no self-respecting movie actor or actress would touch it.

Of course, gradually that changed. Quality improved; even if it hadn't, more and more actors would have come to understand that there was a pot of gold at the base of that TV antenna. Television was obviously here to stay. And, as the TV audience increased astronomically, it quickly became a medium well worth their consideration.

As the audiences grew and the number (and cost) of commercials grew, the money the networks could offer grew, too. Even the pride of actors can swiftly crumble before the onslaught of serious money.

I think the most heated arguments Rock and I ever had were about whether or not he should do television. While I recognized TV's flaws, and they were many and serious, I had handled *Dr. Kildare* at MGM and had seen what that show had done for Richard Chamberlain. It had shot him to the skies. So I had seen TV's impact at work.

"No," Rock would say, telling me about yet another offer from a TV network for him to do a series. "I will not do television."

"Why not? Look at Dick Chamberlain. I bet more people see him on *Dr. Kildare* every week than have seen all your pictures in theaters combined." (I could make that statement because it was true; I had seen statistics which proved that one recent telecast of a Shakespeare play had been seen by more people than had seen all of the Bard's plays since he wrote them—combined!)

"What difference does that make?" Rock said. "I don't care how many people see *Dr. Kildare* or Dick Chamberlain. It's still junk. And my name means something to the audience in the theaters. I won't compromise it."

"At least read some of the scripts," I said. "There are some good ones."

"You want to read the scripts, you go ahead and read them. I'm not going to."

So I continued reading them, and, while most of them were, as he said, junk, there were a few good ones salted in. And then the networks began making TV movies; they called them "specials" at first and now they are "miniseries," but the name doesn't matter. Some of those scripts were very good, and then, in 1970, one came in that I really felt had good potential for Rock. I told him it was for a movie, not a series, and that sounded better to him.

"Well, most of my movies end up on TV anyhow," he said, "so I guess it would be OK for me to do one of them. Tell me about it."

It was an NBC Movie of the Week called *Murder By the Book*. A suave police commissioner (Rock) solves crimes himself and has a kind of kooky wife (Stefanie Powers was the actress they wanted to be his co-star) and it would have, they hoped, all the flavor of the old *Thin Man* movies. A surface sophistication. Since those were among Rock's all-time favorites, he listened.

He even read the script, and he liked it. He also liked the idea of working with Stefanie, who was a good friend. They told him they would give him a comfortably long shooting schedule (one argument he had used against TV was that the shooting schedule was so short compromise was inevitable). He felt he needed ample time to rehearse his scenes properly.

So he agreed to dip his feet in the television pond. But then a problem arose. Rock and I had wanted Stefanie Powers very much, and she had been equally eager to do the part. But, before she was contracted for *McMillan*, she had signed to shoot a pilot for a projected series with Roddy McDowall. And that was still alive, still being considered by whatever network had made it. She reluctantly said she was sorry, but she wasn't free and couldn't play Mrs. McMillan. Because Rock had cast approval, of course, they paraded a series of young actresses in and out for his appraisal.

He didn't enjoy that experience—and he had had it quite a few times himself—because he said he was playing God, and he didn't feel qualified for that role. He had survived enough auditions and readings early in his career to know how traumatic they can be for the actor. He hated to be in the position where he was the one who had to say "No, that person won't do." He always said he felt like a Roman emperor turning thumbs down on some poor gladiator about to be killed.

Many girls wanted that part—among them, I remember, was Barbara Feldon, fresh from her triumph on the *Get Smart* comedy series—but when Susan Saint James came in for a reading, Rock liked her immediately. There was a zany innocence to her approach, plus the fact that she was an attractive young woman. I agreed that she was what we were looking for. We both felt that Rock and Susan would work well together. That made Universal very happy, because she was already under contract to the studio. It turned out to be a very good choice.

(Three or four days after Susan was signed, however, and *Mc-Millan* was set to go, that network turned down the pilot Stefanie Powers had done with Roddy McDowall. By then, of course, it was too late for us to change; Susan was a fait accompli.)

In addition to cast approval, Rock had also been given script approval and director approval. NBC had been so eager to get Rock to sign and so anxious for him to do the show, they gave him everything he wanted. And, of course, a huge amount of money, too.

Rock usually deferred to me about scripts. He felt he was not a good judge of what was best for him. So I would read them, as Paul Mason, the first producer, sent them over. Mason was a pro—as was his eventual successor, Jon Epstein—so the scripts were almost always fine. I might make a few notations for possible changes, but those were ordinarily minor. When shooting started, Rock would very often want to make some changes in his own lines, to make himself feel comfortable saying the words, but those were generally minor, too. Mason encouraged Rock, Susan, and the other cast regulars, John Schuck and Nancy Walker, to express their opinions. And they did; actors are not shy about expressing opinions.

Mason continued on the show until he pulled a dirty trick on Rock.

Rock wanted to finish shooting before Christmas, to be free for the holiday season. There was a part in an upcoming script that would be perfect for the comedian Buddy Hackett, and we all wanted him. Mason came to us and said that Hackett was only available Christmas week. So Rock, cooperative gentleman that he was, agreed to work that week so we could have Hackett in the role.

Hackett was a good friend of mine; I had done the unit on *The Love Bug* at Disney, in which Buddy was one of the stars, and I had actually gone on tour with Buddy to promote that film. (Going on tour with Buddy Hackett would be a whole other book.) And, while Buddy was working on the show that week, he mentioned how inconvenient it had been for him to work that week—he was appearing in Las Vegas and, to do the *McMillan* part, he had chartered a plane and had flown back and forth every day.

"But Paul Mason told us this was the only week you were available," Rock said.

"That bastard!" said Buddy. "He told me this was the only week they would be shooting."

Mason, it turned out, had told Hackett one story and told us another story; it developed that he wanted to go deep sea fishing the following week and conned both Rock and Buddy into working on the show when it was inconvenient for them both to do so.

So we asked Universal to replace him as our producer. They suggested Jon Epstein as his successor. Rock and I had met Epstein earlier and had both taken an instant dislike to him. So when we heard that he was about to take over for Mason, we both exploded.

"Not on your life," said Rock. But it happened that we were with Mark Miller, Rock's secretary and good friend, at the time, and Mark and his pal, George Nader, had known Jon Epstein for many years.

"You're nuts, Rock," Miller said. "Jon Epstein happens to be one of the nicest men in the world, one of the most respected men in Hollywood, and one of the best producers you'll ever find. If you turn him down, you're out of your skull."

So Jon Epstein became the producer of *McMillan & Wife* and became a very close friend to us both; he is today my closest friend. (Today, Jon and I are partners in a very informal, generally losing, betting partnership. We are both big pro football fans and every week during the season we pick out the winners, but we seem to bet on the losers.)

Jon made a huge difference on the show, too. He knew that a

happy cast does a better job, and one way to keep actors happy is to make them feel they are contributing something to the creative process. Actors uniformly believe they should have something to say about how their shows (or movies or plays or whatever) are being shaped. Usually, those contributions are worthless. But a clever producer or director lets them have their say, which makes them feel better, then goes ahead and does things the right way anyhow.

So Rock, and to a lesser extent, Susan, John, and Nancy, would tell Epstein how they thought the script could be improved. Mostly, those thoughts concerned their own lines. Rock was very often right, or at least the change he suggested could be utilized noticeably without harming the script.

Murder By the Book was very successful when it first aired. The viewing public loved it. NBC, which knew a good thing when it saw one (and, particularly, when the ratings underscored that opinion), said to Rock, "How about doing a series for us as Stewart McMillan?"

"No way," said Rock, but, of course, they managed to change his mind. Actually, what happened was that he changed their minds on a very important issue.

They wanted *McMillan & Wife* to be a weekly series, but Rock turned that down flat. He had talked to enough stars of weekly series to know how difficult it was to turn out a quality program on a weekly basis.

He said he would do it once a month. That way, he said, there would be enough time to do it properly. But they said there was no such thing as a monthly series. They were at an impasse, an impasse that was broken to everybody's delight when somebody came up with the concept that became known as "the wheel."

That was the notion of having three or four shows that alternated in the same time slot. The network believed, probably correctly, that they had to have continuity to attain and maintain ratings. So they had to have a program with an overall title to induce the public to tune in at the same time every week. The public's viewing of TV is habitual, and the network wanted to play on that tendency by having a regularly scheduled weekly program.

To this end they created the *NBC Mystery Movie*, which would be on every Sunday evening at eight o'clock. *McMillan* would alternate with three other mystery-type shows. They quickly dug out three other shows they had in their closet (Peter Falk's *Columbo*, Dennis Weaver's *McCloud*, and Richard Boone's *Hec Ramsey*) to alternate with Rock Hudson's *McMillan & Wife*.

In a sense, Rock invented that "wheel" concept, or at the very least was the impetus behind its invention. It proved to be very successful, in this case. Because *Hec Ramsey* didn't click with the public, ultimately the three remaining shows stepped up their production a bit and *McMillan*, *Columbo*, and *McCloud* alternated for the subsequent six solid successful seasons.

The year that Rock made his TV debut—1971—was a big year for major movie stars trying to conquer television. Besides Rock, others who made the attempt were Shirley MacLaine ("Shirley's World"), Henry Fonda ("The Smith Family"), Glenn Ford ("Cade's County") and James Stewart ("The Jimmy Stewart Show"). They all failed. Only Rock made it. It is either a tribute to his popularity or to the quality of the show. A little of both, probably.

McMillan & Wife, like *Columbo* and *McCloud*, was ninety minutes long. On a few rare occasions, episodes were expanded to two hours. But even at ninety minutes they were, in effect, movie length. So Rock, who had made perhaps two movies a year, was now making one a month, on average.

Since he liked to work, that part was fine with him. He felt that as long as he had adequate time to rehearse and enough time for reshooting a scene if he felt the first take was not so hot, it would be OK. And it turned out to be more than just OK—it was a big hit.

One reason for its success came when Epstein decided to give the show a first-class appearance. He hired Milton Krasner as the cinematographer. Krasner had won seven or eight Oscars for his work, and he was determined—with Jon Epstein's blessing—to give the show the look of a quality motion picture. He took time to light each scene properly, unlike most TV shows, which use the same lighting for every shot. Rock always said Milton Krasner should have had the credit for making *McMillan & Wife* look so much classier than the run-of-the-TV-screen shows.

The show quickly shot Rock back up to the top again. Now he was as popular with the television audience as he had long been with the moviegoing audience.

Naturally, he was pleased. But even though he enjoyed doing *McMillan,* he still retained the old movie star's attitude toward television in general. He automatically turned down offers to do other TV shows—specials, movies, whatever—that poured in as a result of the success of *McMillan.* He still thought that the average TV show (not his own, of course) was second-rate.

There was always a good rapport between Rock and Susan Saint James on the screen. Their acting styles meshed and the characters created for them meshed, too. But off-screen was something else again.

It wasn't that they disliked each other or had a feud or any really serious disagreements. The problem was simply that Susan was such a rebel. She was the kind of girl who wrapped herself in causes. At Universal, where *McMillan & Wife* was filmed, good causes were not hard to find. The management of that studio was, on the benevolence scale, about halfway between Attila the Hun and a pit bull terrier. So Susan was always charging up to The Black Tower, the black-glass building that housed Universal's corporate headquarters, and demanding something. I sometimes felt she didn't really care what she demanded; it was the mere act of demanding that she found thrilling and necessary.

Of course, she always tried to enlist Rock's aid, comfort, and support in her crusades.

"Rock, look at this," she would say. "Isn't it terrible what they are doing?" And she would hand Rock a petition that, for example, the studio drivers had circulated demanding, perhaps, covers on all limousine steering wheels, or something equally vital.

"How dare they make those poor drivers go around without steering wheel covers!"

And she would leap out of her chair—the star's chair, the one that had SUSAN SAINT JAMES in large letters on the back—and charge off. Eyes flashing, fists clenched, she would say nothing would stop her until she saw Lew Wasserman himself. He was the head of the studio.

"I'm going to get steering wheel covers on all limos by this afternoon."

Then she'd turn to Rock and say, "You are coming with me, aren't you?"

"Well, no," Rock would say. "I really don't give a damn about the drivers and their steering wheel covers."

"Boy, I never realized what an insensitive person you are," she would say, and off she'd go.

Rock would look at me and shake his head.

"Any old cause in a storm," he'd say.

The plight of the drivers was only one of her causes, but it was a particular pet. Once she led a drivers' revolt as they demanded more overtime pay. That led her to consider overtime for everybody on the set as a must.

One night, the company worked especially late to wrap up an episode. Susan kept strict track of the hours, and she said she was going to put in for overtime.

"How about you?" she asked Rock. "You should put in for overtime, too. After all, you're a human being and if they ask you to work these long hours, they should pay you extra. It's only fair."

"Look, Susan," he said. "I'm making a fortune as it is"—he didn't tell her, of course, but he was making something like $125,000 an episode—"so it would be silly for me to ask for overtime."

She raced off, and I think she did apply for overtime; knowing Universal, I doubt that she got it. Rock thought she was being foolish, because she made a pretty good salary, too. And he felt that working late, when necessary, was just part of the business. Sometimes you'd get off early, sometimes you worked late; in his view, it all averaged out.

Susan Saint James has grown out of that phase of her life. Today, since her own series, *Kate & Allie,* has made her into a major star in her own right, and since her marriage to TV executive Dick Ebersole, she is an entirely different person. Maybe not as zany, but more mature.

She is a very establishment kind of person now—a wife and a mother with a house in the Connecticut countryside. But, when she was playing Sally McMillan, she tilted at more windmills than Don Quixote ever even dreamed of.

One joy for Rock (and me) during the *McMillan* years were the two ladies who played the McMillans' housekeeper. Nancy Walker was the first—she played a character named Mildred—and, when she decided to leave, Martha Raye was hired to play another house-keeper, Agatha. Both Rock and I were crazy about those two ladies. I still am; I visit with Nancy and her husband, David Craig, often in Los Angeles and Maggie Raye frequently comes down to my house in the desert when she feels like getting away from it all.

Rock adapted to television easily, despite his early reservations. He had always been a quick study—he learned his lines swiftly and easily—and he really didn't need as much rehearsal time as he used to claim he did. Besides, once he got the character of Stewart McMillan down solidly, the role became his private domain.

The more he did the part, the more he felt he knew—and liked—McMillan. He became very protective of the character.

If a writer created some dialogue Rock felt didn't fit his concept of McMillan, he would ask for a change.

"McMillan would never say that line," he might say. "Look, I know McMillan better than anybody, and he just wouldn't say that. He would say this."

And he would, extemporaneously, offer a new version of the words the writer had written. Jon Epstein almost always went along with Rock on things like that.

But Rock was never unbending, inflexible. He didn't use his star status to become a dictator. He never threatened to walk of the set if the changes he requested were not accepted. If Epstein or the writer gave him a good, logical reason why the original words were better, he would agree.

Rock was always easy to direct. And, just as important, easy on directors. While he technically had director approval, I don't believe he ever exercised that right. He let Epstein choose the directors. There were a few who came back to the show several times but, whoever was the director, Rock smilingly did his work. Mostly, he and the director would wind up becoming good friends. Rock had that knack for making friends easily.

So, by and large, the *McMillan* years—roughly 1970 to 1976—were good years. Productive years. Pleasant years. And very profitable years.

Despite the success of *McMillan & Wife,* and the fact that it was a pleasant experience, neither Rock nor I thought it was outstanding entertainment. I suspect we had both been spoiled by the intrinsically higher quality of movies. We were delighted that the public liked it and surprised when most of the critics liked it, too. But we always felt it was passable, at best.

We had a big laugh when, some years later, Robert Wagner and Stefanie Powers—both good friends—came out with their series, *Hart To Hart.* More than one critic said in their reviews: "*Hart To Hart* is a poor man's *McMillan & Wife.*"

The blunt truth is that, measured against a movie, a television show simply cannot compare. There is a very logical reason: A television show, because of the exigencies of time and budget, most shoot, on average, ten to fifteen pages of the script a day. On a movie set, even a modestly budgeted one, you shoot at the most two or three pages a day. Obviously, then, you have more time on the movie to try for better lighting and better camera angles, more time for reshooting if a take isn't exactly right, more time to let the actors rehearse and let the director think and let all the technical people strive for perfection. More time to be good.

On *McMillan,* since it was part of that "wheel" concept, we had more time than the average television show, but still much less time than if it had been a theatrical motion picture. We were always compromising, always saying, "Well, it isn't great, but it will have to do."

The amazing thing about television isn't how bad it is, but how good it is, considering that it has two and seven-eighths strikes against it. Given the conditions under which the average television show is manufactured, it is really incredible that it gets made at all.

Rock Hudson had been a major movie superstar for many years by the time he succumbed and began his television career. What TV did for Rock was perpetuate that major superstardom and bring him a new generation of fans as well. Had he done what he was inclined to do—ignore television completely—he would have been gone from that top spot in a few quick years.

The truth is that movies are not the big source for stars they once were. If they come at all nowadays, they come from television and (another category of stars completely) from what passes for popular music now.

But Rock did do television and, as a result, his name and face remained high on the public's fan list.

When Susan Saint James left, the show was never quite the same. Even so, NBC begged Rock to continue, but after a year we realized that the end was at hand. I had convinced Rock to do it; now I counseled him that enough was enough. He agreed with me, and that was that.

He was, of course, deluged with offers to do other TV series. But you should never overestimate the intelligence of TV executives. Most—in fact, all—of those offers were for series in which Rock was asked to play a variation on the Stewart McMillan character. How original! How creative!

Television executives have a bandwagon mentality. When one successful series ends, they immediately want to put the star(s) in another series that closely approximates the old one. They defend that policy by saying that the public wants to see its idols in familiar roles, that TV's brief history has shown that when a star tries doing a show that is totally different from the old hit show, it invariably flops.

Still, it seemed to Rock and me that the offers that were coming in by the bucketful showed a total lack of imagination and inventiveness. They would have had him playing, perhaps, a mayor instead of a police commissioner, or he would have been the head of a large corporation with a zany wife. There were always one or two elements borrowed liberally from the *McMillan & Wife* format.

And Rock, who wasn't anxious to do another series in the first place, was certainly not going to play Stewart McMillan again, no matter how they tried to disguise him.

I read all the scripts that came in, and there was nothing in the series area that I could recommend to Rock. But Flo Allen, still his agent, and I did find a few very excellent TV movies that I was able to persuade Rock to do. They included *Wheels* and *The Martian Chronicles* and *World War III*. In that period between series, too, he also squeezed in a few movies that were not so good: the disaster movie *Avalanche*, which was the one he had been so eager to do, and *The Mirror Crack'd.*

Then along came *The Devlin Connection.*

You may well ask why, if Rock was so eager to steer clear of a character like Stewart McMillan, he accepted the role of Brian Devlin, who was very much stamped from the McMillan mold. Like Mc-

Millan, Devlin was public-spirited (he was director of the Los Angeles Cultural Arts Center). Like McMillan, Devlin had a kooky family member (his recently discovered son, Nick Corsello, wanted to be a detective). And, again like McMillan, Devlin got involved in the solving of crimes.

The answer was that the deal Rock was offered was such that he would have been a fool to decline it, no matter how similar the character was to that of Stewart McMillan.

It began when Fred Silverman took over the reins at NBC and wanted some smash shows. His concept was to bring back big blockbuster stars to TV series—James Garner for one, Rock Hudson for another. He had this show, which ultimately became *The Devlin Connection*, and he liked the idea a lot, especially with Rock playing Devlin. So he put together a deal he presented to Flo Allen—who, in turn, presented it to us.

Neither Rock nor I liked the idea of the show very much, but we were impressed with Silverman's enthusiasm—it is always helpful when the head of the network is gung ho for your show—and even more impressed with his willingness to give us everything we asked for. For one thing, Mammoth would wind up owning the show after the episodes had aired on NBC twice. If the show was a hit, that could be a true bonanza: Mammoth (our company) would get all the money from all the reruns.

Silverman also agreed to pay Rock an enormous sum of money (and threw in an extra $10,000 a show for my services), allowed him control over virtually everything to do with the production, agreed to all sorts of concessions and conditions.

I believe that the deal Rock got for *The Devlin Connection* was probably the best a star had ever received from a network until then. Maybe until now. Rock was given total—100 percent—creative control. That had never been heard of before. And on and on went the list of things they would do for him.

But he was still hesitant. He still had that nagging belief that TV was a second-rate medium and, besides, he shared my feeling that *The Devlin Connection* was second-rate television. That's not what we told Fred Silverman and NBC, of course. We gave as a reason for Rock's reluctance the fact that he found the TV schedule too exhausting. We told NBC that Rock needed an easier working schedule than he had had on *McMillan & Wife*.

"No problem," said the NBC deal-makers. "Tell you what we're going to do."

And they sweetened the deal with an arrangement whereby Rock only worked a four-day week. He would work ten hours each of those four days, but that time was clocked from the moment he arrived at the make-up department, not from when he reported on the set.

When those ten hours were up—right on the button—I was authorized to pull the plug. I would be the heavy and come down to the set and say "That's it for today, gentlemen. Rock's time is up. See you tomorrow." I would, of course, let them finish whatever scene they were shooting, but they would not be able to start a new one.

We worked it that way because both Rock and I knew he was not the type to walk off a set. He was so good-hearted that if a director asked him to do "just one more scene," he would do it. But, under the arrangement we worked out, I would see to it that that didn't happen. This way, he could just shrug—it wasn't his doing—and walk off with me.

With all those inducements, Rock simply couldn't say no. And, in 1981, he signed to do *The Devlin Connection*.

We all agreed on John Wilder as producer. He had great credits and we liked him and, besides, he was one of the new breed known as hyphenates. That meant he did something else in addition to producing; he was a producer-writer, and the use of that hyphen and his ability to do two jobs qualified him as a hyphenate. To us, it meant that Wilder would not only produce but, as a writer, would write many of the episodes himself and oversee those that he did not actually write. It was an arrangement many TV shows used.

In fact, the widespread use of producer-writers on TV was what made people say that TV was a producers' medium, as opposed to movies (a directors' medium) and the stage (an actors' medium).

We made the deal in the spring and TV production generally starts in early summer to make it possible to stockpile episodes and to go on the air in the fall. We met with Wilder and he outlined the thirteen shows NBC had guaranteed they would make. He had all thirteen planned.

"I've got a lot of time to write them," Wilder said. "This is a luxury I don't think I've ever had before. We're in great shape, so everything should be marvelous when you start shooting in June."

Rock and I beamed. The thirteen shows Wilder had outlined sounded great. We talked, idly, about the guest stars who might fit the various roles he was going to write, and we even talked about possible locations.

Everything seemed rosy, but then trouble came along. That was the year of the writers' strike. Because Wilder was a good member of the Writers Guild, when they struck, he struck. As the weeks wore on and the scheduled day to start shooting approached, not a word of a script was yet on paper. Wilder was on the picket line, marching.

Finally, with just a couple of weeks to go before our shooting was to begin, the strike was settled. Wilder scurried to his typewriter but, we later learned, he was going through a messy divorce proceeding that had pushed him to the edge of a nervous breakdown. But he was a man of his word, and he had told us he was going to have scripts ready. He cranked up the old machine and he ground out scripts. By the pound.

They read like they were ground out, too. They were terrible. Awful. Abysmal.

"What'll we do?" Rock said, as we read them at home a few days before the cameras were supposed to start rolling. "I can't do this crap."

"Nothing else we can do," I said. "You have to shoot these scripts. You simply have no other choice."

That's the television trap. The commitment has been made, and the network and the advertisers must have product to put on the air. The public is eagerly waiting because the network's publicity people have spewed out press releases and the promotion department has filled the air with announcements of the coming show. And the public was eagerly waiting to see Rock Hudson's new show, which left Rock with, as I said, no other choice.

Crap or not, he had to shoot it.

He shot the first three, and was in the middle of the fourth when he had a heart attack warning. I believe that his feeling that he was working with material he didn't think was very good, plus all the stress he was under, contributed to that almost-heart-attack he had.

Production was, of course, shut down immediately. In fact, we were in the middle of the fourth episode when we had to stop abruptly, leaving that episode unfinished.

For a time, of course, neither Rock nor I thought anything about *The Devlin Connection* or about television at all. Our entire mental and emotional efforts were directed toward the state of Rock's health. So we were unaware of the wheels-within-wheels spinning away at NBC while Rock was hospitalized and, later, while he was recuperating.

Only afterward did we find out that, during the period of Rock's illness, NBC had gone through a major executive shake-up. Fred Silverman, who had been the impetus behind our deal, was out. Brandon Tartikoff was now the man who was running the entertainment division.

Understandably, any new chief executive officer almost automatically feels compelled to throw out everything from the previous regime. Tartikoff, as he examined the programs and commitments he had inherited from Silverman, came to the contract between NBC and Rock Hudson for *The Devlin Connection.* It was, as I have said, a terrific deal—for Rock. Tartikoff didn't think it was so terrific for NBC.

"We can't live with this," Tartikoff told Flo Allen, who was still Rock's agent.

But, if they wanted Rock and that show, the network had no choice. Tartikoff tried to persuade Flo to renegotiate, but she naturally refused. While all this was going on, Rock and I were away. I had taken Rock on a cruise, as part of the recuperative process— the last trip he took for quite a while. Claire Trevor Bren accompanied us, and it was a good, relaxed—and very necessary—time.

The only thing that marred the cruise was that we read some scripts John Wilder had written. During Rock's hospitalization he had gone back to his typewriter and had done six new *Devlin* scripts and had given them to us to read on our cruise. We read them with dismay, however, because it seemed to both of us they were absolutely unplayable.

Rock was so distressed that he called Flo on the ship-to-shore phone.

"I cannot say these lousy words," he said to her. "These scripts are worthless, completely worthless."

"You're exaggerating," she said. "They can't be that bad. After all, Wilder is a pro."

"That's what Tom and I thought," Rock said, "but he's lost it."

The day we got back from the cruise, Flo called and said she had to see us. She came to the house that Sunday afternoon, and Rock had been planning to go back to work the next day, Monday morning. The idea was that he would finish the episode he'd been in the middle of when he had the heart attack.

She said that the network agreed. Wilder would have to go. We were pleased about that, because we had become very disturbed with the way things were going: the scripts were bad and, consequently, the shows had turned out badly. It wasn't the show we had set out to do.

Fortunately, while we were happy that Wilder was on his way out, although we both personally liked him very much, we were both pleased that it was the network that had decided to do it, not us. Rock would have hated to have that on his conscience. This way, if Wilder or anyone questioned him, he could always say— with total honesty—that he had not suggested the replacement.

Flo said they were talking about Jerry Thorpe as the new producer.

"I know Jerry," I said. "I knew both him and his father when they both worked at MGM. He's a good guy." The same afternoon we met with Jerry at the Polo Lounge. Rock and he seemed to have a rapport, and they shook hands, and we reported back to Flo that Jerry Thorpe was acceptable.

But there was, first, the painful process of going back into the studio and finishing that interrupted episode. John Wilder was still there, unaware that he was being booted out. So Rock had to work for him, while that episode was finished, and keep the secret. It was a very uncomfortable four or five days.

Thorpe reported to the studio and with him we viewed the three finished episodes and a rough cut of the fourth one, the one Rock was shooting when he had his attack. He also read the other scripts Wilder had written. He said it was hopeless.

"You have a great concept for a show here," he said, "but I will not go ahead and film these scripts."

Tartikoff was behind us, but very anxious and concerned about the way things were going. He wanted to make the show right, make it succeed. And yet those scripts represented a heavy investment for NBC; to junk them was throwing money away. Besides, the network had penciled the show in to start airing in a few weeks, and if those scripts were not utilized, there was no way that date could be met.

But Thorpe stood his ground. And Rock and I backed him. We all held out for making a fresh start, which meant putting the whole thing off for several months.

Finally Tartikoff agreed. After all, he wanted a good show—not even the most crass network executive deliberately sets out to make a bad show, no matter how often it looks like they do. So NBC postponed *The Devlin Connection* until the following fall. Thus, once again, the show went on hiatus.

There is something about any creative process that suffers from delays. When a project is newly created, it generates an excitement of its own. The longer things are delayed, the more that excitement wanes.

And so it was with *The Devlin Connection*. We did go back into production the following summer, and we did make a redebut, with a great deal of hoopla and hope, that next September. But it really wasn't a new show, nor was it a revival, nor was it an old show re-turning as a result of public demand. It was neither fish nor fowl.

In retrospect, Rock and I often said that *The Devlin Connection* was doomed from the moment John Wilder decided that his conscience wouldn't let him write those first scripts while the writers were on strike. If he had, chances are the show would have been a solid hit, because it was a good, workable concept; the public was eager to see Rock again; and the network was pushing it.

But it was just one of those things.

And it was the end for Rock Hudson, television star, other than his desperate final fling on *Dynasty*, and one last TV movie, the lamentable *Las Vegas Strip Wars*, in 1984, when the imprint of his fatal illness was already on his face.

The Heart Attack?

One Sunday morning, I woke up much earlier than I usually did. I suppose believers in extrasensory perception, or other quaint customs, would say that my waking up so early was entirely due to some subconscious message I had received. But, in truth, what woke me so early was nothing more mysterious than the fact that Rock was awake and stirring.

Those unusual sounds were what roused me.

I sat up and looked over and there was Rock, sitting by the side of my bed, just looking at me.

I looked at the clock.

"My God, Rock," I said. "It's only five o'clock in the morning, and you're up and dressed. What's wrong?"

"I think maybe I should go to the hospital," he said.

That was enough for me to jump out of bed and get dressed as quickly as I could. Rock was not an alarmist. He went to see his doctor regularly—all motion picture and television contracts demand periodic physical examinations—but only because it was required of him. He was always in great physical condition, and never complained about anything. He rarely caught cold, and even more rarely had a headache or any ache.

The poor guy had been sitting there, by the side of my bed, waiting patiently for me to wake up. It never would have occurred to him to wake me, no matter how lousy he felt. And, apparently, he felt exceptionally lousy that morning. He told me, as I drove him to Cedars-Sinai Hospital that what had wakened him in the middle of the night had been a severe pain in his chest. It had frightened him, so he had gotten up, dressed, and then sat by my bedside, waiting for me to wake up.

Before we left the house, I called his doctor—Dr. Rex Kennamer—and he was waiting for us when we arrived. Rex was known as Doctor to the Stars because so many Hollywood celebrities were his patients.

With Kennamer and the hospital staff taking over, I felt somewhat relieved. I could not conceive that Rock, the absolute picture of radiant health, could be seriously ill. I thought it must have been a severe case of indigestion. At the worst, maybe food poisoning. I tried to remember what we had eaten the night before. Whatever it was, I realized, I had eaten it, too, and I was fine, so I ruled out food poisoning. But I also ruled out any heart problems, because Rock had been checked out not long before and everything, Kennamer said, was fine. Heart included.

I also wondered what I should do about the press, about his series, about his friends. I decided to wait. It was, fortunately, a Sunday. He wasn't due on the set until tomorrow morning. Maybe it was something minor and he'd be able to work the next day. No point in crossing the bridge until somebody had, at least, dug the river.

As for the press, they would undoubtedly find out. Large hospitals, such as Cedars, although they may not be aware of it, frequently seem to have some informants—paid by the press—hidden somewhere on their staffs. Chances are some orderly or nurse or clerk had already called his or her employer—one of the papers or television stations—and tipped them off that Rock Hudson was in the hospital. I prepared for an onslaught of reporters and photographers, and I wasn't disappointed. I managed to fend them off. The press wasn't my only worry. The hosptial had received some death threats—a nut who siad he was going to kill Rock Hudson while he was there—and they insisted we hire guards to protect him. So I hired guards.

I sat in the waiting room for several hours before I was allowed to go into Rock's room. They had run many tests on him. Kennamer was there, at Rock's bedside, when I came into the room.

"Bad news, boys," the doctor said. "It looks like there is a blockage in the arteries. Those pains were not a heart attack per se, but a warning that a heart attack was coming. I want you to have open heart surgery, as soon as possible—Tuesday morning, probably."

We discussed it, but Kennamer was adamant. The operation was absolutely essential, he said. A matter of life or death. The only alternative was a genuine heart attack, which could be a killer. We said that Rock was in the middle of an episode, which would be finished in five days, maybe four if we rushed. Couldn't it wait until that episode was in the can?

No, said the doctor. Not if you value your life. And he did put it in just that simple an equation: your life is at stake.

Rock was scared. I'd never seen him frightened, but he was frightened by the prospect of heart surgery. I was scared, too. But when we looked at each other, we understood that it had to be done. There was really nothing more to discuss. Rock said, "OK, Rex. Make the arrangements."

The next morning I went to the studio to give them all the bad news: production would be shut down indefinitely.

"Rock is in the hospital," I told the assembled actors and crew. They gasped. Nobody had had any indication that he was ill in any way, or even feeling poorly.

"He will be having open heart surgery tomorrow," I continued. "We hope that he will be back, ready to go, in a month or so." (That was strictly an improvisation on my part; I had no idea how long it might take and the doctor had not said and I had not asked him).

He was operated on early Tuesday morning, after he had been prepped most of Monday afternoon.

Open heart surgery has become almost routine but, still, it is surgery on the heart and it can be risky. The operation itself is perilous and there is always the possibility of complications. I sat there for the hours he was in the operating room, trying to remember the prayers I had learned when I was a boy back in Oklahoma City. Finally, I just ad-libbed a few words with God, asking for His mercy on this critical occasion.

And He was merciful. The operation was long—it seemed a lifetime to me—but it went smoothly. The surgeon, Dr. Matlock, and Dr. Kennamer came out to tell me that it had been successful. Rock was now out of danger, they reported, and would make a full recovery.

When Rock was taken to the recovery room, both Matlock and Kennamer came out again to talk to me.

"He's OK," Matlock said. "He's doing just fine. We anticipate no problems."

"But, Tom, we want to prepare you for something," Rex Kennamer said. My imagination immediately conjured up all kinds of dire developments. I had seen enough movies and had been through all of those *Dr. Kildare* episodes, so I was fully prepared for what was coming. Rock is paralyzed. Rock will have lost his sight or his hearing or both. Rock will have lost his memory. Rock's hair will have turned snow-white. One of those four.

"What is it?" I said, sitting down and gripping the arms of the chair firmly. I was ready for the bad news.

"Now it may or may not happen," Kennamer said, "but it does happen very often after open heart surgery. And that is that the patient exhibits a distinct personality change. As I said, some patients never show it. But many do."

"What sort of personality change?"

"Can't say. And it is not necessarily a change for the worse. It could be a change for the better. But we just wanted you to be prepared: the Rock Hudson who comes home from the hospital may not be exactly the same Rock Hudson who went into the hospital."

He went on to say, with Matlock nodding agreement, that if such a change did occur, it probably was only temporary. These personality changes, he said, did not last. Maybe a month or so, maybe three or four. No more than that. Maybe much less. And maybe nothing at all.

I went to the studio after that, to tell the show's production team that the surgery had gone well. And there were a few details I had to take care of. As it turned out, I stayed at the studio until after dinner. I left about 8:30 in the evening and decided to stop in at the hospital on my way home.

So it was about nine o'clock when I tiptoed into Rock's space in the Intensive Care Unit. I was sure he would still be out of it. After all, he had had five bypasses, he had been on the operating table for somewhere around six hours, he must still be totally sedated.

I slowly, quietly opened the door of his room. And I peeked in, expecting to see a figure prone on the bed.

But there he was, sitting up.

"Hi, Tom," he called, with a smile, as though it was just another day. "Come on in. Been wondering when you were going to show up."

But he was nodding off even as he was speaking, and I didn't stay long. I left feeling a great sense of relief, because I could see he would recover quickly. And I marveled at his constitution.

The next morning, a phone call from Kennamer woke me up.

"Sorry to wake you, Tom," the doctor said, "but I just thought you'd like to know how well Rock is doing. You won't believe this— I wouldn't have believed it if I hadn't seen it with my own eyes— but when I went into his room just now there he was, sitting up, smiling and eating breakfast."

He had such a strong, basically healthy system that he bounced back from that open heart surgery like it was nothing more serious than the removal of a wart.

Maybe because of that ultrarapid recovery, he (and I) never gave a thought to his mortality. Perhaps he may have had such thoughts in the privacy of his own mind, but I doubt it. We shared everything, even private thoughts, and I believe I would have known.

Most people, facing anything as potentially serious as open heart surgery, begin to think about the proximity of death. They start philosophizing, perhaps find religion, possibly revise their wills, begin to wonder openly about the next world, reassess their lives and consider their souls. But if any such thoughts ever entered Rock's head—and I really don't believe they did—he never spoke them aloud.

But there was that personality change that the two doctors had warned me about.

It is very difficult to describe that change or, rather, those changes, because it wasn't just one thing, but several. It was nothing I could put my finger on. Instead, it was a series of minor alterations in the Rock Hudson I had known for so long.

He behaved in ways he never behaved in the past. He said things he never would have said before the operation.

Those were not necessarily bad, merely different.

I wasn't alone in noticing the changes, although, being closest to him, I noticed them first. Mark Miller, his secretary and friend, would catch my eye and shake his head. And occasionally, when we were out, I'd hear his friends whispering, "Is Rock really OK? He seems, I don't know, not quite himself."

And he wasn't quite himself. I thought, well, this too will pass—the doctors had said that any personality change would only be temporary—and I kept waiting for it to pass, for the old Rock Hudson to return. But it never did pass. Rock was a different man from the time of his surgery until his death.

There was, however, one very distinct change in Rock's personality, one noticeable change. That was his new, revised attitude toward travel. All through our association, his one overriding passion had been traveling. Give him a ticket and he was gone.

After the operation, all that changed. He did go on that one cruise but, that trip aside, he no longer traveled, although he never would admit that he didn't. In fact, he still planned trips as enthusiastically as before. Now, however, he wouldn't take them.

We would plan trips and I would make all the arrangements and then, at the last minute, Rock would find some excuse not to go. And I would have to cancel all those plans.

A few months after he came home from the hospital Rock was invited to attend the Berlin Film Festival. We both were very excited. For some reason, neither of us had ever been to Berlin. We had been all over Germany, but we had missed Berlin.

And our hosts were going all-out. They had arranged for us to stay at the finest hotel in Berlin, supposedly one of the finest in all of Europe. They had planned a side trip for us to go behind the Iron Curtain into East Berlin. Plus many other pleasant perks.

I was on the phone almost every day for weeks with the people in Germany, checking and rechecking plans and details. Everything was fine-tuned so we would travel with the minimum problems and the maximum luxury. It was going to be a wonderful trip. And they were overjoyed that Rock was coming. Money was no object; they were laying it on thick.

About a week before we were to leave, Rock turned to me one evening and said, "I don't think we should go to Berlin, Tom."

"Why not, for heaven's sake?"

"Well, it's just too cold there at this time of year."

I was unable to change his mind. The old Rock Hudson would never have even thought about what the weather might be. That thought would not even have crossed his mind. We had gone places where it was very cold and places where it was very hot, and the temperature never daunted him.

But now the possibility that it might be cold in Berlin was enough to cancel the whole thing. I realized that the cold was just an excuse, but I wasn't sure what the real reason was.

That sort of thing happened three or four more times within the space of a few months. Fortunately, it was easy for me to get us out of those travel commitments. Whenever we planned a trip, I always insisted on a contingency: in case Rock is required to work, we reserve the right to cancel the arrangements. So it was a simple matter of invoking that contingency.

But that didn't make me any happier. We might be able to back out of our trip, but it left me wondering. So I went to see Dr. Rex Kennamer and asked him if this fear of traveling might be one of those personality changes he warned me about.

"Very possible," he said. "You know, after an operation as serious as the one Rock went through, there is a fear of leaving the womb, so to speak. There is a fear of being too far away from his doctor. Who knows what goes on in somebody's head? It all could be a part of it."

That business of not wanting to travel lasted, I would estimate, about a year. During that year, he canceled—always at the last minute—plans he had helped me make with tremendous excitement. And his excuses for canceling them were always as flimsy and nonsensical as the fact that it might be too cold to go to Berlin at that time of year.

Once we even canceled a trip to New York. And our New York jaunts were the easiest possible trips for us—we didn't even have to pack, since we had duplicates of everything, even toothbrushes, in our New York apartment. And we always had a limousine to take us to the airport in Los Angeles and to meet us at the airport in New York. This time we were scheduled to attend the opening of a show. Again, all the arrangements had been made. It was a very easy trip, and it was one we had made dozens of times before.

Not this time. This time, he canceled a few days before we were set to go. Said he just didn't feel like it.

Then, about a year after the operation, that changed again. We made plans for a trip once more. Even though I fully expected, judging from recent experience, that it would never happen, I went through the motions because he enjoyed planning it so much. But this time—surprise!—we actually went. I was so startled that I was caught unpacked; I had been so sure he was going to cancel that I hadn't packed. I had to jam some things into a suitcase quickly an hour before we left.

So that change passed. There was one change I had been hoping would happen that never came to pass. I had hoped that Rock would quit smoking.

Naturally, Kennamer and every other doctor Rock saw advised him strongly to give up his cigarette habit. They went so far as to say that, in all probability, it had been his heavy smoking that had caused his arteries to harden, necessitating the surgery to unblock them.

He should have stopped then and there, and he knew it, but he couldn't, or wouldn't, so he didn't.

I was a heavy smoker, and I knew if he was to quit, I had to quit—or at least give the appearance of having quit. So I never smoked in his presence then, or for many months after his operation. I would go outside the room, or, better still, outside the house, when I lit up.

"Hey, Tom," he said to me one day. "Who do you think you're kidding? I know you're still smoking. I know you go outside to smoke. I can smell it on your breath. Might as well smoke in front of me."

So I did, and pretty soon he was smoking just as heavily as he ever did. The doctors were very angry with him.

Of course, as it turned out, it wasn't smoking that killed him. And I keep thinking, even today, that if he had forced himself to stop smoking, what good would it have done? All it would have done would be to have made his last few years less enjoyable. So, in retrospect, I am not sad he kept on smoking. At least it gave him pleasure.

CHAPTER ELEVEN
In New York

I f you're connected with show business in any way, you inevitably have to go to two places—New York and Los Angeles. New York has always been the theatrical center of America. Los Angeles is the film center. But, even if you are solely into film, you have to visit New York occasionally because that's where the money is and, largely, that's where the deals are made.

And that's where the shows are. If you want to be *au courant* with the theatrical scene, you have to see the current crop of Broadway shows.

So, once or twice a year, Rock and I would go back to New York and see all the latest hits. While we were there we would visit friends, perhaps have one or two business meetings, do some shopping. Almost like tourists, except on a slightly different level.

We would always stay at the Plaza, and always in a corner suite that Rock particularly enjoyed. And we always made it a point to have at least one dinner in the Oak Room at the Plaza, where Rock would hold court, as everybody who was anybody (and a lot of people who would have liked to have been somebody) came over to our table to say hello. It was old home week, away from home.

But each time we went to New York, we had virtually the same conversation:

"Do we have to go?"

"Yes, I think we should go."

"But I hate that city so damned much."

"I know. So do I. We both hate it—all the dirt and the people pushing and shoving."

"So let's just not go."

"We have to go. We have to see *Hello, Dolly* (or whatever the huge hit-of-the-moment happened to be) and we have to meet So-and-So."

"Well, let's go and come back as quick as we can."

(The dialogue had interchangeable parts; either of us could have spoken any of the lines).

So we would go. And we would keep telling each other how much we hated it as we went, while we were there, and on the way home.

In 1977, we made yet another trip, hating every inch of the way. We stayed in that same corner suite at the Plaza, had one more lovely dinner in the Oak Room, saw a few shows, entertained and were entertained.

One thing Rock and I always had in common was that we were both last-minute people. If we had to catch a nine o'clock plane and it takes an hour to get from midtown Manhattan to the airport, we could check out of the hotel at five minutes to eight and tell the limo driver to step on it.

That meant that I always spent as little time as possible in the checking-out process. I would call the front desk, tell them we were about to leave, and, as we headed out the front door, scrawl my signature on the bill without looking at it and stuff my copy in my pocket and run for the limo. The car would be moving and I'd leap through the open door and we'd speed off for the airport.

On that particular trip, in '77, we had been rather frugal—for us—much more frugal than usual. We had had a small dinner party in the Edwardian Room, just two guests, and we had invited about ten people for cocktails one evening in the Oak Bar. And, unusual for us, we had not once ordered anything from room service. When we were safely on the plane, and airborne, I finally had a chance to look at the bill I had so hastily signed.

It was huge. Absolutely astronomical. I showed it to Rock. We had been there only three nights, had done that small amount of entertaining, and the total was somewhere around $3500.

"Did we spend that much?" he asked.

"Must be a mistake," I said. "No way we spent that much. They'll fix it. I'll get Wally to check it out."

Wally was our mutual business manager, Wally Sheft.

When I got back home, I called Wally, explained the situation. All the bills went to him, anyhow, and I just said that this one from the Plaza was obviously wrong, and when the bill came in, would he please double-check it with the hotel's accounting office?

He did, and reported back to me a week or so later that the total had been correct. No mistake. New York hotels had become so expensive that we did spend around $3500 in three days without being overly extravagant.

"Maybe you shouldn't be such a big tipper," Wally said to me, half in jest.

"You know I have to tip big," I said, with no jest at all. "We've been over that before."

I automatically added 20 percent to every bill. If movie stars tip less, they get the reputation of being stingy and tight, and that reputation can haunt a star forever. (Look at Cary Grant.) Being a movie star can be an expensive trade.

When Rock was cast in *Camelot*, in 1977, we told Bill Ross, the producer, that part of the deal would be that Rock would not have to rehearse in New York. (That was when he still hated New York so.) We went to New York for the casting, then brought the principals back to Los Angeles and they all rehearsed there. It wasn't until the final two weeks that Rock and the other leads went back to New York and began working with the chorus and the sets and costumes there.

It was during those two weeks, when *Camelot* was being put together, that Rock and I both fell madly in love with New York. The city was cleaner than we had ever seen it, and everybody we met was pleasant to us and fun to be with. It seemed like an entirely new—and lovely—city.

We began to think about perhaps getting an apartment. The specter of that $3500 bill at the Plaza Hotel for three days hung over our heads.

When we came East again, as Rock rehearsed his part in *On the Twentieth Century*, we translated that thought into action. Rock was always concerned with my welfare. He worried about what I would do with myself during the many hours he would be occupied with rehearsing the show. So he suggested that maybe I could spend some time looking for an apartment.

"It would give you something to do," he said. "You don't want to hang around the theater all day while I'm rehearsing."

I watched a couple of days of rehearsal, then took his advice. I turned my attention to looking for an apartment we could buy.

I put myself in the hands of a terrific real estate lady and told her exactly what we wanted. We had settled on some absolute requirements.

We wanted to be on the West Side of Manhattan, which may not be quite as fashionable as the East Side, but we were oriented toward the theater district and that's on the West Side. At least, if you're on the West Side, you don't have to worry about going crosstown in a cab when the traffic makes that trip the Gridlock Gaieties. We would sacrifice a little fashion for some convenience.

Another requirement Rock and I had discussed was that we wanted an apartment with personality.

"Not just a bunch of square, boxy little rooms," I told the real estate agent. "It must be interesting."

She wrote it all down without batting an eye. I suppose in her career she'd met all kinds, so people who didn't want square, boxy little rooms were just another type of crazy.

"One more thing," I said. She looked up, pencil and notebook at the ready. "We're Californians, you know, so we need to have an outdoors of some kind. A terrace or a balcony or something like that."

"OK," she said, jotting away. "Terrace or balcony. Right. Anything else?"

"Well, maybe it would be a good idea not to mention that you're representing Rock Hudson. You know how it is—if a Hollywood star's name is bandied about, the price goes up like a rocket."

"I've already thought of that," she said.

So, for the next few weeks, while Rock was rehearsing, she took me around every day and showed me every apartment that was available in the entire borough of Manhattan.

Nothing even remotely close to what we wanted. She even showed me Barbra Streisand's apartment, which was up for sale, but it didn't work for me. Very discouraging.

While I was out pounding the pavements, Rock was enjoying himself immensely. He was so excited about the work, about being in with the Broadway crowd, that he was hyper. At night, we'd compare notes; I'd be footsore and down in the dumps, he'd be walking on air with his head in the clouds. He was so hyper that he couldn't slow down, couldn't sleep, drank and smoked much too much.

We made friends. Rock was always gregarious, always easy to get to know and like. Among our new friends were Marty Richards and his wife, Mary Lea Johnson Richards. She wasn't just any Johnson—she was part of the Johnson & Johnson Johnsons, who had more money than Band-Aids, and they have a whole passel of Band-Aids. She was one of the co-producers of Rock's show.

"We've been invited out to the Richards' place on the Island for the weekend," Rock told me one Friday. I happened to be attending the rehearsal.

"That's great," I said. "I've heard about their place—it's supposed to be absolutely incredible."

"That's what I hear, too. Should be fun. They'll send a car for us after rehearsal tomorrow."

The company only rehearsed for a few hours on Saturday mornings, so we would have a nice weekend on Long Island at the Richards'. It would be short, but sweet.

Later that same Friday, I got a call at the theater from the real estate lady. She said an apartment had just come on the market. It was in the Beresford.

"Where's the Beresford?" I asked. And then I remembered that Sherry Mathis, who was Guinevere in the production of *Camelot*, had told me, when I had mentioned we were looking for an apartment, that the Beresford was one of the finest buildings in the city.

"If you ever get a shot at a place in the Beresford," she had said, "grab it."

So I was immediately interested. The real estate lady was starting to tell me where the Beresford was, but I stopped her.

"I remember now that I know the building," I said. "I'd like to see it, but we're going away for the weekend."

"That's too bad," she said. "Things at the Beresford go very quickly. No chance of seeing it later this afternoon?"

"Well, sure, I guess I could."

So at five o'clock that Friday afternoon she took me over to the Beresford—a grand old building at the corner of Central Park West and 81st Street—and showed me the apartment that had become available on the nineteenth floor.

It was the most hideously decorated place I have ever seen, in all my years. And, believe me, I have been in some hideously decorated places. After all, I've been in the homes of many Hollywood superstars.

But this place took the cake, and the pie, too. It had been built, originally, with beautiful parquet floors. The last occupant had painted all those glorious wooden floors a vibrant pink. The ceiling had an edging of wonderful moldings, and this same boor had painted all those moldings jet black. Everything about the place reeked of bad taste.

But the bare bones were there. It was a corner apartment with two terraces—one on the Central Park West side (with a grand, unobstructed view across Central Park) and a big terrace on the 81st Street side (with an even better view all the way down Manhattan as far as the World Trade Center).

It had interesting, nonboxy rooms. And it even had that rarest of touches in mid-Manhattan, an honest-to-God working fireplace.

I was excited. This was definitely it. And so, that night, when

Rock came back from rehearsal, I told him he had to see the place. I knew he would love it and I knew that he, too, would be able to see beyond the pink floors and the black ceiling moldings and visualize what it could be, properly redecorated.

"We should look at it together tomorrow," I said.

"Well, you know I can't. Rehearsal in the morning and then we're going out to the Richards' on Long Island. We can't back out of that. You'll just have to tell the lady I'll ask for an hour or so off on Monday morning, and I'll look at it with you then."

"Monday may be too late," I said. "Things like this apartment go fast. The real estate lady says that other people are scheduled to see it tomorrow morning."

"We'll just have to take our chances," Rock said. "There's nothing I can do. I'm boxed in for tomorrow."

I thought we had lost it, but fate took a hand. The next morning a tremendous rainstorm lashed the Eastern seaboard, and Mary Lea Richards called Rock up at the theater to say there was no point in coming out to the Island, not in this weather.

"I'll take a rain check," Rock said, and Mary Lea agreed that if ever a rain check was appropriate it was on that particular wet and wild Saturday.

So we had the weekend in the city, after all. I tried all that morning to reach the real estate lady, but she was out. It wasn't until Sunday morning—which dawned clear and sparkling, the way New York can be after a rainstorm—that she returned my calls. She said she thought we were away, but she would try to see if we could see the apartment that afternoon. She called back to say it was OK, and we arranged to meet her at the Beresford.

The apartment Rock and I were staying in was on East 54th Street, near First Avenue. It was such a glorious day that Rock and I walked from 54th Street to 81st Street, through the Park, and over to the Beresford.

The people who were selling the apartment were having a late brunch on the terrace when we arrived. They were, of course, stunned to have Rock Hudson walk in and say hello, right in the middle of their scrambled eggs. I thought, well, there goes the big secret; up goes the price.

Happily, there wasn't much they could do about the price then. It was too late. The ads had all quoted the price: $375,000. Rock liked it as much as I did, and I know he saw its potential too.

We called Wally Sheft as soon as we got back to the place we were staying. His reaction whenever we wanted to buy anything major and expensive, or make any large investment, was always to say no automatically.

"No," he said. "You can't afford it right now. You're going to be doing a Broadway show, and while that may be fun for you, it isn't very lucrative, comparably. Your income is down. No. It's out of the question."

"I'm glad you said that," Rock said. "Thanks for your permission. We're going to buy it, then."

I called the real estate lady. She said that she had just learned another looker had offered the owners $365,000, and they had turned it down.

"Those people are scheduled to see the place again tonight," she said. "I'm sure they're going to offer the asking price, $375,000. If you really want it, I suggest you come in right now with that full price."

I explained to Rock what she had said, and he nodded.

"OK," I said. "We want it. We'll go $375,000. How do we go about it?"

In New York real estate transactions, lawyers play a part. In California, it's all done through real estate people and escrow people, but New York requires lawyers. The real estate lady said that, by coincidence, her "gentleman friend," who was a lawyer, happened to be there with her. He would draw up a letter of agreement and make our offer for the apartment official.

That's what happened. The letter of agreement was rushed by messenger to the sellers, who accepted it and signed it, then rushed back to Rock, and he signed it. And so the deal was consummated that Sunday afternoon.

The next day, the real estate lady later told us, the other buyer (the one who had offered $365,000) had called her in hysterics. He wanted the apartment and was willing to pay $390,000 for it. So Rock could have made $15,000 in a day, without having put a penny down.

I've always said that the Baby Jesus really meant for us to have that apartment. He made it rain, so we didn't go out to Long Island that Saturday. He arranged it so the real estate lady had stayed around that Sunday, and that her gentleman friend just happened to be a lawyer and just happened to be there. He arranged it so the other potential buyer quibbled over $10,000 on his offer.

We spent $200,000 in redecorating and renovating and generally fixing the place up. We spent a lot of great times in that apartment. When Rock and I split up, that apartment was my home for more than a year. And when Rock died, it was sold by his estate for two million dollars.

It was a wonderful place. The building was, as Sherry Mathis had said, special to begin with. When we moved in, we acquired some very special neighbors. Among them was Beverly Sills. We had known her, but once we were neighbors, we got to know her much better. Her first reaction, when we saw her in the elevator, was one of anger. Not genuine anger, but mock anger.

"Oh, I'm so mad at you I could spit," she said, doing a good imitation of the temperamental soprano.

"Whatever for?"

"For getting that apartment, that's whatever for. I simply cannot believe you got that apartment. I've always wanted one on your side of the building. I'm on the other side, and your side is much the better side."

"We didn't know that," I said, truthfully.

"There, you see what I mean? I should have had your apartment, and you should have had my apartment. Why didn't they tell me the apartment you got was on the market? Oh, the cruelty and injustice of it all!"

And then she laughed, and a Sills laugh is almost like a concert. It soars; if I had been a glass, I am sure I would have trembled. Maybe even shattered. Her laugh deserves a standing ovation.

Now that we had the apartment, we had to redecorate it and furnish it. Obviously, we couldn't spend even one night there—not with those pink floors—until something drastic was done to the place.

Rock's mother had died about two years before, and all her furniture had been put in storage. So we sent for it, and that was our nucleus. We also had some things in the Beverly Hills house we could spare, as well. The only major items we had to buy were the beds and everything we wanted for the library. That room had to be furnished entirely from scratch.

We hired a well-recommended decorator-contractor to depink the floors, deblack the ceiling moldings, and generally make the place look civilized and habitable. While he was doing his thing, Rock and I were mostly on tour with *On The Twentieth Century.* But I flew back to New York twice over the next couple of months to make sure things were coming along the way we wanted.

I ordered carpets and drapes—Rock trusted my taste, since our tastes coincided remarkably well—on those two visits back to New York.

Our decorator-contractor had told us we could be in by the first of the year. But you know how it is with the promises of anybody in the building trades. The tour ended in San Francisco in the middle of November. We decided to go on a cruise then—the first such adventure for either of us.

It was a twenty-five-day cruise, a leisurely sail on the *Royal Viking,* a marvelous ship. We sailed from Los Angeles down the Mexican coast, across the Pacific Ocean to Hawaii, back to San Francisco, and finally docked back home in Los Angeles again. We had a terrific time, and we had many of our own good friends with us, including Ross Hunter, and the ship was luxurious and everyone was pleasant. Besides, we had our new apartment in New York to look forward to.

Soon after New Year's we flew back to New York, fully expecting to move into the apartment. But it was a shambles—our furniture stacked in piles in one room while the workmen were hammering and painting and plastering in the others. We got right back on the next plane and went home to Beverly Hills. It was at least another month before we got the word that the place was finally ready for us.

And so it really wasn't until the following fall, the fall of 1979, that we made full use of that apartment. That year we stayed in it from September through January and, for the first time, we began to feel as though we were real New Yorkers.

We were both great walkers, and we walked all over the city. New York is possibly the best city in the world for walking, and we took advantage of it. We explored every north-south avenue, and many of the east-west streets.

We saw every show that opened that season. We got to know everybody in every show. Because of Rock's recent stage work, he was accepted by the Broadway crowd as one of them, not some Hollywood outsider.

Milton Goldman, the Roddy McDowall of New York, is the city's prime party host. He welcomed us with open arms—we were another excuse for him to throw a party. He gave a huge, lavish party and introduced us to the New Yorkers worth knowing.

So, suddenly, we were as much a part of the New York theatrical scene as we were part of the Hollywood film scene. We began to hobnob with people like Hal and Judy Prince, Ruthie Mitchell (Prince's capable right arm), Stephen Sondheim, ex-mayor John Lindsay and his wife Mary, and that whole group. We liked them, and they seemed to like us, too.

They opened their homes, and their hearts, to us—we were the new kids on the block. Of course, we both realized that Rock's name and reputation were great door-openers for us, but we had to believe that we were also both very likable chaps.

By that time Claire Trevor Bren had moved back to New York. We introduced her to our friends and she introduced us to her friends, and now we were all swimming in the biggest pond of them all—New York, New York. It was a heady experience for Rock and me, two essentially naive boys from the Midwest.

We were invited to many parties and, since we both loved to entertain, we reciprocated. We gave a Christmas party that year that was a real knockout. If the building had fallen down that night, it would have been the end for the New York theater for years—everybody of any consequence was at our party. There were many people from the New York social set as well as celebrities such as Beverly Sills, Hal Prince, Betty Comden, Adolph Green and Phyllis Newman, Claire Trevor, Joan Bennett, Hermione Gingold, Lauren Bacall, Ethel Merman, Marilyn Horne, Myrna Loy, Cliff Robertson, and Dina Merrill—and on and on.

Right across the street from our building was the American Museum of Natural History. I am thoroughly ashamed of myself, but I never even set foot in the place. Rock, to his everlasting credit, got up one morning and said, "Tom, get out of bed, you lazy lout—we are going to go across the street and spend the day in the museum."

"I have a cold," I said. "I don't want to give my cold to all those dinosaurs."

I didn't have a cold, but I just had no great desire to traipse around a museum all day. So I stayed in bed and Rock went across the street and traipsed for a few hours—not the whole day, as I was quick to remind him when he came back. He said he enjoyed it, but he had to say that. He never did go back, however.

We were also directly across the Park from the great old Metropolitan Museum of Art. We went there one day for an hour or so. The thing was that neither one of us was really a museum person. The idea of a museum appealed to us theoretically, but when it came to actually going inside a museum door, the flesh was weak. We would much rather go to a movie, I must shamefully confess.

As a matter of fact, during all our trips to Italy—and Rock, of course, spent much more time there than I did, because he filmed there for months on end—he never even saw the Sistine Chapel. In all our visits to Paris, we only went to the Louvre once, and that time stayed at the most an hour. We simply were not the classic American tourists.

But in New York, we saw a great deal the classic tourist never sees. Walking all over, as we did, gave us the chance to see out-of-the-way places—curious stores, odd churches, quaint architecture—that are not featured in any guidebook.

We also often rode the subway. When we mentioned it to our New York friends, they were horrified.

"You actually went down those stairs and rode in one of those filthy subway trains?" one of them said to Rock and me one day. "You two are idiots—a person can get killed down there."

But we were big boys, and nobody bothered us. The subway station was right at our corner, and we were only four stops—maybe ten minutes—from the 42nd Street station. We could be in our seats in the theater in twenty minutes, a trip that might take thirty to forty nervous minutes in a taxicab. I wouldn't recommend the subway to the timid, or to unescorted women, but Rock and I found it a very handy way of getting around the city.

We often found ourselves being stared at in the subway. I could see the wheels turning in people's heads:

"Gee, that tall guy over there looks a lot like Rock Hudson. Could it possibly be Rock Hudson? Nah, Rock Hudson wouldn't be riding in the subway."

But what we never could figure out was why, of all the people who looked and stared, the only ones who ever approached Rock were black men. Always polite, always courteous.

"Mr. Hudson," they would say, "I just want to say hello and tell you how much I've enjoyed your work on the screen all these years."

But it was only black men. Never black women. Never white people of either sex. Just black men, and Rock and I found that most curious.

Among our new friends were many who had country homes— places in Connecticut or upstate New York or on Long Island. And we spent many lovely weekends with them in the country.

Adolph Green and his wife, Phyllis Newman, lived in our building—we very quickly began referring to the Beresford as "our building"—and became good friends. Their terrace abutted our Central Park West terrace. Angela Lansbury and her husband, Peter Shaw, had an apartment near ours, and we saw a lot of them, too.

We had an ever-expanding circle of friends. And we soon began to feel part of the neighborhood, as well. We had our favorite food store, our dry cleaners, our bookstore, our liquor store, and it was almost like small-town Oklahoma. New York is a gigantic metropolis, but it is really just a bunch of individual neighborhoods and, within each neighborhood, there is a lot of the small-town feel to it. It was pleasant to be able to stroll down Columbus Avenue, stop in stores and have the clerks give you a big smile and say "Hi, Mr. Clark, how goes it?" It was nice to wave at people in passing, like I did back home.

We were, of course, the mecca for all the visitors from Los Angeles. Whenever any of our California friends came east, they would stay with us. We seemed to be busy around the clock and yet, looking back on it, we really didn't do much of anything. As far as I'm concerned, that's the finest kind of busy.

At least once a week we would stop in to see Wally Sheft, our business manager. That took up most of the day because, as a rule, we walked both ways. Our apartment was at Central Park West and 81st, his office at the corner of Fifth Avenue and 42nd Street. We generally would walk from our building through the Park at an angle and come out near the Plaza Hotel, then continue down on Fifth or Madison or Park, to 42nd Street. Going back we would take a different route, perhaps going straight up Fifth and cutting across the Park uptown. It took probably an hour or so each way, as we stopped often to look at buildings or people and we did a lot of window shopping. We would often stop for lunch at any place that seemed interesting.

We established a pattern, which we stuck to as closely as we could for the next few years. Often, something would come up to interfere, but basically our plan was to spend a few months in the spring and fall in New York. It was so beautiful to sit on our terrace and watch the Park leap into life in the spring and then, when autumn came, to watch the leaves turn red and gold and see the first snowfall of winter.

We were fortunate in having found a marvelous houseman, Arthur Green, who came in every day. And, when we were back in California, he still came in every day and took care of the place. When we returned, the apartment was immaculate. Arthur Green was a black man from Harlem who had never in his entire life been outside the borough of Manhattan.

While that first snowfall may have been a thing of beauty and aesthetically pleasing to the soul, winter in New York can become a drag after the sixth or seventh snowfall. So we would go back to California, usually in time for Christmas, and spend the winter sitting by the pool and reading all about the blizzards and subzero temperatures and the wind chill factor. All we would have to worry about was whether or not we had enough sun-tan lotion on our sizzling noses.

We loved our stays in New York but always considered California our home. The one thing California had that New York never had was the dogs. We thought about bringing a couple of them to New York with us, because we missed them terribly, but New York is no place for dogs. I know New Yorkers will leap at my throat for saying that, and many of our New York friends did have dogs, but both Rock and I always felt sorry for those poor city dogs. Always on a leash outside, no dirt to dig up, no place to bury a bone, nowhere to run—in fact, what you would have to call a dog's life.

So we kept the dogs back in California, with James, and he took good care of them, and maybe a little vice versa.

We might not have been so eager to spend the fall in New York a few years earlier, when we had been such big football fans, but we had stopped going to both the Rams and the USC games. When the Rams moved away—from Los Angeles to Anaheim—we lost interest. We thought it was unfair that they were still called the Los Angeles Rams, even though they no longer had any connection with L.A. We immediately severed our allegiance.

What's more, because he felt so close to USC, he had left them a sizable bequest in his will, a gesture that they were well aware of.

And so we were shocked to get a letter from USC one year, just after we had sent for our usual annual tickets to the games, telling us that we couldn't have those tickets unless we joined the Trojan Club. The fee for joining was $100.

It wasn't the money. To Rock—and to me, too, at that time—$100 was chicken feed. But it was the idea that, after all Rock had done for the school and after all those years when we had had those same season tickets, now they were being petty.

Right then, we ceased being USC fans. Rock never gave them another bit of equipment. And, what's more, he threatened to take them out of his will. (But he never carried through that threat, and the university remains in the will. It includes a bequest to give some drama student a full, four-year scholarship.)

We became able to spend football season in New York without any remorse at being away from California and switched our allegiance to the Giants.

Those New York years together were marvelous years. Later, when Rock and I split up, I naturally took myself to New York. It had become a second home to me. I felt comfortable there. I had friends; I had my things in the apartment; I was secure there.

When Rock died, the executor of his estate, at the behest of the IRS, sealed the place. Then everything that was in it was sold. Many of the things were mine.

CHAPTER TWELVE
On the Stage

E very actor who considers himself a real, honest-to-God actor and not just a pretty face wants to work on the stage. After all, that is acting in its purest form.

Rock was a normal actor in that way. For years, he kept saying "Boy, I wish I could do a Broadway show!" And he let it be known to his agents, and to me, and to the Broadway theater people that that is what he wanted to do. Nobody took him seriously.

Until Carol Burnett.

One Sunday in 1973, Rock and I were sitting by the pool. Joy came out to say there was a phone call for Rock, and he went inside to take it.

About ten minutes later he came out with a big grin on his face.

"That was Carol Burnett," he said. "She wants me to do *I Do! I Do!* with her at the Huntington Hartford this summer." (The Huntington Hartford is the major legitimate theater in Hollywood). Carol Burnett had obviously taken Rock and his oft-expressed desire to do a stage play very seriously, bless her heart.

But Rock's reaction, at first, was mildly negative.

"As I remember it," he said, "that's an awful show."

"I think we have the album," I said. "Let's listen to it."

We went into the theater and I found the original cast album, with Mary Martin and Robert Preston in the roles they had created on Broadway. Rock began laughing at all the right places.

"This is a very funny show," he said. "I don't know where I got the idea it was a turkey."

"I think it's because Mary Martin and Bob Preston, bless them, were just too old for the early scenes," I suggested. "It's better when you have younger actors who age than older actors who try to act young."

Rock and I listened to it two or three times that day, and he decided he would love to do it. So he called Carol back and said, yes, it sounded very interesting to him. "You sure you want me?" he asked her. "I've never even set foot on a stage."

"I know you can do it," Carol said. And I told him the same thing, because I knew that that was what he wanted to do more than anything. And I was also confident that he could do it, and do it well.

"But I've never been on a stage in my life," he said again.

"Has to be a first time," I said, and Carol said something of the same sort. He was still hesitant—anxious to do it, yet doubtful of his own ability and a bit scared—but Carol kept talking and I kept talking and eventually he said OK, he would be very happy to be her co-star in that production. I could hear her delighted squeal.

I could certainly understand Rock's reluctance. While he desperately wanted to appear on stage, consider the situation. This was a two-character play, meaning that he would be onstage virtually continuously and wouldn't have the comfort of a large cast to help him; he would be playing in Los Angeles, in front of friends and neighbors and people in the business, and that can be the toughest audience of all; and his co-star would be the very experienced and stage-wise Carol Burnett.

But he had fallen in love with the idea of appearing on stage. And, with Gower Champion directing, he knew he was in good hands. They allowed him, after he requested it fervently, an out-of-town tryout, so he wouldn't have to open cold in Los Angeles. That out-of-town wasn't very far out-of-town, as it turned out; it was at the California Theater in San Bernardino, but they did have four nights there before the curtain went up at the Huntington Hartford. San Bernardino could be considered out-of-town only by the skin of your atlas.

As you can imagine, the opening night audience in L.A. was what Hollywood columnists like to call "glittering." And it was an audience packed with stars and high-powered Hollywood executives. Doris Day was in the front row, and later Rock told me that the first thing he saw when the curtain came up was Doris there in the front row, beaming up at him with her high-powered smile. It helped.

After the show, Doris came backstage and threw herself in Rock's arms and cried and cried. Everybody was crying. It had been a stupendous success, and the audience applauded for a full ten minutes. Rock still couldn't sing very well, but he sold the seventeen songs he had beautifully. Of those songs, only one, "My Cup Runneth Over", was a true ballad. The others were simple, undemanding songs. Rock and Carol took so many bows that Carol later said she had to have somebody straighten out her back.

They played five sell-out weeks. It was all designed to raise money for ANTA and the Plumstead Playhouse, another reason Rock had agreed to do it. It was such a hit that Carol's husband, Joe Hamilton, got dollar signs in his eyes and his mind started clicking and he suggested that they do it for real money.

By now, Rock was totally hooked. He had loved being on a stage, loved the heady feeling of audience laughter and audience applause, and he would have played *Getting Gertie's Garter* if somebody had asked him. So he didn't hesitate when Joe asked him.

"Yes," he said. "Anytime, anyplace, anywhere."

The anywhere turned out to be the Fairgrounds in Dallas, an immense place—3200 seats, to be exact. It was a theater more suited to a three-ring circus with twenty elephants than to an intimate two-character play, but it didn't matter. They were a sellout and a socko success in Dallas, as they had been in Los Angeles.

Then they moved on to the Kennedy Center in Washington—another smash—and to the Muni in St. Louis—ditto. Wherever they played they were sold out well in advance, and the audience loved them. Rock was in his glory.

Naturally, a thing like that string of sellouts did not go unnoticed in theatrical circles. Suddenly, Rock was a hot stage property. I began getting nibbles and offers.

One came from a man named Stockton Briggle. With a name like that, I always thought he should have been a character in an Oscar Wilde play or a Dickens novel, but he was actually a very nice young man, and he was full of big plans and bigger schemes and the biggest ideas.

He called me the next year, when Rock was back doing the *McMillan & Wife* series, with the idea for a summer tour in a musical while *McMillan* was on hiatus. He asked if Rock would have lunch with him.

"I'm too wrapped up in the series," Rock said. "You meet him and see what he's got in mind."

So I had lunch with Briggle, who brought along Bill Ross. I knew Ross to be a Broadway character, a producer and director and stage manager. We had lunch at Scandia, and when they mentioned their idea, I was disappointed.

"We see Rock as Nathan Detroit in *Guys and Dolls*," Ross said, and leaned back with a satisfied expression. I think they both expected me to jump up and down and clap my hands at the audacity of that notion. But the truth was that people had been after Rock to play that part for years and he didn't like it, and I agreed with him. It was a flashy part but not right for Rock.

"Sorry," I said. "I can tell you positively that Rock will never do it. Anything else?"

"How about *Camelot?*" Bill Ross said without a moment's hesitation.

"Wow!" I said. This time, I almost felt like jumping up and down and clapping my hands. What an idea! "That is a terrific idea. Let me talk to Rock."

So I went and told Rock that they wanted him to do a summer tour in *Camelot.*

"Wow!" he said. He took to the idea immediately. And, when

McMillan ended for the season that spring (it was now 1977), we took the next plane for New York. That was the beginning of what, I still think, was one of the happiest times of Rock's life. He loved being in *Camelot,* and it was a triumph from the very beginning.

They did everything they could to make Rock happy and to make him feel comfortable in the role of the King. It had been written originally for Richard Burton, who was no singer, either. Like Burton, Rock was not a great singer, but they both sang with a sincerity that transcended mere vocal quality. They were both great sellers of songs.

Rock sold those marvelous Rodgers and Hammerstein songs magnificently—and he looked so very regal.

They gave him cast approval, so we sat in the theater in New York while dozens of singers and actors paraded by on the stage to audition for Rock and the others. They agreed on Jerry Lanning as Lancelot and Sherry Mathis as Guinevere, which turned out to be a double-header of a choice. Not only were they both great in their roles but, during the course of the tour, they fell in love and eventually were married. They both called Rock "Cupid" after that and remained good friends—and they are still my good friends, today.

Stockton Briggle had somehow gotten hold of the original script—I think he got it from Roddy McDowall—and rewrote much of the show to conform to that script, departing from the one that had been played so often. It built up Rock's role as King Arthur. Briggle also was the director; Rock had his choice and he said "Let Stockton do it."

The tour opened in Dallas, and the record Rock and Carol had set with *I Do! I Do!* was broken the first week with *Camelot.* As the tour rolled on, records were broken all over that summer, and I believe the record they set in Atlanta still stands.

Rock was really a superb King Arthur. To begin with, of course, he looked so magnificently kingly, so tall and commanding. He fit the part as though it had been written with him in mind. He had a speech—the "Proposition" speech—at the end of the first act, that left the audience cheering as the first-act curtain fell. And the dramatic scene at the climax of the play left the audience literally sobbing.

We were booked to play in Hyannisport, Massachusetts. This was in 1977, long after John Kennedy (whose administration had often been called the Camelot administration) had been assassinated. The Kennedys were still, of course, the first family of Hyannisport. The show was playing in a tent there, a typical summer stock theater, and I happened to be wandering around outside when I saw Rose, Teddy, and Ethel Kennedy standing in line to buy tickets.

Now I had a problem. Should I tell Rock that the Kennedys would be in the audience that night? If I did tell him, it might make him nervous and upset. And yet if I didn't tell him and he happened to spot them in the middle of the show, that could possibly throw him. I finally decided that not telling him was the lesser of the two potential dangers, so I didn't tell him and crossed my fingers up to the wrist.

Rock made his exit, at the end of the first act, by walking right through the audience, striding regally up the aisle. That night, as he made that exit, he spotted the massed Kennedys sitting in the last row. (They had bought their tickets at the last minute, so there weren't many good seats left, and they hadn't tried to pull any strings to get better ones).

"I damn near died," Rock said to me after the show. "I look up as I'm walking out, and there is Teddy Kennedy smiling at me, and on one side of him is Rose and on the other side is Ethel. And all three of them have big grins on their faces. Did you know they were going to be there?"

I had to admit that I did.

"Why didn't you tell me? No, I take that back. I'm glad you didn't tell me. I would have been so nervous I would have peed in my armor."

We both had a great summer touring in *Camelot*. We got to know everybody in the company, and it was a large company. Rock always made it a point—in that show and in every show he did—to become acquainted with all the people, from the stars down to the kids in the chorus. I helped him memorize their names and faces and, because he knew them all by name (and, surprisingly, that is unusual in stage productions) he was greatly loved by everybody in every show.

He also made it his practice to give at least one big party for the whole company at some point during the run. At that party he would circulate and spend a few minutes with every person, chatting and finding out about them and their families. It wasn't anything put on falsely, either; Rock liked people and liked to get to know them, and his times touring with stage productions were fun because he did get to know everybody. In Hollywood he had done the same thing on movie locations. It was second nature for him to make friends with the whole company.

It made for a happy company. Many stars, I found out, stayed distant, aloof, remote. They might say a perfunctory "Good evening" in passing or nod casually, but they would never engage the kids in the chorus in genuine conversation. So everybody loved Rock, and he reciprocated that love. He was in his element with a touring stage company. He thrived in that atmosphere—the camaraderie, the joking, the us-against-the-world attitude. To him, it was all stimulating and it enriched his spirit.

Both movie location companies and touring theatrical companies are microcosms of a larger society. They are both small, integrated, self-sufficient groups that, during the course of the making of the movie or the tour of that play, see romances and enmities develop, cliques form, a pecking order established and be frequently revised.

I've often thought that a sociologist could write a marvelous thesis or book about a movie location company or a theatrical touring company, because both are such unique social forms.

I think one large reason Rock loved that environment so much was because he was, of course, the undisputed king of the companies with which he toured. Because he was the unquestioned star, he was able to stand back and observe all the goings-on among his subjects. He would smile tolerantly at their carryings-on, watch the liaisons bud and flower and, sometimes, wither and die. He and I would often discuss the people in the company and have fun analyzing their characters and making small wagers on whether the young juvenile would succeed in getting the red-headed chorus girl he had a crush on to go to bed with him or not.

We often took some of them out to dinner with us after the show, and we got to know many of them very well over the course of the weeks or months we were together.

Even before the *Camelot* triumph, Rock had tried his hand at some deadly serious acting. At the time—this was 1975—I was running Mammoth, Rock's company, as well as serving as his manager. I was fielding all the calls, offers, and feelers that came in. There were many from the stage area after the *I Do! I Do!* success. A man named James Fitzgerald, Jane Powell's husband, came to see me with one more proposition. This one sounded good.

He was putting together, he said, a production of Stephen Vincent Benet's *John Brown's Body*. I knew that would appeal to Rock, because it was something dramatic and, after the light romantic musical that was *I Do! I Do!*, I knew he wanted to soak his whole body and soul in the dramatic pond.

"I've got John Houseman to direct," Fitzgerald said, "and Joseph Cotten as John Brown and Colleen Dewhurst for the woman. And I want Rock, too."

It was, he said, going to be part of the '76 Bicentennial Summer celebration. It all sounded fine, so I tentatively committed Rock to do it. It was in the future and all somewhat indefinite. Meanwhile, there was the *McMillan* season to finish and we also had a commitment for Rock to do a production of *I Do! I Do!* in London for three months. We were looking forward to that, but there was one thing we didn't have—a leading lady. Carol Burnett was not available.

Mark Mordo, a personal manager I knew, called and asked if we would consider his client, Juliet Prowse, for the part. We knew her to be a sensational dancer, although neither of us had ever seen her work in person. Mordo invited us to Las Vegas, where Juliet was appearing, and we went and she was as terrific as we had assumed she would be.

During her performance, Rock leaned over to me and whispered, "Do you realize what we're doing here? We have the nerve to be auditioning a genuine headliner."

"Yes, but we have to see her," I said.

"Still, it's dumb," he said. "We knew all along she was a sensational dancer, so what's the point? Let's go back after the show and talk to her."

So we went backstage and met Juliet, and we both found her delightful. She was also tall enough not to look like a dwarf next to Rock, as some of the girls who had been suggested would have.

We agreed right then that she would do the part with Rock in London, and we had a happy celebration dinner together.

There was an offer for Rock to repeat his role as King Arthur in *Camelot* in London after the *I Do! I Do!* run, but I said no to that very quickly. Rock was disappointed.

"Why not?" he said. "I love that part."

"You have to be out of your cotton-picking mind," I said. "An American can't play King Arthur in England. You'd be hooted off the stage."

I explained to him that even Charlton Heston, who has never been accused of lacking nerve, backed out of a proposed production of *Macbeth*, that was going to be one of the plays in the same series as *I Do! I Do!*

"Chuck Heston had enough sense," I said, "to realize that he couldn't play *Macbeth* in England, and you can't play King Arthur in England, either. Trust me."

And he trusted me, and agreed not to do it.

We flew to London the day after Christmas and had a big river-view suite in our favorite hotel, the grand old Savoy.

It was as though we had never left home, so many old friends happened to be staying at the Savoy at that time. We ran into Elaine Stritch in the lobby—she was actually living at the Savoy then—and bumped into Jean Simmons in the elevator. She was in London doing *A Little Night Music.* And Rock and I had a couple of marvelous friends, Sarah Marshall and Carl Held, who were living in London then.

"We should have a party," Rock said. It didn't take much to get Rock started thinking about hosting a party. Almost any old excuse would do.

"How about a New Year's Eve party?" I suggested. We had never been particularly wild about New Year's Eve; as holidays go, we ranked it somewhere between Arbor Day and Genghis Khan's birthday. But I knew Rock liked to have a peg to hang his parties on, and December 31 was coming up very soon, so why not?

"Great idea! Marvelous! We'll have a New Year's Eve party for all the Americans in London."

The wheels started turning in his head. We could see Big Ben, London's historic old clock, from our hotel window. That, Rock said, would be the focal point of our party. We would all stand at the windows as midnight approached, glasses on high, and when Big Ben tolled the twelve notes to signal the birth of the new year, we would toast that historic moment.

We had the hotel set up a bar in our suite and assign a bartender. We spent a few happy hours in Harrod's great food department, buying all sorts of cheeses and assorted delicacies. We sent out invitations and, on New Year's Eve, we had around thirty people in our suite, awaiting Big Ben's bombastic boom. Among those who shared that evening with us were Lee Remick, Jean Simmons, Elaine Stritch, Juliet Prowse, Sarah Marshall (the daughter of Herbert Marshall and Edna Best), and several people from the company.

And there we were, at 11:59 P.M., thirty Americans in various stages of inebriation, hanging out the windows, singing crazy old songs, and anticipating the big moment.

"Quiet, everybody," Rock said. The hands of the old clock in the tower were almost straight up. "It's time." Everybody was quiet, for the first time that night. We waited for Big Ben to strike.

Nothing happened. Not a sound.

"Excuse me, Mr. 'udson," said the bartender. "You wanted to hear Big Ben?"

"What the hell happened? Why didn't Big Ben go boom?"

"Oh, I thought everyone knew, Mr. 'udson, sir," the bartender said. "The clock don't ring after ten-o'clock. The neighbors used to complain about how the ringing kept them awake, so they shut the old clock down after the ten-o'clock ring."

So we saw the new year in without Big Ben's assistance. In the long run, it really didn't matter.

I Do! I Do! was a moderate London success. Not anywhere near the smash it had been back home, but it had a very respectable run nevertheless. The reviews were uniformly bad, but the London public wanted to see Rock and Juliet anyhow, so enough of them came to make it a fair success.

Some of those reviews were shameful. London critics can be cruel, and cruel in a very personal way. One of them wrote a line that had everybody in the whole London theatrical community seeing red. In fact, many of our English friends called up to apologize to Rock for the nastiness of the reviewer who wrote:

"Rock Hudson wasn't nearly as bad as we had hoped he would be."

That was the kind of gratuitous rottenness that went far beyond decency. It was so deliberately unkind that we ended up laughing at it. In fact, eventually Rock considered it something of a compliment. He had had so many bad reviews that, by now, they rolled off his back as though they were nothing.

But that particular sentence in that particular review may have contributed to his illness. During the run of *I Do! I Do!* he came down with a particularly rough case of flu and couldn't go on for about a week. The public had paid to see him, so they asked for their money back.

Since the show was only in London for a limited run, the loss of that week's revenue was something the producers could not recoup. They asked Rock to do them a favor: Would he play two weeks in Canada so they could make their money back? Rock agreed and, later that year, we did play for a week in Hamilton and a week in Toronto, and those two very successful weeks helped the producers clean up—and our end of the take was decent, too.

While we were in London, James Fitzgerald called to talk about the *John Brown's Body* production.

"Would you do me a big favor, Tom?" Fitzgerald asked. "Would you call Joe Cotten—I know he's in London right now—and ask him if he'd do *John Brown's Body* with Rock?"

"I thought you told me you already had him," I said.

"Well, I do, or I mean I did." He was blustering, always a bad sign. "It's as good as set, you know, but I just want to nail it down. You know how it is."

Oh, I knew how it was, all right. He had told us he had Cotten and Dewhurst to get Rock. And he had probably told Cotten that he had Rock and Colleen, and he had probably told Colleen that he had Rock and Joe. With enough chutzpa a man can rule the world—or put a production together.

"Look, Fitz," I said. "I'm not the producer. You are. It's not my job to talk to Joseph Cotten or anybody else. As a matter of fact, I do not even know Mr. Cotten, so I have absolutely no intention of talking to him for you."

He was miffed, but I could care less. I wasn't about to do his job for him. A few days later, he called again.

"Good news and bad news," he said. "It looks like we've lost Colleen Dewhurst. That's the bad news. But the good news is that we've got Diane Baker."

"Terrific," I said. "Now here's some more bad news for you— you've just lost Rock Hudson."

Diane Baker may be a very lovely lady, but she is hardly the stage presence Colleen Dewhurst is, and Colleen Dewhurst was an integral part of the package that Fitzgerald had presented to us originally.

"Look," I said, "Rock and I bought a package of Houseman directing, and Cotten, Dewhurst, and Hudson acting. Now you tell me that Cotten isn't firm and you have lost Dewhurst. I am not about to let Rock do a production with Diane Baker and Mr. X. No way."

I knew what I should have done right then was get on a plane and fly back and straighten it all out. But I wasn't feeling too well—just over a particularly bad case of the galloping jet lag— and, besides, I had to keep an eye on the *I Do! I Do!* box office. It was my practice to monitor the box office of every show Rock did, and a good thing, too. Once my little survey unearthed fifty people who were in on "press passes," and not one of them had ever even read a newspaper. So I counted the house of every one of Rock's shows every night to make sure he was getting a fair shake.

Fitzgerald and I had several more long and often heated phone conversations. At one point he said he had Irene Worth for the woman, which was great—she is a tremendous stage actress. But then he called and said, no, that deal had fallen through too.

He did get Leif Erickson for the John Brown part, which was fine with us. Not a major name, but he was always a fine actor, and he fit that part well. But he still had no woman and, without a woman he could respect, Rock would not do it. The woman's role in that work is pivotal, and very difficult—she ages from a young girl to an old woman, runs the gamut of emotions from A to way past Z.

Finally, Fitzgerald was exhausted.

"Look, Tom," he said. "Who do you and Rock want to play the woman?"

I asked Rock if he had any ideas, and he immediately said "Claire." So I said to Fitzgerald, "Rock would like you to get Claire Trevor."

Claire and Rock had always talked idly about how someday they would like to work together, but both of us knew that she would never go on the road. So there was method in our mad suggestion to Fitzgerald that he get Claire: we knew she wouldn't do it, and that would be our nice, convenient way to back out of the deal.

"She would be great in the role," I said to Rock, after I hung up the phone. "It's just too bad that she won't do it."

I decided to call Claire, in Newport Beach, to prepare her to expect a call from Fitzgerald. When I reached her, she told me that Fitzgerald had already called her—and she had agreed to do the part.

"As soon as he said that Rock Hudson wanted me," Claire said, "I jumped at it. It will be such fun!"

So it finally came to pass. Houseman, a brilliant director but an out-and-out tyrant, had some great ideas for the production. Always before, *John Brown's Body* had been done as a reading, with the principals standing behind lecterns, books open, reading the long and intricate speeches Benét had written.

"I want you to memorize it all," Houseman said.

That was a monumental task. Rock, in particular, had to commit extremely long speeches to memory—one, a description of a Civil War battle, ran twenty-six pages. Without a break or an interruption of any kind.

Rock, Claire, Milton Bren, and I went to Cabo San Lucas, at the tip of the Baja California peninsula, for a week while Rock and Claire memorized that long, long script. Milton would work with Claire and I would work with Rock, then the two of them would meet and work together.

They wound up hating Houseman—"a pompous ass" is the way Rock described him—but he got a wonderful performance out of the group.

Fitzgerald had booked a tour of college campuses, so they wound up playing in gyms and college chapels. The bookings had been made very unprofessionally, however. It was summer, and college populations are way down in the summer months. They were booked into a college gym in Bakersfield on the same night the Los Angeles Philharmonic Orchestra was playing in the town's auditorium. Nobody came to see *John Brown's Body.*

Besides the three principals, Houseman had had the idea of a Greek chorus behind, and Fitzgerald had hired a good-sized group of young people. With the prospect of a lengthy tour in front of them, many of these kids had given up their apartments to come with us.

The box office was slim, but the reviews were fat. Bill Edwards, wrote in *Variety:* "Rock Hudson is now ready to take his place as one of our foremost dramatic stage actors." You can imagine how happy that made Rock feel; he couldn't have read any words that would have pleased him more. Flo Allen read the review to us over the phone.

We toured for a month or so. The bookings continued to be strange. We played in the Masonic Temple in San Francisco, a gigantic place that seats thousands. The next night we might be in a college chapel holding maybe two hundred. Then, after playing in Denver, Fitzgerald said that was that. He was closing the production down. Many of the kids in the chorus had nowhere to go. Rock invited them all to come home with us, so we had some sixteen kids bunking in the house for the next few weeks. Rock, ever the soul of propriety, kept the sexes separate—a boys' dorm and a girls' dorm, one in one of the living rooms, one in the theater. James and the other servants were not too happy at having all those youngsters around, with sleeping bags all over the floor of those two rooms, and I had to use a lot of psychology to keep the staff from quitting.

Then, out of the clear blue bonanza, I got a call from Zev Bufman, an entrepreneur who owns a couple of theaters in Florida. He had read all those good reviews—particularly Bill Edwards' in *Variety*—and he had also read about the tour's collapse.

"Do you think you could get everybody together again and come down and play my theaters?" he asked.

"Everybody is already together," I said. "As a matter of fact, they're all eating lunch on the terrace even as we speak."

So we went to Florida, played a week in one of Bufman's theaters, and then a week in the other one.

Both weeks were sold-out smashes, and the *John Brown's Body* experience ended on an upbeat note. There was actually a week between the two weeks we played in Florida, and Bufman generously paid for everybody to stay in Miami Beach for that week.

By now, Rock had contracted a virulent case of stage fever. He desperately, hungrily wanted to do a show on Broadway. So he reached for any straw that might prove to be that Broadway opportunity.

During the *Camelot* tour, the backstage grapevine had brought rumors that there was a musical version of the old *Twentieth Century* in the works. The grapevine added a raisin to the report: Rock was ideally suited to play the lead in that production. We tracked the rumor down, and some of it was true. Producer Bobby Fryer and director Hal Prince were, indeed, at work on assembling that production.

Rock and I went and rented a copy of the old movie of *On the 20th Century*, with John Barrymore in the starring role, to see what it was all about. It was hard to imagine Rock in the role Barrymore had played, but the whole thing could have been revised for the musical stage.

The drums kept on giving us jungle information. Hal Prince would be coming to see Rock in *Camelot*, while the show was playing at Westbury, on Long Island. We never knew if he actually came or not; if he did, he did not reveal his presence to us. The next thing we heard, the show was going to go on—with John Cullum in the lead.

Another bubble burst. But Rock shrugged off burst bubbles with the greatest of ease. In the acting business, life is one continual series of burst bubbles and terrible disappointments. Anybody who is discouraged by rejection should find another line of work.

So Rock and I forgot about *On the Twentieth Century*, and life went on for a year or so. And then, in 1979, Bobby Fryer called and said they would be putting together a national company to do *On the Twentieth Century* on the road; would Rock be interested in the part?

"Well, we'd like to see the show before we give you an answer," I said. I'd heard conflicting reports about the show; it was moderately successful, but the reviews had been mixed.

"Of course," Fryer said. "I'll fly you both to New York and you can see the show a couple of times."

"Thanks, but we'll make the arrangements ourselves," I said. I didn't want us to feel obligated to Fryer in any way, at least not at that point.

So we booked our flight and made our hotel reservations—this was before we had the apartment—and went back. Fryer did set aside tickets for us on two successive nights, and we accepted them.

We went to see the show, and I sat there, getting sicker and sicker. It was just plain bad.

"It's terrible, Rock," I said at the first intermission. "And it's definitely not for you."

"Wasn't Imogene terrific?" he said. Yes, Imogene Coca had been terrific. And so was Judy Kaye (who later went on to become a major Broadway star, playing the diva in *Phantom of the Opera*.) "It would be marvelous fun to work with somebody like her."

I could tell that, even though he must have realized how poor the show was, the idea of doing a show—almost any show—was causing him to ignore the faults and concentrate on the good things. He kept saying how it would be great to work with Imogene Coca.

The fact was—I could see it in his eyes—he wanted to do the show, no matter how bad it was. It was a big, flashy production, and he saw only the fun of being part of all that flash. He didn't understand that there has to be some substance to hold the glitter together.

We went to Sardi's afterward for a late supper. By coincidence—or was it?—Imogene Coca was there, with her husband King Donovan. And by another coincidence—hah!—we were given the booth next to theirs. Imogene is a little wren of a lady, and she spotted Rock and twittered. "Oh, Mr. Hudson, I hear you may be joining us on tour. I do hope you will do it. We'd have such a great time! It's such a fun show to be part of."

We were talking to Imogene and King when Judy Kaye came into the restaurant. If Imogene is a wren, Judy is a hawk. She soared over to our table, squeezed in next to Rock, and punched him playfully on the arm.

"Hey, Rock!" she said. "You just gotta do this show with us. We will have a genuine ball, I promise you. You just gotta do it!"

"I've just decided," Rock said, as I knew he was going to say. "I'm going to do it."

I heard that in a cloud of dismay. I shook my head, but I knew he was gone. He had fallen for the camaraderie of it all, the jolly good fellowship of Imogene and Judy, the idea of being part of that spiffy production with its train chugging away onstage and all the flashing lights and the gaudy effects. The fact that it was a bad show never entered into his consideration of it. He had no interest in the cons, not when the pros were such fun.

I knew that, camaraderie and flash aside, it was a terrible show, and simply not right for him.

"Hooray!" said Imogene.

"Hooray!" said Judy.

And somebody ordered champagne, and they all toasted each other and they toasted the production and I think they even toasted Mother Teresa and Kareem Abdul-Jabbar before the night was over.

Rock realized I was not putting my heart and soul into my toasting and drinking. He knew I thought he was making a very large mistake.

"What the hell, Tom," he said to me at some point during the evening's festivities. "I have nothing else to do this summer, so why not?"

"Why not? I'll tell you why not. Because it's a lousy show, that's why not. Because the part is not right for you, that's why not. Because it'll hurt you in the long run. How's that for some why nots?"

"Well, maybe all that's true," he said. "But it will be fun. After all, isn't that what it's all about?"

I made him promise me that, before he signed anything, he would at least ask for one of his "artistic meetings." I said he should meet with Hal Prince and Ruthie Mitchell (Hal's top assistant) and ask them to rework the score so he could handle the songs.

"Tell them, at least, to put the songs in your key, whatever the hell that is," I said.

So he did ask for, and got, a meeting with Prince, Mitchell, and the composer, Cy Coleman. The meeting was at Coleman's studio. Cy accompanied Rock on the piano while he tried some of the songs. Adolph Green and Betty Comden, who had written the lyrics, were there too.

Ruthie Mitchell never opens her mouth in Hal Prince's presence, but when he's not there she really takes over. And he doesn't do anything or say anything without checking with her first. At that meeting, Prince did most of the talking, with Ruthie nodding away behind him.

"We will rework the entire score to fit your voice, Rock," he said. "Cy will rearrange everything so it's in your key, right, Cy?"

"No problem," said Coleman.

"And Betty and Adolph will change the lyrics, if it's necessary, so you can sing them easily, right?"

Betty and Adolph said, sure, certainly, absolutely.

"And I will restage the entire production so it's your show from beginning to end. As a matter of fact, I've already thought of just how I'm going to do it."

Rock was more than satisfied. He turned to me with a little smile on his face, as if to say "See? And you thought I was silly to say I'd do this show. Look at all they are going to do for me."

So he signed the contract. We went back to Los Angeles while they were revamping the show to fit Rock, restaging and rearranging and rewriting and reworking. Then we went back to New York a couple of months later, and Rock went into rehearsal. I sat quietly in the rehearsal hall and watched.

They had not done one thing. Not a note of music had been changed. Not a comma in the lyrics had been altered. Not a single bit of the staging had been reworked. The show was exactly as it had been.

"They haven't done a blessed thing for you, Rock," I said to him after his first day of rehearsing.

"Well," said Rock, ever the optimist, "I guess they figured it was right the way it was. After all, they are the Broadway experts, not me. I'll fit in OK."

He had the time of his life, during that rehearsal period. He was working with Hal Prince, one of the all-time giants of the Broadway stage. He was the star of a major Broadway musical even though he wouldn't be appearing on Broadway. He was part of all that giddy hoopla, the top banana in a big cast, he would sing with a big orchestra backing him up, he had dance numbers to learn and dialogue to perfect and songs to rehearse.

"I told you it would be fun," he kept saying to me. "And, Tom, I'm having more fun than I've ever had."

I was happy for him, of course, so I wasn't going to be the one to spoil his fun. The show was still a dog, as far as I was concerned. I knew it was going to have a rough time on tour. But let him have fun, let him enjoy it all as long as he could.

But it was not fun and not enjoyable for anybody, especially Rock, when the show opened for business. The first stop was Detroit, and that set the tone. The reviews were bad and the audience, as the old saying has it, stayed away in droves.

"I can't understand it," Rock said. "When I was in *Camelot*, the people came and they loved me."

"My friend," I said, "you are learning a very valuable lesson. And that is that it is one thing to tour in a vehicle like *Camelot*, which the public knows and loves, and it is quite another thing to tour in *On the Twentieth Century*, which the public has never heard of and doesn't like very much when they see it."

And Rock's eager but basically mediocre voice simply could not handle a couple of the ballads, and he was outmatched in his duets with Judy Kaye, who has a beautiful voice. Maybe if they had done what they promised him they would do—rearrange the songs to fit his voice—it would have been passable. But without that assistance, the results were lamentable.

The critics were actually kinder to him than I expected but the reviews were still poor. For once, I felt the critics were justified in those raps.

After a few weeks of this, Rock was dejected. But he was never a brooder, and he took solace in the fact that he was with people he liked, and he enjoyed being part of a talented group, and they treated him as an equal, one of the bunch.

He was also very honest with himself. And one night, after playing to an audience that was exceptionally sparse and somewhat hostile to boot, he admitted to me that he had made a mistake.

"From now on," he said, "I am going to listen to you. If I ever say no to you again, remind me of this conversation. Remind me that you were the one who told me not to do *On the Twentieth Century*. I hate people who say 'I told you so,' but in this case you have my permission. Go ahead, say it."

And I did say it, but I also said that he might as well relax and enjoy it. Have fun—and he did.

I must admit, however, that from then on, as long as we were together, he pretty much took my advice on professional matters. I read every script that was submitted to him, and I screened all the offers and all the feelers that came his way. I tried to weed out the wheat from the crap.

I would read a script and toss it aside and he'd say "How was it?" and I'd say "It was rotten," and he'd say "Oh," and that would be the end of that script. Only in rare cases—like the one with *Avalanche*—did he ever again go off on his own and do something I advised him against doing.

Because of all the theater he did, he and I toured all over the United States, as well as those forays into England and Canada. While playing on tour is pretty time consuming, we often had some hours to enjoy ourselves, and we got to see a lot of America and have some good times.

When we took *I Do! I Do!* to Washington, in 1974, Betty Ford— Gerald was vice president at the time—came backstage to meet Rock. She is a great movie buff and had been a longtime Rock Hudson fan. A cousin of mine who was very big in Republican women's organizations arranged for tours for all of us in the company. We saw the House and Senate in session and had a backstage White House tour.

While we were in Dallas with *I Do! I Do!*, both Rock and Carol rented houses for the duration. Each house had a swimming pool. On our days off, those pools were the sites for parties for everyone connected with the show. (Even though there were only two in the cast, a lot of people were involved in the backstage and front office operations.)

I have a cousin in Dallas, too (I have a lot of relatives), and this cousin is rich as Croesus. They entertained Rock and me and Carol and Joe often during our weeks there.

After the show, we would usually all go out together. Rock would get so keyed up for a performance that he just couldn't eat anything for several hours after the curtain went down. He would have to have a few drinks to pull himself together before he could manage to eat. So my cousins, when they came to understand how things were, would organize dinner parties starting at one o'clock in the morning. Staid old Dallas was stood on its collective ear when they began getting invitations to dinner parties at 1:00 A.M.

During the Dallas run we got to know Tom Hughes, who operates the huge theater where we were playing. He is a marvelously flamboyant man and, on opening night, he always makes a splash, wearing a flowing cape and carrying a cane with a silver eagle on the handle.

We were listening backstage to his fiery opening talk, which climaxed with:

"And, finally, ladies and gentlemen, I would like to introduce you to a gentleman who is in our audience tonight. This gentleman will be starring in our next production. It is my extreme pleasure to introduce you to Mr. Gene Kelly!"

Poor Rock freaked out. In *I Do! I Do!*, he was required to do a little dance number—in top hat and tails, yet—and it had always given him trouble. And now he would have to do it while the master, Gene Kelly, was watching. He asked me to go to Tom Hughes and ask him never to do that again. I told Hughes that neither Rock nor Carol liked to know when somebody important was in the audience.

Actually, Carol is passionate on that point. If she spots somebody during the course of the show, that doesn't bother her somehow, but she gets livid if she is told ahead of time that there will be a particular person in the audience. Especially a *BIG* particular person.

Rock didn't like to know, either. And, once the curtain went up, he was safe because, without his glasses, he couldn't see well enough to make out any faces clearly. Only close up—such as that time in Hyannisport when he recognized the Kennedys—could he distinguish people.

It wasn't Rock's fault that *On the Twentieth Century* was derailed. Actually, except for those ballads that were beyond him, he did a remarkable job with a poor role.

In truth, he had become a fine stage actor. Some people have gone so far as to say that he eventually became a much better stage actor than he was a screen actor.

I believe *John Brown's Body* was his finest work on stage. His reviews were excellent. Actually, unless a particular review was called to his attention, he never read any review—good or bad. I would read them all and read to him any that I felt contained any valid criticism which could help his work. I think the bad reviews he had received early in his career had hurt him deeply, and his defense was to ignore them all.

Being recognized as a competent stage actor—and perhaps even considerably better than merely competent—brightened his life. He felt that now he could hold his head up in any company of actors. A movie actor carries a certain stigma forever—not quite an actor, not quite a professional—and that was especially true for Rock, because of his name and because he was so handsome. Nobody that good-looking could possibly be a good actor, too. Rock was always aware of that stigma and so his emergence as a stage actor of significance was meaningful to him. That stigma was forgotten, at least by his peers.

And so his years as part of the theater were good years. Had he lived, I have no doubt that one day he would have done a Broadway show. That was the dream that never happened.

CHAPTER THIRTEEN
Aging Gracefully

Rock and I often talked about the future—his, mine, ours—but it was idle talk, theoretical talk. It wasn't practical talk because, to us at the time, the future was some very remote and distant horizon. We were relatively young, and the notion of our mortality was something which we would deal with tomorrow.

I eventually became the vice president of Mammoth Films, Rock's own production company, and the president of Gibraltar Films, a development company we started but which never developed anything beyond the letterhead. Mammoth's only asset was Rock Hudson, but that was a considerable asset, so the company was very busy. Since most of Rock's movies during the latter years of his career were all co-productions—Mammoth teaming up with whatever other company was involved—I was kept very busy.

Most of our discussions about the future revolved around the roles Mammoth and Gibraltar would play in that future. We had big dreams. We eventually wanted the two companies to produce films and television programs in which Rock was not involved as an actor. Perhaps he might do some directing or producing, that's all.

He wanted to direct. What actor doesn't?

Whenever he was on a picture, he would watch the director, study his actions, and observe his philosophy. He was building up a reservoir of knowledge because someday, he kept saying, he was going to direct. But he vowed he would never direct himself.

"I can't understand these actors who direct themselves," he would say. "Each job is big enough, without trying to do two big jobs at once. When I direct, I'll direct. Period."

Milton Krasner, the cinematographer on *McMillan & Wife*, was one of the best; he had won an Academy Award for his work on *Three Coins In the Fountain,* among others. I had worked with Krasner at MGM, so I knew him well and, of course, he and Rock became good friends during the years that they were together on the *McMillan* show.

On a television show there is usually a new director each week. But, as a rule, the cinematographer stays. That is done on purpose, to give the finished product a continuity, a consistency, to make each week's episode bear some resemblance to every other week's.

Krasner provided that continuity. And, week after week, Rock would talk to him, ask questions, learn about cinema techniques. He had been in enough movies to have seen many different directors at work, but that had always been from his spot in front of the camera. With Krasner's help, he began to see how it looked from behind the camera.

Many TV stars—Michael Landon on *Bonanza,* Alan Alda on *M.A.S.H.*, Chad Everett on *Medical Center,* to name a few—had begun directing careers on their own shows. I kept suggesting to Rock that he break in as a director with an episode of *McMillan & Wife.*

"Jon would be happy if you would," I said. I'd spoken to Jon Epstein, the producer, and he had said, yes, any time. "He'll have an episode written in which your character is light, and you can direct it. Milton Krasner will help you. You couldn't ask for a better time or a better place to get your feet wet than this."

"No," he said. "I've told you: I won't direct myself, no matter how light my character is in the episode. I think it's wrong. I think I would be doing myself an injustice, both as an actor and as a director, and I think I will be hurting the production, too. I'll wait."

I started looking for scripts I thought we could make—scripts for movies Mammoth could produce and Rock could direct. Dozens of scripts were submitted to us, but they were all for Rock as an actor. Nobody thought of him as a director, which was understandable. After all, he had never directed anything.

It never happened. I think that was another of the regrets of his life. And I think he would have been a good director, because he always had a good eye. He would often say to me, at home in the evening, that he had shot a scene that day which would have been better if the director had shot it from a different angle.

But he was always a director's dream as an actor, because he never volunteered his opinion. Sometimes young directors were hired for a *McMillan* or a *Devlin Connection* episode, and I could see Rock burning while they fiddled. Rock, with all his experience, could have told them what to do in a few easy minutes, but he politely kept his mouth shut. He would never intrude on their prerogatives.

"Come on, Rock," Milton Krasner would say, "why don't you do an episode? I'll be at your side, I'll help you. We'll all help you. I know you'll do a fine job."

"Go ahead, do it," I'd say. "You know you want to, and this is the perfect time."

"Any time you want, Rock, just say the word," said Jon Epstein. "I can have an episode written where you are sick and Susan does all the work, so it'll be a cinch to direct. You won't be in it hardly at all."

We all worked on him, but he continued to refuse. He had his integrity and his principles and he simply did not feel an actor should ever direct himself, and he never would.

Rock was looking forward to a long career. He was gradually moving from leading man roles to character roles, a transition he was pleased about.

By far the best roles are written for character actors and actresses. Not necessarily the largest roles, but the best ones. Leading men and leading ladies may have the biggest roles, the starring roles, the best-paid roles but, by and large, those parts are dull. Heroes are dull. It is the villains who have the meatiest parts.

So, many real actors and actresses look forward to the day when their faces—those beautiful faces which brought them fame and fortune originally—begin to show signs of maturity. Only then can they begin to have more fun, playing roles that are exciting and challenging.

After all, what is acting but playing make-believe? And that is a better game when you can make believe you are somebody totally removed from yourself. Those parts are the ones reserved for character actors.

So Rock was looking forward to the time when he could be cast in those good, meaty, mature character parts.

And he was aging beautifully. His face was still handsome—it always would have been, had his health permitted—but it was beginning to show some signs of age. To most observers those signs only enhanced and strengthened his appeal. Had he lived, I think he would today be playing marvelous character parts and be recognized as one of the greatest of actors.

When he was in *Wheels*, he worked with Ralph Bellamy. Earlier, Bellamy had been a leading man. Now, with advancing years, he had become a brilliant character man, and Rock often said to me that he hoped his career would parallel Bellamy's as he got older.

He and I went to see the movie *Being There*, based on the Jerzy Kosinski novel. Peter Sellers played a retarded man who worked as a gardener. His childlike remarks about his garden were taken by others—including Melvyn Douglas as a major political wheeler-dealer—as very profound.

We didn't like the picture very much, but afterward it had an effect on Rock.

"My God," he said. "Isn't it exciting? I think in a few years, I'll be ready to play parts like that one Melvyn Douglas had." Douglas too had been a leading man when he was younger, and Rock continued to think he wanted to model his later career on Bellamy, Douglas, and others of that stature.

He was so thrilled at the prospect that he talked about it constantly. We went out to dinner after seeing *Being There,* but Rock couldn't eat. He sat there, and all he could do was talk about that Melvyn Douglas part, and Ralph Bellamy in *Wheels,* and how he might be playing those parts in another ten or fifteen years.

"Do you think they'll give me parts like that?" he said as eagerly as a boy asking if someday he could have a puppy.

"Rock, there is no way you won't get parts like that," I said. He smiled; I had told him he could have the puppy. "Look, my friend, your name is always going to mean something, always. Your name means something on TV and it means something in the theaters. You remember what Roddy McDowall said the other day?"

Roddy McDowall had told us that he had read somewhere that, of all the big Hollywood names, Rock's movies played on TV more than anybody else's.

"So you'll be in demand forever," I said. "And they'll be happy to give you any part you want."

"Tom, I just can't wait!" he said. "I think the future is going to be great fun."

It wasn't.

CHAPTER FOURTEEN
The Split

I had fought hard to get Rock those great contractual delights in his deal to do *The Devlin Connection*. When he went back to work after the open heart surgery, I was particularly glad I had.

What was, I felt, especially important to his physical well-being was the clause which permitted me to go down on the set, at five o'clock (actually, it was ten hours after he reported to the make-up department, and that worked out usually to be around five) and pull the plug.

I was never dictatorial and abrupt about it. I would go to the director and say, "I hope you understand about Rock's contract. He can only work ten hours and, today, that means he'll have to leave about five. Of course, if you're in the middle of a scene, it's OK if you go another fifteen minutes or so, but don't count on starting anything new after five."

I never would come down, on the stroke of five, and say, "That's it. Cut. Rock's out of here." I would just tell the director at the beginning of shooting in the morning, and usually remind him during the lunch break, as well. Then I'd show up around five and catch his eye, and it would work out. Or it should have worked out. But I had a problem I had not foreseen: Rock.

Rock was the thorn in the ointment. I would have all my arguments ready to use on the director, in case he showed signs of wanting to do just one more scene. They were cogent arguments— not only the black-and-white words of the contract but also the commonsense consideration of Rock's health. After all, he had only recently had an operation on his heart and really shouldn't work too hard.

But it was Rock who would say "Tom, if we can do one more scene tonight, we'll be way ahead of the game."

Another way I was supposed to protect Rock—and he had insisted on this during the contract negotiations—was to sit in on all production meetings. I would be there when the next week's script would be analyzed. That was the usual procedure on any TV show: the whole production team would get together and figure out how many hours they would need for this scene, how many hours for that scene, and so on through the entire script.

I was at those meetings representing Rock, and very often I would say "That's not enough time for Rock to do that scene. It's a tough physical scene for him, and I want him to have more time. You'll have to rearrange the schedule so he has a break both before and after he does that scene."

I was being tough, but it was all for Rock's own good. I would make them understand that we were talking about a man who was still recuperating from open heart surgery and just couldn't be worked too hard.

The *Devlin* production team was terrific. They went along with all my suggestions without serious argument. They even volunteered to arrange the shooting schedule so Rock could have an hour's rest period after lunch every day. They bent over backward to accommodate him. If there was a scene that even remotely seemed strenuous—even such an innocuous scene as going up a flight of stairs—they would check with me to see if I felt he could handle it. Or should they get a stunt double to do it?

The production staff was cooperative. Rock kept shooting me

down. If I said he shouldn't do a scene because it would be too much for him, he would publicly pooh-pooh my concern. If I suggested that they rearrange the shooting schedule to give him a break after a long and difficult scene, he would say "Oh, come on, stop trying to baby me."

Between that and his insistence on working past the agreed-on quitting time, I often found myself standing there with an omelet on my face. And all the production people would be staring at me as though I were the enemy. The star was willing to work, so who is this other guy who keeps wanting him to quit or to take it easy?

I was the bad guy.

To make matters worse, *The Devlin Connection* was doing poorly in the ratings. The whole concept of the show had changed somewhere along the way. Originally, the idea had been to shoot it in New York. The concept was to show the glamorous side of New York, to film at all the fanciest restaurants—The Four Seasons, The Russian Tea Room—and let the rest of the country see New York's glamour and glitz.

But NBC said that would be too expensive and persuaded us to shift it back to Los Angeles. We never should have given in, because much of the show's potential was wrapped up in that original premise. So I suggested that, at least, we show the glamorous side of L.A. Let's have Rock—and there was nobody who could look as elegant as Rock Hudson—in black tie, going to the Music Center, at the Polo Lounge, strolling down Rodeo Drive, and exuding oodles of high-tone culture. But that didn't happen either. And the show never did find its niche, or its audience.

Rock blamed me for the fact that *The Devlin Connection* was falling on its face.

I didn't feel he was justified in blaming me. We had both gone along with the concept for the show, even though neither of us had been overwhelmed by it, because of the terrific deal we had managed to get from NBC. The real problem was those bad scripts, and certainly they were not my fault any more than they were Rock's fault.

Rock had never had a television failure before, and he apparently had to blame somebody. And I was convenient.

McMillan & Wife had been a blockbuster. His TV movies and miniseries had all been very well received; even *The Martian Chronicles*, his least popular TV effort until then, had had very respectable numbers. And *Wheels* had gone through the roof. It wiped the country out those four or five nights it was on. We learned, firsthand, just what kind of impact it had had on the nation.

A day or so after it aired we went back to New York and, with two women friends, went to see the play *Dracula*, with Frank Langella. We had gone to hundreds of plays in New York through the years and were used to being stared at and, occasionally, accosted by people asking for autographs or just wanting to shake Rock's hand. It was no big deal. But that night, at intermission, we got up to go outside for a smoke and the audience spotted Rock—and it was frightening. Our dates were scared to death, because of the way the people descended on him. And it was all because of the excitement *Wheels* had generated. We had to leave the theater.

So Rock was used to television successes, and now the network was talking about dropping *Devlin*. And then NBC had another management shake-up and we were confronted by another new team of executives. Naturally, the new boys automatically wanted to sweep away all vestiges of what the old boys had done. Especially old vestiges—such as *The Devlin Connection*—that were not pulling their weight.

We finished thirteen episodes and Rock and I went back to New York. On the plane, we talked about it.

"I think that's it for *Devlin*," I said. I had been talking to the new network brass, and I could see the handwriting on the ratings. "In the first place, we both know that the show isn't what we had hoped it would be. It just didn't jell, not since Wilder went on strike."

"Well, you should have got me out of it right then," he said in a petulant tone that was unlike him. I chalked it up to one of those personality changes the doctors had warned me might occur following the heart operation.

"What's past is past," I said, trying to mollify him. "It's too damn bad. We had such high hopes for it, too. But the new boys at

NBC tell me they can't live with your contract, either—too rich for their blood, I guess. So I expect when we get back to California, we'll get our cancellation notice."

"Maybe. Maybe not," Rock said. "Maybe we can still do something to save it. Change the format. Maybe add a girl."

"I'm afraid it's too late for that. Let's face it, our goose is cooked. If we were number one or even in the top ten, they'd keep us. But we're way down the list. And, with that contract, it makes the show just too expensive. So better prepare yourself for the axe."

I don't think he believed they would drop him or his show. But when we got back to California it happened, as I had known it would. Again, he blamed me. He said I hadn't taken care of him as well as I should have.

"It's all your fault, Tom," he said. And he said it in a harsh, unfamiliar tone. "If you had been watching out for my interests the way you should have, this never would have happened."

That, again, was unlike him. Before the operation he would have been depressed by the cancellation, but he never would have lashed out at me or anyone else. In ten minutes he would have shrugged it off and said something like "Well, on to the next adventure." But this time he looked at me with unfriendly eyes and went up to his room and closed the door and brooded for hours.

I thought a new project would bring him out of it. And, fortunately, at the time there were several interesting scripts I had read.

"No," he said, and he still had that brusque tone. "I don't want to work any more."

I spoke to Mark Miller, and we compared notes about this new, unlikable Rock Hudson. Mark had noticed the change, too. We both figured it was that postsurgical personality change, but I remembered the doctors had said it wouldn't last long. And this was lasting quite a while.

He kept to his room, mostly. He didn't want to do anything or see anyone. No more parties. No more fun. And no more work, even though I had some pretty decent scripts for him, which I urged him to consider.

I was left with nothing to do. My jobs as vice president of Mammoth and president of Gibraltar were really empty since both companies had only one asset—Rock Hudson—and now the only asset was mostly sulking up in his room.

So I rattled around the house for a couple of weeks, with no purpose in life. Rock and I ate our meals together, but that's about all. Only rudimentary conversation, about the necessities of life. The spark was gone from his eyes and my life.

Eventually I just said to myself "Well, screw this. Rock is going through a phase and there's no point in my hanging around here. I'll split."

Claire Trevor happened to be visiting us. He was polite to her because she was one of his favorite people, but there was no warmth, even for her. She noticed it and we talked about it. When she was ready to go back to New York, I decided to go with her.

I told Rock I was going back to New York for a while.

"Fine," he said.

"So I'll see you soon," I said.

"OK. See you soon."

But the next time I saw him he was dying.

We had no harsh words, no fight, just that simple exchange of brief sentences. In my mind, our separation was temporary. It never crossed my mind that it might be permanent. I went back to New York mostly because I felt so useless in Los Angeles. I figured I'd stay maybe a month, two at the most, then come back.

Rock told me he didn't want me to move out. He tried to persuade me to stay, but I felt an overpowering need to get away by myself for a while. I explained that I wasn't leaving, just going to New York for a change of scenery.

People have written about our relationship and have said we "split up" at that time. As it turned out, it was a long time before we saw each other again, but it wasn't a split—that word implies an end, a permanent separation, usually after a fight or an argument. This was not that at all. I was going away for a little while. In neither Rock's mind nor my mind was this an end.

This was in September 1983. On the plane back to New York with Claire, I felt empty, as though part of me was missing. Yet, in a way, I felt relieved. Rock and I had been together for seventeen years—a long time, not matter who or how. We had drifted apart, but I was sure the drift was caused mostly by that surgery-induced personality change. I believed what the doctors had told me about the change being temporary. So I felt certain that, after I had been in New York for a weeks or so, I'd get a call from Rock. He would be back in his normal good spirits, and we would joke and I'd grab the next plane back to the coast.

I did get a call—the first of many, as it turned out—but the first one was Rock was merely asking me to do him a favor. He wanted me to negotiate his contract for that terrible picture *The Ambassador*, which I had advised him against doing. I said sure, of course, send the contracts along and I'd be happy to look them over. He did, and I did.

He called often from Israel, too, when he went there to film *The Ambassador*. Pleasant calls, in which I asked him how the filming was going and he asked me about our mutual friends in New York. Just nice, chatty calls, the kind two old friends would normally have.

As it turned out, I stayed in New York about six months. Those mutual friends of ours were now my very good friends. I didn't do much of anything: I went for long walks, saw plays, went to parties, spent weekends in the country with people like Betty Lee Hunt, the Broadway publicist, and Mary Lea Johnson Richards and Ruthie Mitchell.

As the filming in Israel neared its end, Rock called to say he would be returning via New York and looked forward to seeing me. He said something about "ironing out our differences," which rather surprised me, because I wasn't aware of any wrinkled differences that needed ironing out. But I ignored that; I was willing to grab the old iron and smooth away if that was the way he wanted it.

I knew we had always had some joint financial dealings that needed to be attended to periodically—documents to be signed, that sort of thing—and perhaps that was what he was referring to.

We talked very often over the next few months, as winter came. I spent Christmas with the Smiths in Harrisburg, Pennsylvania. It was the first time in years Rock and I had not been together for that holiday and so, over the phone, we exchanged "merrys" and other appropriate holiday sentiments. He was still in Israel that Christmas and found it a very interesting experience.

He had told me he would be stopping in New York on his way home, but then he called. From California. He had bypassed New York and in so doing had bypassed me, too. He told me he was just so homesick that he didn't want to take the time to stop in New York. He had taken the polar route back to Los Angeles.

In one of his calls, just before he had left for Israel Rock had mentioned a new friend, a young man named Marc Christian.

"I met him at the health club," Rock said. (Later, incidentally Christian said he had met Rock at a fund-raiser for Gore Vidal, Rock told me he met him when he went to this health club in his continuing search for comfort for his always-aching back, and Christian had spotted him there and had arranged to meet him.) "The poor guy has nowhere to sleep—right now, he is crashing on some lady's sofa—so what would you say if I asked him to stay in the house while I'm in Israel?"

"I'd rather you wouldn't," I said. "After all, I've got all my things there [When I'd gone to New York, I had taken nothing except the clothes on my back and the book I was reading] and what do you know about this guy?"

"Trust me," Rock said. "It'll be OK."

But, of course, it wasn't. In letting Marc Christian into the house, Rock paved the way for what eventually turned out to be the dreadful and horrifying lawsuit, in which Rock was portrayed as a man who continued to have sex with Christian after he knew he had contracted AIDS.

But even before that lawsuit, which I firmly believe was a terrible miscarriage of justice, things at the house turned unpleasant as soon as Marc Christian came in the door.

What I feared happened. My things vanished, never to be seen again. Among the missing were items I treasured, such as some gold-and-lapis studs and cufflinks Rock had given me for my birthday.

In his calls after he got back from Israel, Rock began to intimate that Marc Christian was becoming a nuisance and, in fact, a danger.

First, he complained about the young man's personal habits.

"You wouldn't believe this house," Rock said to me. "He leaves his dirty clothes all over. He never cleans up. I don't think he's particularly clean, either."

Another time: "You wouldn't believe what that asshole has done now." (I forget what it was he had done—broken something—but I'll never forget Rock's indignation.)

"Well, get rid of him," I said. "Get him out of the house."

"It's not that easy," Rock said.

"Why not?"

"Well, he's making threats," Rock said, which was the first intimation I had that there might be a blackmail plot brewing.

"Oh, Rock, you can deal with that," I said.

"It's more than just that," Rock said. "I'm afraid physically. This guy really scares me. I think he's nuts."

The threats came out in testimony during Marc Christian's suit against the Hudson estate. Mark Miller testified Rock had told him, "Christian has letters. Give him anything he wants." You'll hear more about those letters shortly.

Christian had also made threats against Rock and his exercise man, Ron Channell. James Wright testified at the trial that Christian had said, "I'll see those two in the papers." And Mark Miller, also in trial testimony, quoted Christian as saying, "I'll see them in the Enquirer and don't think I don't know the press, because I do."

I worried, but there wasn't anything I could do long-distance, and Rock still had not come out and asked me to come back.

So I stayed in New York. One thing I did was work closely with our business manager, Wally Sheft, on some of those sticky financial arrangements Rock and I shared. And one day Wally told me that Rock had cut me out of his will.

Years earlier, Rock and I had drawn up joint wills. We both felt that, since we traveled together so much, we might one day be killed together in a plane crash. If we were going to go together, we reasoned, we should have our wills together.

At the time those wills were written we were in the process of changing both our legal and our financial representation. Rock had had a business manager who, after two fantastically lucrative years with *McMillan & Wife,* had called to tell him, calmly, that he was broke. "Bankrupt," was the precise word he had used. I don't know if Rock was literally bankrupt or not, but I do know that money was very scarce. Fortunately, that period was brief. It coincided with the continued success of *McMillan & Wife,* and that quickly put Rock back in the black—solidly.

So we began looking for a new business manager. I found Wally Sheft through, of all people, Buddy Hackett—a good pal since we had worked together on *The Love Bug* at Disney. I mentioned to Buddy the problems with our business manager.

"Wally Sheft has been with me since Day One," Hackett said. "We never even had a contract. Talk to him."

So we did. Sheft, whose office is in New York, happened to be in Los Angeles and came to the house to see us. Within an hour we were convinced he was the man for us. And, as it turned out, he was.

In a few years' time, he built Rock's estate until it was worth somewhere around ten million, then twelve, then fifteen. When Rock died, nobody knew how big it was—certainly not Rock. It included a lot of valuable real estate. It included a piece of the famed Pritikin Institute; Rock had a large piece and I had a small piece (and, in fact, I still do). It included a large chunk of a rest home in Westwood, which was always full of elderly folks and was therefore very profitable.

We used to joke that, with our Pritikin and his rest home investments, if the one didn't save us, we could always go and live in the other.

Rock had no heirs. His mother was gone and the remote family members he had didn't thrill him, certainly not to the point where he wanted to bequeath them any of his millions. Not even a token thousand.

In those joint wills, we were each other's executors. Paul Sherman was the attorney who did the work with us. One day when we were both in New York, Sherman came and had lunch with us at the Plaza.

"Look, Tom," Sherman said, "I don't think it is wise for you to be Rock's executor. I think it would be much too much work for you in the event that he predeceases you. His estate is getting to be enormous, and the executor has to be someone with the know-how to handle a huge and complex estate."

I could have cared less about being executor. (I have since learned that an executor of a big estate makes a great deal of money, but I didn't know that then.) So I said sure, no skin off my nose, put somebody else down. Who would he suggest? He said he thought our business manager, Wally Sheft, would be the ideal person to be the executor. So the change was made.

When Sheft told me that Rock had written a new will, eliminating me as his beneficiary. I shrugged it off. I was surprised but not devastated. Since we had had no harsh words, no fight, not even a minor dispute, I knew that his action was not motivated by any ill will toward me. It wasn't as though he were saying "Go, and never darken my doorstep again."

I never discussed it with Rock. When I saw him again he was dying, and I didn't want to burden him with anything that might cause him even minor distress.

On reflection long after the fact, I believe that he was motivated by my well-being. I think that, because he believed Marc Christian was making threats, the threats Mark Miller and James Wright later testified to, he anticipated that his estate would be the subject of litigation and, by writing me out of the will, he was sparing me the hassle and ugliness he knew would be coming. That, of course, is only theory and supposition, but it is the only theory and supposition that makes any sense to me.

Rock also was aware of an unwritten agreement among Mark Miller, George Nader, and myself. We would take care of each other. When I was the chief beneficiary, I had agreed to take care of Mark and George out of my share of the estate, assuming that Rock predeceased me. And, later, when George replaced me as the chief beneficiary, I knew he would do the same for me when the time came.

The will, as Sheft explained it to me, provided for a cap on the money George could receive—$500,000 annually. Whatever the estate earns in interest over and above that $500,000, goes back into the estate. There are bequests, too, to the Motion Picture Country Home (something I pushed for, telling Rock he really should give money back to the industry that gave it to him), the USC Film Department, and a charity he was active with, the Foundation for the Blind.

Because of our being physically apart and because of my being dropped from the will, the popular perception was that Rock and I had had a major falling out. But that was simply not true. During those six months I was in New York we talked very often on the phone, friendly and warm calls and, like the song says, there never was heard a discouraging word.

I stayed in the New York apartment for those six months, until the inactivity bored me to death. I was still on the Mammoth payroll during that period—the weekly paychecks never stopped; and I felt I earned them when I negotiated Rock's contract for *The Ambassador*—so money was no problem. But boredom was a big one. You can walk and window-shop and go to plays and parties only so long; after that, your mind hungers to be active.

I began thinking about looking for a job, but I already had a job—with Mammoth—and I was certain that, any day now, Rock would call with work for me to do. So I waited. I did get a call, but it wasn't from Rock—it was from MGM.

"We're in a bind," Marsha Robertson, then the head of the studio publicity department, said. "We've got a picture about ready to shoot, and it's a problem picture."

To Hollywood publicity people, a problem picture is one in which somebody—director or producer or star, or maybe a combination of the above—is difficult to work with. In this case, the picture was called *Fever* (eventually released as *Fever Pitch*) and the problems were manifold. There was a problem producer (Freddie Fields), a problem director (Richard Brooks), and a problem star (Ryan O'Neal).

"With those three," Marsha said, "I can't get any publicist to take the job. I know you get along with Brooks, so that's a start. And I know you're at loose ends—so how about it?"

Actually, not only do I get along with Brooks, but I am very fond of him. I like Richard Brooks a lot. I knew Fields' reputation for being difficult. And O'Neal was, I also knew, no bed of roses for a publicist. But I'd worked with a lot of thorny people in the past.

Marsha was right in that I was at loose ends. In fact my ends were so loose they were positively drooping. So it really didn't take much persuasion on her part.

I went over to see Richard Brooks, to get a handle on the production. Brooks writes all his own scripts and he is a bit paranoid about letting them out of his sight—in fact, a lot paranoid. So I had to sit in his office while I read the *Fever* script with him watching me like an especially alert hawk, to make sure I didn't have a portable Xerox machine in my pocket and wasn't copying his precious words. Of all the Hollywood execs I worked with, he was the only one who kept a shredder next to his desk and used it constantly.

Brooks is so concerned about his script getting into the wrong hands that he never lets his cast read the whole script. Each one sees only the sides that has his lines on them.

So I sat there and read that script. Then he asked me what I thought.

"It's really great, Richard," I said, and I wasn't lying. It was truly a really great script. "But I do have one problem with it. I can't see Ryan O'Neal in this part."

"That's my problem," Brooks said. "You just watch."

And I did watch, and it was amazing. Most of the picture was shot in Las Vegas—it was about a compulsive gambler—and Ryan O'Neal gave the performance of his life. Brooks got him to act, as he had done in *Paper Moon*, but never once since then. I told Brooks that I thought this was going to mean an Oscar for both him and O'Neal, and Richard didn't disagree.

When the picture came out, I was back with my dying friend and had little interest in motion pictures of any kind. But I had enough curiosity to call a friend at the studio the morning after *Fever Pitch* had its first rough screening to ask him what he thought about it.

"Tom, you won't believe that film," my friend said. "It is the worst piece of shit I have ever seen."

I have never seen it, so I don't know what happened. From what I have heard, however, I gather Richard Brooks decided on a pseudo-documentary approach, edited it in that fashion, and somehow it didn't work.

But it nevertheless did me a world of good. It kept my mind occupied through the winter of 1984 well into the spring of 1985. It also helped me financially, because the union scale for motion picture unit publicists had gone through the roof. When I did *Fever Pitch*, MGM was paying me $1200 a week, a per diem expense account while we were in Las Vegas, and other good stuff. Of course, because unit publicists work only sporadically, they have to make it while they can, but that is still some very worthwhile money.

Throughout my work on that film I continued to speak to Rock frequently. He continued to tell me stories about Marc Christian, emphasizing his fear of the man. He continually used the expression "He's really nuts."

I think he meant it literally. Rock intimated, time and again, that Christian was threatening him, and he told me there had been some letters.

Apparently, uncharacteristically, he had written some letters to Christian while he was in Israel.

"They're really nothing letters," he said, "but still he's using them."

Christian had apparently said he would release the letters to the press exposing their relationship if Rock carried out his threat to kick him out of the house. When I came back to Los Angeles after finishing my work on *Fever Pitch*, we talked about my coming back to the house, but Rock said he wanted to get Christian out first. The letters were standing in the way.

Those letters surfaced during the trial, in which Christian won his big judgment against the Hudson estate. Somebody showed me one, and it was a very curious document.

That one letter I saw was not in Rock's handwriting—I had seen Rock's handwriting often enough to know that letter had been written by somebody elese. Furthermore, the phrasing was not Rock's. The way it was written was totally alien to Rock's writing style, such as it was. And, most important, it was signed "R.H." Every letter Rock ever wrote to a friend was signed "Me;" he never signed anything "R.H." in his life. Anybody who ever received a letter from Rock Hudson knows that.

Still, that was one of the letters with which, somehow, Christian was threatening Rock. Perhaps he had inadvertently disposed of Rock's real letters and had these made up as substitutes, and never actually showed them to Rock, but merely waved them under his nose.

Whatever it was, it served the purpose. Rock would not kick Christian out of the house. But, even though Christian continued to live there, he was merely a presence, not a person of importance in Rock's life.

"I don't even know what that asshole is doing," Rock said to me during one of our conversations. "And I sure as hell don't care."

If they ever had an affair it was short-lived. Christian's big claim, during the trial, was that he was exposed to AIDS when he and Rock continued their affair after Rock was diagnosed as having the disease. But that is absurd.

Rock's condition was diagnosed in the summer of 1984. I was back in Los Angeles then, but sadly oblivious to the tragedy that had befallen my friend. By Easter, several months earlier, he wasn't even talking to Christian any more, much less having a love affair with him. So Christian's claim of being in danger was, at the very least, an overstatement.

He was a dangerous man, as Rock feared. One of Rock's good friends was an actor, the late Dean Dittmann, who had been in the cast of *On the Twentieth Century* and had been kind to Rock when he was adjusting to that difficult part.

Dittmann was a short, heavy-set character actor—there could have been no sexual attraction there. When I went to New York, he spent some time with Rock and was there when Christian moved in. When Rock became ill, Dittmann told me, he received a visit from Christian.

"I'm going to sue Rock," Christian said.

"What for?"

"I'll think of something. My lawyer's working on it. But, look, if you come in with me, and back me up, you can have a piece of the action."

Dittmann was furious.

"Get out of my house, you whore," Dittmann yelled at Christian. And Christian left.

A week later, Dittmann's house was fire-bombed, and he lost everything. While there could be some other explanation behind that tragedy, Dittman told Mark Miller that he was convinced that Christian was behind that attack. But there was never enough evidence for the police to take action.

In his deposition, according to Mark Miller who saw it, Christian told how Rock had taken him everywhere, had introduced him to his friends, including Martha Raye. But Maggie in her depositions, said she had never heard of Marc Christian and certainly had never met him with Rock.

He claimed he continued to have sex with Rock after the AIDS diagnosis. The servants, led by James, testified that was not so—and you can't fool servants. (I have no idea where the trial jury was during that testimony). James even testified that Christian had many other young men up to his room (my room!) during that period.

When I left the New York apartment to take the *Fever* unit job, I made the mistake of leaving many of my own personal possessions there. Later, when Rock died, the apartment was sealed and then the executor of the estate, under the direction of the IRS, had everything auctioned off, including things which had belonged to me personally. But that possibility had never occurred to me. I went back to a house in Los Angeles Rock and I owned jointly, a house that was high up on Mulholland Drive, with views of both the city to the south and the mountains to the north.

But it was too big for me alone. I was rattling around in it. So I sold it—half the proceeds went to me, half to Rock—and bought a small condo in the city.

I was living there when I read, in Army Archerd's column in *Daily Variety*, just like the rest of the world, that Rock Hudson had flown to Paris.

He was, the report said, seeking treatment for AIDS.

By then his relationship with Marc Christian was long over, according to what Rock told me. It had been over and done with, he said, for several months and, by the time the AIDS diagnosis was made, Rock hated Christian and was no longer even talking to him, much less having any sexual relationship with him. Christian insists Rock was enamored of him—but if that was the case, why did Rock never take him with him on his trips? He went to Hawaii—and took a friend. He went to Paris and took his exercise man. He went to New York several times—and never took Marc Christian.

Why wasn't all this brought out in court, during Christian's lawsuit?

A fair question. Some of it was. As I have said, James and the other servants testified that there was no longer anything between Rock and Christian, but the jury either wasn't listening or chose to ignore it.

But most of it, for whatever reason, did not become part of the testimony.

Exhibit A: The famous letters Rock supposedly wrote to Marc Christian.

As I wrote earlier, I believe them to be forgeries and the lawyers for the estate, having consulted a noted handwriting expert, felt the same. But the defense legal team, rather than expose them as forgeries, chose to bring them up themselves, in an attempt to prove that Christian was blackmailing Rock. They didn't actually introduce the letters but, instead, questioned Christian about them.

He testified that he had nothing to do with them, and then said that he had found them after Rock died, in his desk. At that point, the defense lawyers should have called me to testify, because I would have said—and Nurse Tammy Nu would have corroborated that testimony—that after Rock died his desk was totally empty. As a matter of fact, the desk in question was my desk, not Rock's, and some days before Rock's death I had cleaned it out—with Tammy Nu assisting.

They didn't call me to testify.

They didn't call Tammy Nu, or the other nurses, who could have stated their belief that Christian never saw Rock, as he claimed he did, while Rock was on his deathbed.

They didn't call Elizabeth Taylor or any of the other stars Christian claimed to have met with Rock, who would have said he never did.

They didn't call Linda Evans, who had sworn in a deposition that the controversial kiss Rock gave her on the set of *Dynasty* was a tight-lipped, side-of-the-mouth peck and not the big, juicy, dangerous kiss Christian said that Rock bragged about giving her.

They of course, couldn't call Dean Dittmann—he had passed away—who could have told of that incident when Marc Christian asked him to participate in a lawsuit against Rock and later came to believe that Christian masterminded the fire-bombing of his house.

They didn't call a certain individual who had pictures he has said he was willing to produce—if they were subpoenaed—showing Marc Christian in Paris participating in an orgy with a young Norwegian boy. This, at the time Christian was supposedly in Paris for tests to see if he had AIDS.

And, lastly, they didn't call a friend of Mark Christian's who worked for Dr. Gottlieb, who had been one of Rock's physicians. It was, in fact, Gottlieb who diagnosed Rock as having AIDS. The friend had told the lawyers that, ten days after Gottlieb had made the diagnosis, Christian told him that Rock had AIDS. Christian probably knew Rock had AIDS as soon as Rock found out, or perhaps before. And, moreover, Rock was through with him long before that awful diagnosis.

None of this will help Rock, of course. But I do believe it will help the public conception of him, the public memory, to bring out these facts. The lawsuit created a picture in the public's consciousness of a man who didn't care if he infected somebody or not. That was not the real Rock Hudson. That was not the real man.

CHAPTER FIFTEEN
Illness

I had gone to New York by myself in the autumn of 1983. From then until the summer of 1984 I saw Rock in person only once, and then only for a few minutes, although we had many telephone conversations over that period.

Some people had been telling me he didn't look well, that he had lost a lot of weight, that he had a gaunt appearance. So, whenever he called, I would always ask him how he was feeling.

"Oh, I'm fine," he would say.

"But Mark Miller [or whoever it had been] told me you look a touch peaked." That was Oklahoma talk, and he always got a kick out of it when I talked Oklahomese.

"No, I'm not peaked, Tom. I'm really OK, no matter what Mark [or whoever] told you."

Then, once, he admitted he was a little anemic.

"I just can't believe you're anemic," I said that time. "Not with your appetite. You eat like a cayuse." More Oklahoma talk.

"Well, I don't seem to have much of an appetite these days. And the doctor tells me it's anemia."

So I thought that was it. Just a little anemia, maybe brought on by the exhausting shooting schedule in Israel, or the extreme heat over there in the Middle East, or a bit of both. Nothing serious. Some tonic or something and some rest and good food, and that would be the end of it. I wasn't worried, because Rock had always been so vibrantly healthy. I could not conceive of anything serious having a chance in that sturdy body.

When I came back to California in May 1984, and was staying in the Mulholland Drive house, I was very lonesome for the dogs. So I called Rock one day and asked him if I could have them for a weekend. He said sure, so I drove down to the house to pick up the dogs. I saw him that day, but only for three or four minutes at the most. We were both in a hurry.

At that time, I thought he looked thin and somehow unhealthy. I asked him if he was OK.

"Yeah, I'm OK," he said. "But I just don't seem to be able to shake this damned anemia."

"Have you seen Rex [Kennamer]?"

"Sure."

"What does he say?"

"Only that it's anemia and I should eat more. But I have no appetite any more."

So I said he should try and eat, and he said he would, and I left with the dogs. When I brought them back the following Monday, he wasn't there, so I never saw him again until he was on his deathbed.

That was May. By the summer I had read in the papers and heard on television of his frantic flight to Paris, where he thought there was some new treatment for AIDS.

AIDS?

I simply could not believe what I was reading and hearing. AIDS was a disease which—as I understood it then—was confined to the promiscuously homosexual community and to Haitians.

Rock was neither.

I will go to my grave convinced that Rock got AIDS from contaminated blood during a transfusion. There is no other explanation, in my mind. He was never promiscuous. And he certainly wasn't Haitian.

When he came back to California from Paris in October—and I wept when I saw the shots of him carried from the plane and put in the ambulance—I went immediately to the hospital, UCLA Medical Center.

At first I couldn't see him. He was only allowed two visitors a day—one in the morning and one in the afternoon—and I wasn't on the list. In fact, Mark Miller told me that Rock had said he didn't want to see me. That, of course, hurt me deeply because, despite our recent separation, I knew that, deep down, we still meant a lot to each other.

I sat in the waiting room. That afternoon's visitor happened to be Juliet Prowse. She had been unaware of the fact that Rock and I had split up and, when she went into Rock's room, her first innocent question was "Where's Tom?"

"I don't know where he is," Rock said. "Mark, see if you can find Tom."

"He's right outside, Rock," Miller said, and so I went in and was with him from then until he died.

Mark and the nurse, Tammy Nu, were there that first day I returned. And Jon Epstein was allowed in, too. And all three of them later said they noticed what I felt so very strongly—an almost tangible sensation, something like an electric flash.

It was as though the two years that we had been apart never happened.

I truly believe he had always wanted to see me again but had told Mark he didn't because he was embarrassed. He didn't want me to see him looking that way. Then, when Juliet asked him where I was, he suddenly decided the hell with embarrassment, he wanted his best friend there.

Once I was there, Mark Miller asked me to take over at the hospital. He had been trying to run the house and at the same time schedule Rock's visitors at the hospital and handle press inquiries and all that. So I gladly became the man on the scene at the hospital.

I slept in a couch in Rock's room. Mark Miller had made the necessary security arrangements (a guard was posted outside the door around the clock and I helped him). Until Mark had taken over, there had been too many unauthorized visitors trooping in and out of his room. We kept a tight rein on all visitors—just two a day were allowed—and we got in touch with people we knew he would want to see. Even before I got there, Elizabeth Taylor and Carol Burnett had been in to see him, and there was a steady stream, but it was a carefully screened and well-regulated stream. With so many reporters and photographers around, Mark had set up a system for Rock's visitors to use a back door when they came in and left.

I was with him there at the hospital, for several weeks. It seemed to me to be cruel and unusual punishment. Because there was nothing that could be done for him and I knew he would be happier at home, I pleaded with Kennamer to let me take him back to the house.

Rock would sit up in his hospital bed and look out the window, and he could see the house up there in the hills in the distance.

"Why can't I go home?" he would say. "Tom, see if you can get them to let me go home."

But for weeks they kept him there.

I think the reason for that was that the hospital physician on the case, Dr. Gottlieb, the doctor who had made the AIDS diagnosis, seemed to be enjoying the publicity. He was holding daily press conferences, at which he would learnedly discuss Rock's condition. Stripped of all the medical jargon, the essence of his daily message was always the same: there really is nothing we can do for this man.

So I kept working on Kennamer to release him. I said that we would hire competent nurses. We had an excellent cook—Rock was still eating fairly well then, although that didn't last much longer—who could prepare meals according to the doctor's dictates. I said there was nothing they were doing for him at the hospital that we couldn't do for him at home—and, most importantly, he wanted to go home.

Meanwhile, I had another problem to contend with: my friends, who thought I was foolhardy and a stupid jerk to move back in with Rock.

"After the way he treated you, why should you go back and risk your life to be with him?" That seemed to be the consensus of informed opinion among my circle of friends.

"Because he needs me," I'd say. I said it so often to so many people I almost had handbills printed up with the words BECAUSE HE NEEDS ME printed on them.

"Because he is my best friend. Because if the situation was reversed, and I was the one who was sick, I know damned well he'd come and take care of me."

Many of my friends remain convinced that I was nuts to do what I did. In fact, a few of them felt so strongly about it that they stopped talking to me.

But I had no choice. After all we had meant to each other for so long, after all we had been through together, there was no way I could abandon him now. I could not leave him alone in that hospital room—or, later, in the house—with only servants to care for him.

A man who is dying needs love.

When I came into the room that first day at the hospital, he was glad to see me. He gave me a big hug.

"I feel better already," he said.

The first thing he asked me to do was keep Marc Christian away from him. It was obvious to all of us that he was very agitated and disturbed at the prospect of having to face Christian again. The problem, however, was how to make Christian disappear.

At first, Mark Miller was the one who told Marc Christian that Rock wanted him out of the house. Christian, according to Miller, said he wouldn't believe it until he heard it from Rock's own lips. But Rock had put Christian's name on the list of people he didn't want to see at the hospital.

Miller told Rock that Christian wouldn't get out of the house until he heard it from him. So Rock said, OK, let him come to my room and I'll tell him.

The next day Christian showed up. I was in the room; so was Claire Ziega, who was in charge of celebrity relations at the hospital. We both left when Christian showed up, and he was in the room alone with Rock for perhaps five minutes.

When he came out, he said to Claire and me, "Well, Rock asked me to move out, so I'm moving out." Mark Miller and Tammy Nu, the nurse, also heard him say those words—words he later denied he ever said.

"Please move out today," I said. "I want to bring Rock home, and he doesn't want to come home while you're still there—you upset him too much."

"OK, I'll move out today," he said.

I told Kennamer and he said, "Fine, then you can take Rock home today."

With the press there in droves, getting Rock out would not be easy. I had devised a circuitous route for what I thought of almost as "the escape." In the afternoon, when James called to say that Marc Christian had gone, I gave the word and we began implementing my plan.

We hustled the gurney through the hall, down a rear elevator to a little-used entrance, where our getaway car was parked. We were blocks away before the press knew we were gone.

"Slow down," Rock said. "You're driving too fast." I had never heard him complain about excess speed before.

He was delighted to be home—so delighted the nurses and I had a tough time persuading him to go to bed. He wanted to romp with the dogs, he wanted to touch all of his favorite things, he wanted to stay out on the deck and see the view he loved.

But we finally got him to bed, and I collapsed in my own bed soon after. I was exhausted and slept like that well-known log. The next morning I went into the kitchen for my usual first-thing cup of coffee. The door to the dining room opened and in walked Marc Christian. He had moved back in in the dead of night.

And he refused to leave again until Rock died.

My first thought was to throw him out bodily, but when I mentioned that to Mark Miller, he told me he had wanted to do that, too, but had been advised by our lawyers that that was not a wise course to follow, satisfying though it might be to the inner man. The lawyer said that he had lived there for a year (unfortunately, that was true) so it was legally his domicile, and he was therefore entitled to be there. Much later I heard a conflicting opinion from another lawyer, but by then it was too late. I took the first lawyer's advice and didn't throw him out.

But I did say that he was never, under any circumstances, to go upstairs. And, if Rock should come downstairs, he was to make himself scarce. I said I didn't want Rock to know he was in the house at all. Fortunately, because it was a large house, Rock never did learn that Marc Christian was still there. He slept in the theater, and I made sure he stayed as far away from both Rock and me as possible.

The first time I had met Marc Christian was a few weeks before, when I had again come to the house on a dog-borrowing mission. I was taking Bo, the big Doberman, for the weekend. When I got to the house, Marc Christian was there.

We sat on the patio and chatted a while. Just casual talk about the weather, the dogs, the baseball season.

When I moved back in there were continual problems with him. It wasn't bad enough that I had my dying friend to minister to; I had to play hide-and-seek with this character. For one thing, I knew Rock didn't want to see him. For another, peace and quiet had been prescribed for him, and Christian's presence would be anything but peaceful and quiet. Christian eventually came to accept the fact that he wasn't going to see Rock, but it took a lot of vigorous persuasion before he did.

We hired nurses, of course, and one of their instructions—from the doctors as well as from me—was never, under any circumstances, to let that person up to see Rock. So, I doubt that he ever saw Rock Hudson again. The nurses—and one of them was on duty around the clock—had been instructed not to let him in the room, and they insist they didn't. I was there ninety percent of the time, and he never entered the room. Anything is possible, but if he did sneak by us, it could only have been for a few seconds.

One Sunday, when Rock was sleeping and Marc Christian was out somewhere, I called his mother.

"Mrs. Christian," I said, "your son is complicating Rock's life very much. Rock doesn't want him here, but Marc insists on staying. He is bothering Rock and Rock, as I am sure you are aware, is a very sick man."

"My son is a very good boy," she said, coolly. "He would not stay where he was not wanted. I'm sure if he is staying, it is because he thinks he can be of some help. He is not the kind of young man to cause any problems."

But he was causing me problems. He was, in fact, a royal pain in the butt. He wouldn't leave; he just kept hanging on and hanging around. He would stay in the theater, downstairs, all day, playing records—most of them were my records, which further infuriated me.

The important thing, however, was Rock's health. I would not accept the premise that he was dying. That, to me, was unthinkable. He could not die. It was not in our plans. All through our years together, if the subject of death had ever come up, Rock had always brushed it aside.

"They talk about going to your just reward," I remember him saying once. "I don't want any reward, just or unjust. They can keep it. I'm not buying that jazz."

He was being flip, of course. He knew that death was inevitable. The deaths of his mother and Marilyn Maxwell had affected him very deeply. But he felt that, for him, death was something very remote and nothing for him to concern himself with for many years to come.

"I want to live to be the grand old man of the movie business," he said to me more than once. And he would have made a grand grand old man, if he had lived.

I was not at all surprised, when I came back, to see him still smoking, as he had continued to do after his heart surgery. It was a habit I didn't think he could ever kick. I knew he should have quit long ago (as I should have), especially with his health in the precarious state it was. Surely, smoking couldn't help him—and yet, when I considered it, the way things were going with him now, it couldn't hurt him very much, either.

Cigarettes hadn't caused his problems. And so, when he had visitors—and there was a steady stream—they would almost always say to me, as they were leaving, "But he's still smoking!" I would say "Yes, he's still smoking. What do you want me to do, make him quit now, when he has maybe five minutes left to live?"

I didn't try to get him to quit smoking. If it made his last few months a little more bearable, why the hell not let him smoke? As it turned out, whatever did him in—AIDS or, as it said on his death certificate, cancer of the liver—it wasn't lung cancer.

Actually, the cause of Rock's fatal illness remains something of a mystery. There is some doubt, some confusion, as to whether or not he should be considered a victim of AIDS.

He was diagnosed as having AIDS, then went to Paris when he heard about the successes Dr. Dominique Dormant was having there. In Paris, under the supervision of Dr. Dormant, he was given a series of injections of a substance Dormant called HPA 23. That was in August and September of 1984.

He came back to California on October 4 of that year and was immediately tested by Dr. Kennamer. He told me that, while Rock was still testing positive for AIDS, the AIDS virus could no longer be grown in his blood.

"But don't get your hopes up," Kennamer said. "He's still going to die. His liver is totally shot. In effect, he has no more liver."

Other doctors who examined him, both at the hospital and after he came back to the house, remarked that he did not resemble any AIDS case they had seen.

"He doesn't have the AIDS virus" one very respected doctor told me. "Every AIDS patient I've ever seen is covered with Kaposi's sarcoma [a type of skin lesion] and Rock has none."

On his death certificate, Dr. Kennamer listed the cause of death as cancer of the liver, AIDS related. That may have been the way AIDS expressed itself in his case, but it could also have been caused, I suspect, by his very heavy drinking.

But, as Kennamer pointed out to me at the time, it was all academic. He was doomed, whatever the cause. It didn't matter to him why he was dying.

I made it a point that conversations with me or anyone else were always upbeat talk, happy talk. I would permit no long, sad faces around him. I would countenance no tears and no talk of death or dying. I encouraged visitors (and forced myself) to talk about the future, about movies to be made, about television series in the works, about worlds to conquer and places to see and things to do.

I do not know what was going on in his mind. Rock had never been a philosopher. One night, there might have been something, had I encouraged it or permitted it.

It was one of those hot, dry southern California nights, with the Santa Ana winds puffing desert air over the whole Los Angeles basin. It was so clear you could see forever and from the house, perched as it was high on a hillside, stars were just an arm's length away. And there was a full moon.

Rock was in bed, but I went inside to get him.

"Come on outside with me," I said. "We've got us the kind of night you love."

I told him about the Santa Ana blowing, the stars waiting to be touched, the moon in all its splendor.

So the nurse and I got him up—by now he had great difficulty moving—and we brought him outside. He sat there, with those warm and gentle breezes caressing his thin and weakened body, and he smiled. He could still smile.

He looked up at that glorious sky and then turned to me, and I could tell something serious was on his mind.

"Tom," he said, softly. "You know, I've been thinking about. . . ."

I stopped him.

"No time to talk about heavy stuff," I said.

He sighed and turned away. The moment was gone. I think, had I let him go on and say what was on his mind, he might have told me how he thought about the approach of death.

Perhaps I should have let him talk. But my feeling was then that I didn't want any negative ideas to be voiced. I still had the notion, naive perhaps, that a positive attitude might produce a positive result. If we didn't let the idea of death intrude into our thinking, then death could never happen.

The doctor said he should eat. He said he didn't feel much like eating. So my main purpose in life was to try and to coax him, force him, bribe him, wheedle him into eating more. It was like with a baby: "One more spoonful, and then I'll let you alone."

One night, after he hadn't eaten a thing all day, I went into his room. It must have been about ten o'clock. I told the nurse I'd watch him for a while, and she left. He was so weak he could barely hold his head up.

I climbed onto the bed with Rock and took his hand.

"Look, old friend," I said. "You are not helping me one damn bit.

We have fought a lot of battles together and we have won most of them. And we can win this one, too, but you have got to help me."

"What do you want me to do?" he said. Every word was agony to him; he was so weak that the effort it took to manufacture sound was almost overwhelming.

"You've got to eat."

"I don't care if I eat or not."

That was the first time that I sensed he had given up. It was a distressing realization for me that he was now resigned to the fact that he was dying. And didn't care if he did or didn't.

I was still full of the conviction that I had to keep him thinking in positive terms.

"Sure you care," I said. "You have to care. You can't just give up."

I reached over and shook him. Just a little shake, but enough to get his attention. He looked surprised.

"What do you want me to do?" he asked again.

"Help me. Eat."

"OK. I'll eat if you leave me alone."

The next morning I came up with some soft-boiled eggs. He waved them away.

"Remember our conversation last night?" I said. "You said you'd eat if I left you alone. OK, I left you alone, so now you have to eat. Here."

I held out the spoon, and he ate. And he did eat pretty well the rest of the day.

His friends tried to help me get him to eat, too. One of our friends was Olive Behrendt, a very elegant upper-crusty kind of society lady, always proper, always prim. She had a home in Venice, and whenever we'd gone to Italy we had visited her there and roamed the canals with her—she was the only American woman licensed to operate a speedboat on the Venetian canals.

She was a faithful visitor during Rock's illness. One day after she'd seen him, she came down to the kitchen, where I was, and we looked at each other with tears in our eyes.

"He's so weak," she said.

"He won't eat. I've tried to get him to eat, but he just won't."

"Let me try," she said. "I'll go up and ask him what he'd most like to have and then, whatever it is, I'll go and get it."

So she went up to his room and then, in a few minutes, she was back again. I asked her what he said he wanted. And, in her exquisitely refined voice, she said, "Do you happen to know of a dish called Hot Mother Fucker?"

I had to laugh. Yes, I knew of it because, in fact, I had introduced Rock to it. It came from my days in Houston, when my wife and I were part of a group of young married couples struggling to get by on not very much money. So the gals all had to be ingenious in coming up with ways to save money, and one of them had invented a casserole dish made up of ground beef, Betty Crocker's noodles romanoff, sour cream, cottage cheese, and some other stuff. For some reason it came to be known in our refined circle as Hot Mother Fucker. My mother, who is the God-fearing Methodist of all time, kept the recipe in her file, listed simply as H.M.F. I had taught James how to make it, and Rock loved it.

So Rock had asked elegant Olive for Hot Mother Fucker. I don't know if he honestly wanted it or whether he just wanted to see the expression on Olive's face when he asked her for it. But, like a good soldier, she relayed the request, and James made it but he didn't eat that either.

We all did whatever we could for him, even things we might consider useless and silly.

One very hot autumn day—and autumn can be the worst time in California, the time for forest fires and heat that sears—I was alone in the house with Rock and Tammy Nu. All the servants were out; even Marc had gone out. Rock was very sick that day, mostly not conscious. At lunch time, I went downstairs to the kitchen to fix myself a sandwich. I turned on the TV and was watching an old movie with Sylvia Sidney when the front doorbell rang.

When I opened the door, there was this tall, stately woman who reminded me somewhat of Rock's mother.

"Good afternoon," she said. "I have come to see Mr. Hudson."

"I'm very sorry," I said, "but Mr. Hudson is in no condition to receive visitors."

"Oh, but you don't understand," she said. "Jesus told me to come and see him."

I said to myself, oh-oh, one of those.

"Nevertheless," I said, "it is impossible. He is very sick, and there are no visitors allowed."

She said she had to see him. I politely but firmly said she couldn't. And I closed the door. I went back to the kitchen to finish my lunch and watch some more of the movie. During a commercial break I went to the door and looked through the peephole, and the woman was still standing there. So I opened the door again and told her there was no chance of her seeing Mr. Hudson, so please leave. She turned around and walked up the path, but I saw her find a shady spot by the wall and sit down.

"I know I will see him," she said to me as she walked up the path, "because Jesus told me I would."

I watched the end of the movie and went upstairs to check on Rock. He was breathing peacefully but was not conscious. I sat by his side and read for a while, then I happened to look out the window, and the lady was still sitting there on the wall, just staring at the house. I thought, well, why not? Rock won't know one way or the other. Nobody but Tammy and me was in the house. The woman was obviously sincere, obviously a nice lady, and, besides, there was that resemblance to Rock's mother. As they say, it couldn't hurt.

So I turned to Tammy and said I was going to bring the lady in. (I had told her about the lady.) She shrugged. It couldn't hurt.

"I think she's harmless," I said, "but stay alert in case she's more of a kook than I think she is."

So I went and got her and she said "Thank you" and came in with me. At Rock's bedside, she took his hand and said "Jesus told me to come and tell you that everything is going to be fine. As a matter of fact, Jesus told me to tell you that he has great plans for you."

And Rock opened his eyes and looked at her and said "Thank you very much."

"You're welcome," the lady said, and walked out. I gave her a cold drink in the kitchen and she turned to me and, spontaneously, we fell into each other's arms and began sobbing. It was the only time I cried until Rock died.

"I have had an unbelievable day," she said, and proceeded to tell me about her day.

She said she had talked to Jesus the first thing in the morning—something, she said, she did frequently—and he had said, "Eleanor, I want you to go and see Rock Hudson and tell him he'll be fine and I have great plans for him."

"Jesus, I can't do that," Eleanor had said. "You know me, I'm too shy to do that."

"Eleanor, you must do this."

"But, Jesus, I don't know where he is."

"Don't argue with me, Eleanor, do it."

Well, she suddenly remembered she had read in the newspaper that Rock Hudson was at UCLA Medical Center, so she had gotten in her car and gone there. They told her he had been there, but wasn't there anymore. So she got back in her car.

"Well, Jesus," she said. "I tried. No luck."

"Eleanor, keep trying. You'll find him.

She had no idea where to look, so she began driving around. And she happened on one of those Los Angeles fixtures, a kid selling maps to movie stars' homes. She stopped and bought one. And she eagerly looked for the name of Rock Hudson. But we had carefully kept the address away from the mapmakers, so it wasn't there.

"You see, Jesus, his name isn't here. Can I go home now?"

"No, Eleanor. Keep trying. I have confidence in you."

She was looking at the map, and one name leaped off the page: Pat Boone. She knew he was a person of strong religious convictions. Maybe he could help. So she drove to the Boones' house and range the bell, and Shirley Boone answered. Eleanor explained her mission.

"Come in," said Shirley Boone. "You are not going to believe this, but we are holding a prayer vigil for Rock Hudson right now. Please join us."

So Eleanor went into the house and participated in the prayer vigil, and it was Shirley Boone who gave her the address of Rock's house.

Actually, Pat and Shirley Boone and Gavin and Patty MacLeod

and some other very religious people came to see Rock one evening. I was grasping at straws, and this was another of those it-couldn't-hurt straws.

There were about ten of them, and they knelt around Rock's bed, praying fervently and speaking in tongues, which sounded like gibberish to me. I was on the bed with Rock. Pat Boone led the prayers and he took Rock's hand and prayed hard.

Rock was out of it, but I spoke to him softly.

"Rock," I said, "there are some friends of yours here who are trying to help you."

And, once again, he opened his eyes and said, "Oh, hello. Thank you very much for coming."

As it turned out, they were his last visitors.

Eleanor, that lady who had visited him on Jesus' instructions, came to the house with Shirley Boone (they had become friends) later in the morning, after Rock's death became known. I was downstairs, so I don't know what they said in his room, but they were there a few minutes.

I had tried anything and everything I could think of to help Rock but, of course, nothing could possibly help.

Ministers of several faiths came and prayed.

Well-meaning friends brought home remedies, and we tried them all.

Doctors tried new medications, new drugs. He took pills and had shots and submitted to it all gracefully.

But AIDS (if it was AIDS) was even more a mystery then than it is now. Rock got weaker and weaker, sicker and sicker, closer and closer to the end.

Many of the visitors were my friends as well as Rock's friends, and they worried about my health. They wondered if I was not running a perilous risk by being so close to a man who was infected with that deadly virus.

I worried some, too. But, while Rock was still hospitalized, I had sat down with Dr. Kennamer and asked him to tell me what peril, if any, I was in. He admitted that medical science didn't know that much about AIDS yet. But he said that most doctors believed AIDS was actually a very hard disease to catch; it was far less contagious than a cold or the average run-of-the-virus infection.

"As long as you don't exchange blood or any body fluid with an AIDS patient," he said, "you'll be OK."

So I really was never too concerned. I tried to be careful, of course, but I honestly wasn't worried.

The nurses on duty had had some experience with AIDS, too. And they told me much the same thing. They were particularly careful about covering any open sores or cuts they had on their own bodies, because if any of Rock's blood had gotten into them through such a wound, they might have had a problem. They cautioned me to be careful about that.

Still, I had my moments of concern.

Once, in another attempt to get him to eat, I asked James to make him some tapioca pudding. That had always been one of his favorites. I brought the tapioca pudding up to him, and spooned out a little and held out the spoon and he put it in his mouth.

"Yuch," he said, spitting it out. "Tastes awful."

I had had a little in the kitchen before, so I knew it was fine. And I said so. He tried another spoonful.

"No, it's no good. Here, you try it."

And he took the spoon out of his mouth and thrust it at me.

Now I had a dilemma. Should I put that spoon, which had just been in the mouth of a man who was probably dying of AIDS, in my mouth? If I didn't, I would be rejecting him.

I decided, whatever happened, I could not reject him. So I took the spoon and ate the tapioca pudding and said "Mmmm. It's good," and he did manage to eat a little bit of it after that.

On another day, he said he wanted a shower. But he was obviously too weak to shower by himself. I said the nurse would bathe him, but he would have none of that.

"You take me," he said. "Please."

So I took him into the bathroom and the nurse undressed him and I undressed myself and carried him into the shower with me. I washed him and shampooed his hair. The nurse was standing outside in case I might need some assistance.

Then I heard her gasp, and looked up at her, and she was pointing at my foot. Poor Rock had lost control of his bladder and was urinating, and the stream was hitting my foot. I moved my foot and shrugged at the nurse: What can I do? It's a fait accompli, and she shook her head sadly.

Fortunately, I had no open sores or cuts or anything like that on my foot.

I relied on the advice I had gotten from the doctors and the nurses. If they were right, I was in no danger. Time seems to have proved them right. I suppose I could still come down with it—the researchers have not yet established how long the incubation period for the disease is—but I feel confident that I am OK.

I do admit I had some qualms at the time, but I really had no choice. He was my friend. I had to do what I could to help him when he needed me. What else are friends for?

Later, there was some criticism of Rock for having been cavalier about the disease, especially in some of his contacts. One of his last jobs was on the television soap opera *Dynasty*, the episode that contained the scene in which he kissed Linda Evans.

The story got around that Rock had come home and gloated about the fact that, sick or not, he had given Linda Evans a big, fat, sloppy, juicy kiss.

But that wasn't true. Linda Evans, as I mentioned earlier, has told many people that Rock's kiss was about as chaste as a kiss can be.

"His lips were tight shut," she said, "and he barely touched the side of my mouth. He really cheated the audience with that kiss."

Rock later told me that he had agonized over that kiss and made sure that his lips were dry and that nothing really touched Linda. He only grazed her cheek, nothing more.

Each day, as Rock weakened, my optimism faded. Even in my rosiest moments I could see that he was losing ground steadily. Each day, each hour, he slipped gradually away.

Sometimes, however, as with any disease, there were moments of remission. At those times, miraculously the color would return to his cheeks, the light to his eyes. But those times became rarer as the weeks went by.

More frequently, now, he was out of it. He would lie there, his eyes open but not really looking at anything. He could barely move. Not only could he no longer go downstairs for meals, he was too weak even to get out of bed. Even moving his head was too much for him.

I often got onto the bed with him. He needed comforting. He needed somebody to hold him, to tell him he was going to be all right. Maybe we both knew that was untrue, but I needed to say it and he needed to hear it. So I held him in my arms and told him that everything would be all right. He clung to me; I was the life ring in the ocean, which was full of sharks.

I don't think he was in any great pain. At least, he never complained of hurting. He would often say that he felt weak, that he was tired, but he never spoke of pain.

The strongest pain-killer the doctors prescribed was Darvon. And I think the nurses and I only had to give him one of those pills twice.

When he was feeling good—those times of temporary remission—he would want to watch television. If I couldn't find a program he liked, I would run a movie on the VCR. I had to be very careful about TV—the *National Enquirer*, for example, was running a series of commercials about how he was dying—so I always had the remote control gizmo in my hand, ready to switch channels at the first sign of that ad.

Sometimes, on his best days, we played cards. Our old favorite, Spite and Malice. And, weak or not, he was such a competitive card player that he often beat me. He loved winning, loved to say, "I win!"

We all tried to make him as comfortable as possible, of course. The nurses were marvelous. James and the others on the staff did everything they could for him. And I was there every minute of the day and night. I slept on a sofa in his room.

If there was anything that made me happy during those months it was that Rock was, at least, at home. In his own room, in his own bed. Surrounded by people who were trying to make his life as pleasant as was humanly possible. The doctors often suggested he be taken back to the hospital, but I kept saying "Why?"

"So he'd have professional care in an emergency."

"Is he going to live?"

"No. No, he's not."

"Then what kind of an emergency can there be?"

"Well—."

"Well, at least let him die in his own bed."

Every day I'd bring the dogs up to see him. They would jump on his bed and crawl all over him and lick his face. He was too weak to return their affection, but I knew he loved seeing those animals. It was one of the high spots of his daily routine, such as it was.

And the visitors kept coming.

I would always get him fixed up, to make sure he looked his best. I shaved him every other day. Combed his hair regularly. Saw that he was always in clean pajamas, with a clean robe on.

If you just saw his face—and that is all most of the visitors did see—he had an almost ethereal look, near the end. I would pull his sheets and blankets up around his chin. His face, with the hollow eyes and sunken cheeks, had an almost-haunted, spiritual quality.

It was only when he stood up that you noticed how the skin sagged and how he had become so thin you could literally see his bones beneath the skin. People who saw him then would gasp in shock and horror.

But the usual visitor never saw him like that, and so the usual visitor came away thinking he looked thin but beautiful. It was a different sort of beauty from the former Rock Hudson, the big bursting-with-health-and-vigor Rock Hudson, but it was still a beautiful face.

People would call and ask me if they could come. It depended on how he was feeling that particular day. I didn't let anyone see him when he was in one of his out-of-it days. But if he was OK, if he was conscious, I encouraged visitors. Anything so he could take his mind off himself.

His old movie crew came, one by one. Betty Abbott, the script supervisor. George Robotham, his stunt man. Mark Reedall, the make-up man. Pete Saldutti, the wardrobe man. At the time they were all working on the same picture—*Psycho II*, which Tony Perkins was directing.

One day I got a call asking if they could all come over, en masse, that night after they wrapped for the day. I told Rock to expect a flock of visitors that evening.

"They'll be coming from work?"

"Yes, right after the wrap."

"They'll want a drink, then."

"Yes, I imagine so."

"Get me up, Tom. Get me downstairs. I'll be by the bar when they get here."

So the nurse and I got him up, dressed him, clothes hanging loosely on his toothpick frame, and brought him downstairs. He sat by the bar with his old gang, the people who had been with him on so many movies. They reminisced about the old days and told stories and drank and had a great time.

It was the last time Rock was downstairs. And, of course, it could never have happened if he had still been in the hospital as some of the doctors wanted.

As he became progressively weaker I began thinking about the inevitable—death and its consequences. One of our old friends, Susan Stafford, visited Rock and, afterward, said she thought he should see a priest.

"He was originally a Roman Catholic, wasn't he?"

"Yes."

"Well, then, it's something you have to do for him. He has to have the last rites of the church."

Again, operating on the old it-couldn't-hurt philosophy, I agreed. Susan said she had a good friend, Father Terry Sweeney, who would be happy to come over.

I didn't tell Rock he was coming. At the moment of the priest's arrival, Rock happened to be in one of his better moments. In fact, he had gotten out of bed and was sitting at his desk, trying to write a letter, when Father Sweeney came into the room.

"Rock, here's a friend of Susan Stafford, come to see you."

"Oh, fine," said Rock. "Come on in. Sit down."

Then he saw the man was a priest. Rock looked over at me, but I couldn't tell from his expression if he understood the meaning of the visit or not.

I stayed in the room but said nothing. I just wanted to be sure there would be no trouble, that Rock wouldn't become upset. He didn't. Father Sweeney was very pleasant. So I left.

He stayed about twenty minutes. When he came out, he told me he had heard Rock's confession and had given him communion.

"Did you give him the last rites?" I asked.

"Well, we don't use that terminology any more," the priest said. "We just call it Prayers for the Sick. I prayed with him."

Then I went back into Rock's room. He had gotten back into bed. He looked at me and said "Thanks for that."

Both doctors, Kennamer and Gottlieb, told me that Rock was going to die. Nothing could be done to avoid it.

"How long does he have?"

"Hard to tell." This was Dr. Gottlieb. "He had a very strong constitution, so it won't be for a while yet. He could hang on for several more months, maybe even six months."

This was late in September. So I was prepared for a fairly long siege. Rock's condition seemed to have stabilized. He certainly wasn't improving, but neither was he weakening. I took some solace from that and, actually, began to feel that perhaps the doctors were wrong. Perhaps it had bottomed out. Perhaps he had weathered the crisis point. Perhaps he would confound science and recover.

I don't think I actually believed that, but I think it helped me show a cheerful face to Rock.

On the morning of October 2, I even thought I saw some slight improvement. I had gotten up early, because he did. We were watching the *Today* show. We were having coffee. We were talking about whatever it was on the TV program.

Then I thought I'd get another cup of coffee.

"I'm going down and get another cup of coffee," I said. "How about you? Another cup?"

"No, I don't believe so."

So I went out and, before I went downstairs to the kitchen, I signaled the nurse. She had been sitting outside Rock's door, and as soon as I left, she went in to stay with Rock until I came back.

I was in the kitchen, getting my coffee, when the nurse buzzed on the intercom.

"Mr. Clark, Rock is gone."

I ran upstairs and he was lying in the bed, looking very peaceful. She said that just as soon as I had left the room, he had simply closed his eyes.

CHAPTER SIXTEEN
Saying Goodbye

Marilyn Maxwell's three-ring funeral, with screaming fans and thundering herds of reporters, turned both Rock and me off those big, gaudy, pointless affairs. We had decided that day that if either of us went, the other would preside at a simple cremation. Maybe a little memorial service, for close friends, afterward. Nothing that public or press would be allowed to attend.

I vowed that I would accompany Rock on his final trip to the undertaker and stay with him until the cremation had taken place.

All of Rock's closest friends had tried, during his last weeks, to remain hopeful and optimistic. But we were pragmatic enough to realize that the very worst was probably going to happen, and the doctors had told us that he was certainly going to die. So there were arrangements that had to be made.

Mark Miller had talked to an undertaker and given me his name and phone number. When Rock died, I would call him immediately. He would know what to do.

I made two phone calls—to Dr. Kennamer and then to the undertaker—about ten minutes after nine.

Then I called George Nader (who was in Palm Springs) and Mark Miller (who was in New York) and I told them. That was all. I made it clear to the four people I called at that time that I would handle the press and asked all four not to tell anybody else for the time being.

I stayed in the room, alone with Rock, for ten minutes or so. Then I asked the nurse to come in.

She and I cleaned Rock up, straightened the room, and waited for Kennamer and the undertaker. Then I made a serious mistake. I went downstairs and there was Marc Christian, parked in the theater as usual. I had begun to think of him as "the squatter."

I told him that Rock was dead. Maybe I had the forlorn hope that now he would pack his things and quietly move out of the house and my life. I compounded my mistake by asking him if he would like to come upstairs and say good-bye to Rock.

He did come upstairs with me, stood at Rock's bedside silently for a few moments, then turned and silently walked back downstairs. That was the end of his silence.

I was in the room with Rock, still waiting for the arrival of the doctor and the undertaker, when the phone rang. It was close to ten o'clock; certainly no later, a little less than an hour after Rock had died. The caller was Rona Barrett.

"I understand Rock is dead," the gossip columnist said. "Can you confirm that, Tom?"

"Yes, he is. But how did you know?"

"It was on radio and TV," she said. "The wire services have it."

Later, when I was calmer, I tried to track down where the leak had happened. The four people I called—Kennamer, the undertaker, George Nader, and Mark Miller—all swore that they hadn't leaked the news, and I believe them. Later Mark Miller did some detective work.

He checked the phone bill at the house. On the morning that Rock died, somewhere around ten, a call had been made from the house to a New York number. All the calls I had made were accounted for. My only call to New York had been to Mark Miller, and that was another New York number. So Mark called the number and got the Regency Hotel.

Shortly after Rona Barrett called, Elizabeth Taylor was on the phone. She, too, had heard about Rock's death on the radio and asked if I had taken security precautions. That was one thing I had overlooked, and when I told her that, she said she would send her own security people right over. I realized at that moment that not only had I neglected to think of getting security people but also that the outer gates to the driveway were wide open.

I thanked Elizabeth and ran downstairs, outside, and got to the gates in time. I shut them and locked them.

By the time Elizabeth's security people arrived, dozens of press people were outside, trying to get pictures and quotes. I was very grateful to Elizabeth for thinking about security, but I guess her life has been so traumatic that the first thing she thinks about in a crisis is security.

One precaution we had taken, in our conversations with the undertaker, was to ask him not to send a hearse, but to send a plain-looking van. That way, maybe we could trick the waiting photographers. So a van did arrive and the driver backed into the garage— cars had been moved out to make room for it—and Rock's body was taken out through the garage and placed in the van. The press wasn't fooled; as he left, the driver had to inch his way through the clamoring crowd of reporters and photographers.

The photographers were shooting from everywhere. They climbed up trees, up the gateposts. They used telephoto lenses. Anything to try and get a shot of Rock's body. It was an exercise in extreme ghoulishness.

I tried to stand between the van and the camera people to obscure any possible shot. Even though the body was in a body bag, and the body bag was in the garage, and the van had solid sides, I didn't even want them to get a picture of anything that they could claim was the body, or even the body bag. And then I climbed into the van myself and rode with Rock's body to the funeral home.

The body was cremated and then, according to the plans we had made at the time of Marilyn Maxwell's death, scattered his ashes at sea.

We chartered a boat to go out into Santa Monica Bay. It was a big yacht and many friends and business associates showed up— even Marc Christian and a bunch of his buddies. When we got far enough out into the bay, the ship hove to and I took the container and scattered the ashes into the sea.

I said a few words, silently, and probably some of the others did, too. Then we went back to the dock.

Thus there was no funeral as such. But Elizabeth did say we should have a memorial service and we arranged a lovely one at the house, in the back garden. It was a place he had loved very much, the perfect setting.

Rock and I had always promised each other that, if one or the other died, there would be mariachis and margaritas at whatever service was held. That would help the survivor survive; we knew that the one who had died couldn't care less.

So, at the memorial service, there were mariachis and the margaritas flowed. It was a happy time, lasting about three hours. Elizabeth and I had invited Rock's good friends, of whom there were hundreds, and it was all very informal. Anybody who wanted to get up and say something about Rock was welcome to do so, and dozens of people did. Most of what they said was funny—people were remembering the good times, the happy things—so it was in some respects a cheerful afternoon.

As an example of how strongly the people who knew him felt about him, I will cite one case history.

Susan Saint James, his co-star in "McMillan & Wife," was in New York, shooting her "Kate & Allie" series. She was also pregnant. But she simply had to be at the memorial service for Rock.

So she and her husband, Dick Ebersole, got on the red-eye from New York to Los Angeles after her filming day was over. They stayed for the service and caught the red-eye back to New York later that night.

Afterward I collapsed. I just went back to the house and, for a few days, it was just me and the dogs and total solitude. The dogs were my solace.

Those few days were, however, the calm before the storm. Actually, several storms blew up following Rock's death.

There was a monetary storm, for one.

It was Mark Miller who told me that Rock's estate was enormous, which I already knew, but Miller said that it should have been even greater. I knew, of course, that Rock had always been a soft touch. Any old friend—or even old acquaintance—down on his or her luck could always be sure that Rock would be good for some money. But I was unaware of the extent of his personal charity. Mark Miller told me that, at the time of his death, Rock was owed around $90,000 by people.

This was pretty serious money. Mark had a list of all the debtors. We decided to see if we could get some of it back. Three of the people on the list were dead. Of the others, when we approached them for repayment, they most often said "Rock doesn't need it any more."

We got none of the $90,000 back.

Of course, they were right: he didn't need it any more. But, I have always felt that debts should be repaid, no matter whether the creditor is alive or dead, but not a nickel was returned.

When the will was filed, I was not mentioned. I had known that, of course. But there were still some arrangements regarding me that had to be ironed out.

With our original wills—the ones we wrote together, naming each other as the major beneficiary—we had some unwritten understandings. If Rock predeceased me, my responsibility would be to take care of Rock's mother and George Nader and Mark Miller. George and Mark both knew about that verbal pact and were confident that I would take good care of them. After all, Rock's estate was vast; there was plenty in it for everybody.

But, as it happened, now the shoe was on the other codicil. Now it was George Nader who was Rock's major beneficiary. Now it was George who has promised to take care of both Mark Miller and me. In fact, his good faith has already been demonstrated since he has given me life estate in his home near Palm Springs. He has said that, when the estate is finally settled, he will take care of both Mark and me.

Mark and George, soon after Rock's death, decided to buy a ranch in the Garner Valley, which is in the mountains just north of the desert area where I am presently living. But they didn't have the money to swing the purchase, so I loaned them a third, which makes me a third owner of their ranch. They tired of that life, however, and sold it.

George has bought a home in Hawaii, where he and Mark Miller are comfortable and living the life they enjoy. I live modestly, and happily—I don't require a fortune to make me happy. I know I'll always have sufficient funds to live comfortably, if not luxuriously.

I would like to get back into publicity work, but it's been some years since I last worked; *Fever Pitch* was the last movie unit I did. And, in the publicity business, time races on. It is a business that depends largely on personal contacts, and many of my good friends in the various media have either died or retired. The papers and television programs are run today by a bunch of younger people whose names I don't even know.

All the people who were good friends in the days when Rock and I were together have remained my good friends. It gave me a great glow when, after Rock died, they kept on inviting me to affairs. I had wondered if they would drop me.

We had been close, for example, to Danny Kaye and his wife, Sylvia Fine. When Danny died, I wrote a note to Sylvia, and she answered me with a very lovely note I will always cherish for its warm friendship.

I frequently call Nancy Walker, or she calls me, and I keep in close touch with Carol Burnett. Maggie Raye came and stayed with me in my home after her husband, Nick Condos, died. I have stayed in contact with Elizabeth Taylor. Doris Day telephoned me several times in the months after Rock died.

Looking back on the seventeen years Rock and I were together, it is not enough merely to say that they were the happiest years of my life. That is an oversimplification. Those years made up a block of time that was, in effect, a separate life.

I had a life—a full one, a good one—before I met Rock Hudson. It contained a wonderfully pleasant childhood, college years that were fun and exciting and even somewhat educational, the experience of being a husband and father, a career that was fascinating.

And I fully expect I will have a life—again, a full one and, I hope, a good one—after Rock Hudson died and left me. At the moment, I have no way of knowing what sort of life that will be, where it will take me, who (if anyone) I will share it with. But I am certain it will contain its portion of surprises, its ups and its downs.

Rock Hudson and I knew each other for twenty years and shared our lives for seventeen of them. That period of time constitutes, for me, a life that was an entity in itself, a life apart from what preceded it and what will follow it. It was a life that was chock-full of adventure, laughter, thrills, love, drama, and—most important of all—a deep friendship.

I will always be grateful to Rock for those years. Next to that feeling, other considerations—money or fame or power—mean nothing. Rock gave me the greatest gift one person can give another: the gift of an exciting and happy life.

Index

Abbott, Betty, 260

Adams, Henry, 3

Adams, Julie, 102

Alda, Alan, 220

Allen, Flo, 141-44, 147, 165-66, 169-70, 210

Allen, Rupert, 10, 12-13, 16, 101, 122-23, 135, 137

The Ambassador, 145, 230, 235

Andrews, Julie, 34, 93-97, 101, 149

Ann-Margaret, 57, 64

Archerd, Army, 239

Avalanche, 27, 144, 148, 216

Bacall, Lauren, 106, 191

Baker, Diane, 208

Barrett, Rona, 64, 265

Behrendt, Olive, 38, 252-53

Bellamy, Ralph, 28, 222-23

Ben Hur, 150-51

Bennett, Joan, 191

Bergman, Ingrid, 107

Bogart, Humphrey, 22, 106

Boone, Pat, 255-56

Boone, Shirley, 255-56

Bowers, Lynn, 6

Bren, Milton, 46-47, 83, 124, 209

Briggle, Stockton, 200-201

Brooks, Richard, 235-36

Buffman, Zev, 210-11

Burnett, Carol, 38, 76, 85, 108, 197-99, 201, 204, 216-17, 245, 269
Burton, Richard, 63, 201
Buzzi, Ruth, 115

Camelot, 183, 200-202, 204-5, 211, 215
Cardinale, Claudia, 7
Chamberlain, Richard, 60, 63, 155
Champion, Gower, 198
Chandlee, Esme, 61
Channell, Ron, 232
Christian, Marc, 24, 117, 231-32, 234, 237-41, 246-49, 265-66
Clark, Tom: family, 4, 43-46, 49, 53; as publicist, 5-6, 10, 12-13, 158, 235-37, 239, 269
Coca, Imogene, 38, 212-13
Coleman, Cy, 214
Comden, Betty, 191, 214
Come September, 31
Condos, Nick, 269
Corman, Roger, 144, 148
Cotton, Joseph, 204, 207-8
Craig, David, 38
Crowley, Patricia, 62-63
Cullum, John, 211
Curtis, Tony, 100-102

Darling Lili, 34, 75, 93, 149
Davidson, Sara, 87
Davis, Matthew, 73-75
Day, Doris, 20-21, 54, 99-100, 106, 116, 125, 150, 199, 269
Devlin Connection, 48, 165-67, 169, 171, 224-27
Dewhurst, Colleen, 204, 207-8
Dickinson, Angie, 149
Disney Studios, 12
Dittmann, Dean, 238-39, 241
Dobson, Jimmy, 25
Donovan, King, 212-13
Dormant, Dr. Dominique, 250
Douglas, Melvyn, 222-23
Dracula, 227
Dynasty, 171, 241, 258

The Earth is Mine, 130
Ebersole, Dick, 162, 267
Edwards, Blake, 34, 93-97, 101
Elizabeth II, 107
Embryo, 144
Epstein, Jon, 34, 157-60, 163, 220-21, 244
Erickson, Leif, 208
Evans, Linda, 241, 258
Everett, Chad, 64-65, 220

A Farewell to Arms, 126, 151
Farrow, Mia, 148
Feldon, Barbara, 157
Fever Pitch, 235-37, 239, 269
Fields, Freddie, 235-36
Fine, Sylvia, 269
Fitzgerald, James, 204, 207-10
Fitzgerald, Pat, 5-8, 37, 104
Fitzgerald, Walter (RH's stepfather), 47-49, 79
Ford, Betty, 216

Ford, Glenn, 6, 63
Foreman, John, 148
Foster, David, 12
Foundation for the Blind, 235
Fryer, Bobby, 211-12

Gardner, Ava, 8-9, 51, 139
Garland, Judy, 68, 103
Garrick Club, 16
Garson, Greer, 6, 63-64
Gates, Phyllis, 71-73, 102
Getting Gertie's Garter, 199
Giant, 105
Gibraltar Films, 219, 229
Gingold, Hermione, 191
Goldman, Milton, 191
Gottlieb, Dr., 241, 245
Grant, Cary, 108
Great Lakes Naval Training
    Center, 54
Green, Adolph, 191, 193-94,
    214

Haber, Joyce, 136
Hackett, Buddy, 157-58, 233
Hall, Jon, 56
Hamilton, Joe, 38, 108, 199,
    217
Harper, Valerie, 115
Held, Carl, 205
Hellman, Lillian, 105-6
Heston, Charlton, 57, 147, 205
Hopper, Hedda, 61-62
Horne, Marilyn, 191
Houseman, John, 204, 208-9
Hudson, Rock: awards, 110,
    125; death and funeral, 261-
    67; family 46-49, 51-52,

55, 57, 67, 70-85, 249;
health, 172-79, 242-63; movies, 10-11, 13, 27, 31, 33-
34, 67, 72, 75, 93, 99, 105-6,
114, 125-26, 130-31, 141-
53, 165, 216, 227, 230, 235;
stage work, 25-26, 38, 49,
76, 85, 117, 183-84, 190,
197-218, 238; television
work, 14, 18, 25-28, 34, 48,
114, 142, 149, 154-71,
200-201, 204, 220-27, 233,
241, 258
Hughes, Tom, 217
Hunt, Betty Lee, 230
Hunter, Ross, 101, 190
Hurricane, 56

Ice Station Zebra, 10-11, 13,
    148-49
I Do I Do, 25-26, 76, 85, 117,
    197, 201, 204-8, 216-17
Ingersoll, Rick, 12

James (RH's cook/butler),
    25, 89-92, 94, 98, 117, 124,
    195, 210, 239-40, 247,
    257, 259
John Brown's Body, 26, 204,
    207, 209-11, 218
Johnson, Van, 68
Jones, Jennifer, 151
Joy (RH's housekeeper), 17,
    88-89, 197

Kaye, Danny, 269
Kaye, Judy, 212-13, 215

Kelly, Gene, 217
Kelly, Grace, 135-37
Kennamer, Dr. Rex, 173-76,
    178-79, 243, 245, 247, 250,
    256, 262, 264-65
Kennedy, Ethel, 202
Kennedy, John F., 27, 139-
    40, 202
Kennedy, Rose, 202
Kennedy, Teddy, 202
Kerr, Deborah, 126
Krasner, Milton, 160, 220-21

Landon, Michael, 220
Langella, Frank, 227
Lanning, Jerry, 201
Lansbury, Angela, 105, 193
Las Vegas Strip Wars, 171
Laurie, Piper, 102-3
LeRoy, Mervyn, 135
Lindsay, John, 191
Lollobrigida, Gina, 31, 107
Lover Come Back, 67, 99,
    125, 150
Loy, Myrna, 191

McDowall, Roddy, 38, 107,
    149, 201, 223
McKuen, Rod, 96-99, 101
MacLeod, Gavin, 255
McMillan & Wife, 14, 18,
    25-27, 34, 114, 149, 158,
    160-67, 200-201, 204,
    220-21, 227, 233
Mammoth Films, 16, 123,
    166, 219, 221, 228-29, 235
Manners, Dorothy, 29

Margaret, Princess, 107
Mario (RH's driver), 31, 124
Marshall, Sarah, 205-6
Martian Chronicles, 131,
    165, 227
Marvin, Lee, 96
Mason, Paul, 34, 157-58
Mathis, Sherry, 186, 189, 201
Maxwell, Marilyn, 73-74,
    139, 249, 264, 266
Merman, Ethel, 191
Merrill, Dina, 191
Metro-Goldwyn-Mayer
    (MGM), 5-6, 8, 10-11, 13, 52,
    59-60, 64, 151, 235
Miller, Mark, 3, 15, 24, 117,
    158, 177, 228, 232, 234, 239,
    242, 244-47, 264-65, 267-69
Mills, Juliet, 38
The Mirror Crack'd, 105, 165
Mitchell, Ruthie, 191, 213-
    14, 230
Mitchum, Robert, 142
Montalban, Ricardo, 116
Motion Picture Country
    Home, 235
Murder by the Book, 14, 149,
    156, 159

Nabors, Jim, 66
Nader, George, 3, 15, 158,
    234, 265, 268-69
Newman, Phyllis, 191, 193
New Trier High School, Win-
    netka, Illinois, 50, 57
Nu, Tammy, 240, 244, 246,
    253-54

Oklahoma, University of, 4, 26, 52, 59
Olson, Joe, 79
O'Neal, Ryan, 235-36
On the Twentieth Century, 38, 49, 184, 190, 211-12, 215-16, 218, 238

Parsons, Luella, 29, 61-62
Peck, Gregory, 147
Pillow Talk, 99, 150
Power, Taryn, 104
Power, Tyrone, 104
Power, Tyrone IV (RH's godson), 104
Powers, Stephanie, 114, 156, 164
Preminger, Otto, 128-29
Pretty Maids All In a Row, 33, 149
Prince, Hal, 191, 211, 213-15
Prowse, Juliet, 204, 206, 244

Randall, Tony, 99-101, 125
Ranier, Prince of Monaco, 137
Ransohoff, Marty, 11-12, 148-49
Rayburn, Gene, 117
Raye, Martha, 20, 163, 239, 269
Reagan, Ronald, 26-27, 139
Reedall, Mark, 260
Remick, Lee, 28, 206
Reynolds, Debbie, 63-64
Richards, Mary Lea Johnson, 185, 187, 230
Rivers, Joan, 28-29

Robertson, Cliff, 191
Robertson, Marsha, 236
Robotham, George, 260
Roddenberry, Gene, 149
Royal Driving Club, 16

Saint James, Susan, 157, 159, 161-62, 165, 267
St. Vincent's Church, 19
Saldutti, Pete, 260
Sayonara, 151
Scalia, Jack, 48
Schuck, John, 157, 159
Seconds, 146-48
Sellers, Peter, 222
Send Me No Flowers, 99
Seven Pictures Company, 67-68
Shaw, Peter, 193
Sheft, Wally, 183, 188, 194, 232-34
Shepard, Dick, 11
Sherer, Jerome (RH's uncle), 78, 81
Sherer, Katherine (RH's mother), 46-49, 51-52, 55, 67, 70, 76-81, 83-84, 249
Sherer, Luther (RH's uncle), 77-78
Sherer, Roy, Sr. (RH's father), 47, 57, 79, 82
Sherman, Paul, 233-34
Shore, Dinah, 106
Showdown, 114
Sidney, Sylvia, 253
Sills, Beverly, 189, 191
Silverman, Fred, 166, 169
Simmons, Jean, 205-6

Something of Value, 72
Sondheim, Stephen, 191
Stafford, Susan, 261
Stapleton, Maureen, 103, 105-6
Streisand, Barbra, 96
Strickling, Howard, 5-6, 8, 11-12, 59-62, 64
Stritch, Elaine, 205-6
Sweeney, Fr. Terry, 261-62

Tartikoff, Brandon, 169, 171
Taylor, Elizabeth, 29, 63, 104-5, 139, 240, 245, 265-67, 269
Taylor, Robert, 60, 63
Teamsters Union, 58
Thorpe, Jerry, 170-71
Tobruk, 148
Torchia, Emily, 13, 19-20
Trevor, Claire, 46, 83, 124, 169, 191, 209, 229
Turner, Lana, 6, 8, 13, 51, 68
The Undefeated, 149
Universal Studios, 67, 100
USC Film Department, 235

Vadim, Roger, 149

Vidor, Charles, 151

Wagner, Marion, 18
Wagner, Robert, 164
Walker, Nancy, 18, 20, 38, 157, 159, 162-63, 269
Wayne, John, 22, 96, 149
Weber, Lois, 12
Wheels, 27-28, 142, 165, 222-23, 227
White Elephant Club, 16
Wilder, John, 167-71, 227
Willson, Henry, 65-67, 71-72, 141
Windsor, Duke and Duchess of, 95
World War III, 165
Worth, Irene, 208
Wright, James, 232, 234
Written on the Wind, 106
Wyman, Jane, 139
Wynn, Keenan, 149

Young, Loretta, 19

Ziega, Claire, 246